# The Landscape Of My Memory

By

Richard D. Antti

© Copyright 2008 by Richard Antti

All rights reserved, including the right to reproduce this work in any form whatsoever, without written permission from the publisher.

ISBN Number 978-0-615-25914-7

Published by

CREATIONS

Printed by

Lulu, Inc.
860 Aviation Parkway, Suite 300
Morrisville, NC 27560

Place orders at:  www.Lulu.com

Cover design by Richard Antti

Cover layout by Paul Stewart

# Contents

Preface ................................................................. i
Dedication ............................................................ iii
Acknowledgements ................................................. v
Notes on Format .................................................... vii
The Stage ............................................................... 1
My War Begins ....................................................... 5
October 1966 .......................................................... 11
November 1966 ...................................................... 43
December 1966 ...................................................... 73
January 1967 .......................................................... 99
February 1967 ........................................................ 125
March 1967 ............................................................ 163
April 1967 .............................................................. 185
May 1967 ............................................................... 203
June 1967 .............................................................. 221
July 1967 ............................................................... 239
August 1967 .......................................................... 255
September 1967 ..................................................... 279
October 1967 ......................................................... 299
My War Never Ends ............................................... 307
Epilogue ................................................................ 313
Maps ..................................................................... 314
Battalion Base Camp Layout .................................. 316
Front Cover Artwork .............................................. 317

# Preface

Several months ago I started writing a short story of events in my youth so my children might understand more about me and why I react in certain ways. As it turned out, the more I wrote, the more I remembered. Thus that short story grew into this book. My audience has also expanded to include not only my children, but also you the reader, my family and friends. My aim is to inform and motivate the reader to feel what I felt and to gain a more complete vision of the terror and humor of my war.

This collection of memories represents many of my experiences in a combat line unit in Vietnam. I was there from October 13, 1966 to October 12, 1967, and proud of it. That's where boys became men overnight, especially in a combat unit like the 1st Battalion Mechanized 5th Infantry, 25$^{th}$ Infantry Division!

I will add my apologies for any inaccurate information, because I am bringing up incidents that have heretofore been hidden in my mind for several decades.

I have dug deeply into my mind to bring forth as vivid an image as I could about my year in Vietnam. I pray that the images I portray in this book force the reader to adjust his or her preconceived images of the Vietnam Combat Soldier. I can only hope that the reader will pass from ignorance of our service to knowledge of what we endured. This is not a documentary of facts and figures, but a study of the quality of our lives. We were lowly U.S. Army Infantry Grunts facing the terrors in the jungle of War Zone C & D, in the Republic of South Vietnam.

Please understand, too much misinformation has been given about soldiers in Vietnam. I have tried to give a complete and accurate accounting of our story, sometimes at the risk of exposing some of my own human failings. The names of the people mentioned are not fictional characters; they are real men who had dreams and hopes for a better future.

Come fly with me on the "Airline to the Past", and look down through the breaks in the clouds onto the landscape of my memory.

# Dedication

It is my pleasure and privilege to present this book to all the following:

I could not have been more proud to serve with the Combat men of the 1st Battalion 5$^{th}$ Mechanized Infantry who served in the 25$^{th}$ Infantry Division at Cu Chi, Vietnam from 1966-1967. The unit is a legend among line units in Vietnam. Visit their web site at www.1-5th-m-25th-inf-1966.com.

Our fallen brothers are listed at the end of each chapter. They are the heroes of this book and they hold a mortgage on our freedom!

Most of the families of the guys who didn't walk up the stairs to that jet airliner out of Nam have no idea what their loved ones faced on a daily basis. Without the constant support of our families we soldiers could not have continued the struggle.

Special Dedication
Congressional Medal of Honor
Specialist Fourth Class Daniel Fernandez
Friday, February 18, 1966

While under attack from the Viet Cong and under intense enemy fire, Sp4 Fernandez organized the rescue of a wounded sergeant. While first aid was being administered to the wounded, the intensity of the weapons fire forced them to take cover. As they did, an enemy grenade landed in the midst of the group, although some of the men didn't see it.

Realizing there was no time for the other men to protect themselves from the grenade blast; Danny Fernandez vaulted over the wounded sergeant and landed on the enemy grenade as it exploded. Sp4 Fernandez' profound concern for his fellow soldiers led him to sacrifice his own life. His actions were above and beyond the call of duty and in the highest traditions of the U.S. Army, reflecting great credit upon himself and the Armed Forces of his country.

Danny Fernandez is loved and revered by his brothers in arms and by the citizens of his home town of Los Lunas, New Mexico.

iv

# Acknowledgements

Writing a book, as I found out, is not a one man show. Any attempt to put ideas, thoughts and feelings on paper is a great undertaking, and the further along you go the more help you need. The following people have helped me to complete the Landscape of My Memory.

My wife Raylyn has helped me to persevere in expressing my thoughts and experiences. My children Julie and Jason inspired me to describe the events that define me. My sister Joyce and her husband Rich, my brother Ronald and his wife Marilyn, and my brothers Guy and Steve have encouraged me to complete the book. I have the greatest family! My best friend Brian "Giuseppe" Lane and my great friend Charmona Lloyd have waited with anticipation for the book to be in print. They have my gratitude and thanks.

My Brothers-in-Arms Butch Petit and Tim Fyle helped encourage me, and they provided technical and combat recollection to put events in their proper order. Bob Whaley helped me make sense of the map coordinates, enabling me to locate areas on the two maps on pages 314 and 315. Keith Arnold, an Iraq War veteran, provided some interesting comparisons and perspective. Kim Hoang and Henry Tran, my Vietnam civilian advisors, helped answer my questions about their culture. Jerry and Sherry Bechthold and Mary Peratt read my book with critical eyes. They pushed me to publish it. Thank you all for your support.

Those people who provide help in the technical completion of a book are very valuable. Harry Ferguson, the "Patriotic Poet", provided punctuation expertise, adding impact to my words. Paul Stewart helped me to complete the cover. Thanks guys.

Finally my heartfelt thanks go to Jim Bain for his discerning eye and ability to corral my swift pen and thoughts. The changes have been the crowning-point to the manuscript!

## Notes on Format

This book depicts a year in the life of a combat infantry unit in Vietnam. Since these events occurred over forty years ago, I cannot personally remember details from every day. For that reason I have related the stories in three different styles. The first style comes from "After-Action-Reports" recorded by the U.S. Army. The second is narrative based on my direct memories and recollections of the action. The third style includes personal commentary from my point of view today. I have formatted each of these three styles differently in the book to make it as easy as possible to follow the story.

1. The "After-Action-Reports" are shown in a type style similar to that of an old typewriter of the period. They look like the following:

   ```
   November 6, 1967 the Battalion conducted Search
   and Destroy operations at 8:30am Company B...
   ```

   The "After-Action-Reports" help show the intensity of our daily activities in an official and impersonal manner. They add an interesting dimension to the reading experience.

2. The narrative and memories are written in the regular style font and include the main body of my story.

3. The personal commentary and related information are in the normal style font, but are indented and are enclosed between two bars like the following:

   > It didn't occur to me until decades later what I had experienced and what situations...these are mainly reflective.

   The personal commentary sections allow me to reflect from today's point of view, and frankly rant and rave a bit. Hopefully this gives the reader a direct window into my sometimes frightening soul.

# The Stage

If "All the world's a stage and we the actors on it", then I lay before you the stage on which this adventure will be acted out. Vietnam is a tropical country in Southeast Asia. It extends south from Mainland China in an s-curve bordering Laos and Cambodia to the west. The entire east coast of the country lies along the South China Sea. Vietnam is about the size of California and has about 2½ times the population. Lying on the bottom tip of the continent of Asia, Vietnam has historically been a strategic gateway to China from the South China Sea.

When I arrived in Vietnam in 1966 there were two capitals, one in Saigon (capital of the Republic of South Vietnam), and the other in Hanoi (capital of Communist North Vietnam). The country was in a state of civil war (do these words sound familiar)? The North Vietnam Communist government was supported by the communist governments of China and the USSR (Soviet Russia). So you see the war wasn't really a civil war, rather a Communist takeover. The United States of America had provided aid to support the democratic government in South Vietnamese government since 1953.

As a result of the Geneva Convention in April 1954, Vietnam had been divided into two countries. France and the United States supported South Vietnam, while China and Russia supported the North. Elections were scheduled in 1956, but the North Vietnamese and the South Vietnamese governments couldn't agree on how to conduct elections. In 1957 Communist forces from North and South Vietnam began attacking and terrorizing villages in South Vietnam. Thus began the Vietnam War.

President Harry S. Truman promoted the idea that the United States should fight any Communist takeover in any country. Presidents Eisenhower, Kennedy and Johnson continued this policy. At that time Vietnam was part of the colony of French Indochina. The U.S. provided military aide for the French to defend against the Communist incursions. President John F. Kennedy began supplying military advisors as early as 1961 and supplied troops up to 1963 when he was assassinated. Subsequently, President Johnson increased the number of troops in 1965. The war was going full force by the time I entered the Army on Valentine's Day 1966. President Johnson's time in office accounted for the greatest expansion of U.S. troops.

Richard M. Nixon was president from 1969 to 1974. President Nixon began pulling United States troops out of Vietnam in January 1973. The last troops left on March 29, 1975 when Gerald Ford was President.

The Vietnamese people were and are basically a gracious and

hard-working people. Most live in villages where their families have lived for centuries. These villages are on the coastal plain and river deltas. Living close to water is essential in Vietnam, since their staple foods of rice and vegetables require irrigation. Many people who live near the sea are involved in the fishing industry.

One thing that bothered the GI's was the expansive poverty level we observed, especially in the remote villages. I had always hoped that an end to the war would allow the country to stabilize its economy and provide for the people. I have since wondered if that has occurred.

Some of the basic facts were and are:

- The clothing was mostly made from cotton.
- Housing in the north was primarily made from lightwoods and bamboo with tiled roofs. The houses in the south were made from bamboo, palm leaves or straw. Some houses in the cities were constructed with stone or brick.

- Vietnamese is the official language.

- In Vietnam some of the religions practiced were Buddhism, Confucianism, Taoism, Catholicism and various other Christian faiths.

- The land and climate of Vietnam is tropical since it is on the east coast of the Indochina Peninsula. The tropical climate has monsoons (Seasonal Winds) that affect the weather throughout the year. The summer monsoons bring heavy rains from the southwest. The winter monsoons bring lighter rainfall from the northeast.

- Most of Vietnam has two seasons, a wet, "hot" summer and a drier, "cooler" winter. Southern Vietnam has high humidity throughout the year. The area around Saigon (now called Ho Chi Minh City) receives about 80 inches of rain between April and November, with average temperatures from 79°F to 85°F. December through March the weather is a little cooler with lighter rain.

- The Red River and the Mekong Delta and its branches are important waterways.

- The bicycle ranks as the chief means of transportation in northern Vietnam. The bicycle is also important in the south, but motor scooters like Mopeds and Lambrettas are used there as well.

- Radios and televisions provide the primary means of communication in the southern part of the country. Telephones were in use during the time I was there, mostly in the cities.

Unless I was a wimp, the temperature when I first landed in Saigon was more like 115° F to 120° F, at 3:00 in the morning!

Today the economy depends mostly on agriculture and about two thirds of the people are farmers. All farms, factories and other businesses are now owned and controlled by the Communist government. Crops besides rice include coffee, coconuts, corn, cotton, sugar cane, sweet potatoes, tea, tobacco, rubber, cashew nuts and a tropical plant called cassava.

Vietnam had an extensive transportation system. The system included about 20,000 miles of roads and 2,000 miles of railroad tracks. I know that during the war the US Army engineers worked to improve the road conditions, because we spent some time in August and September 1967 providing Road Security for the Engineer units. The roads were severely damaged from anti tank mines used by the Viet Cong.

The Vietnamese we knew were a poor, struggling people, terrorized by the Viet Cong. They would have been happy to live their lives as their families had for centuries (provided they weren't subjected to the same old Feudal System of the Warlord states).

I must note that South Vietnam continued fighting until April 30, 1975 when they surrendered. The North Vietnam government continues to receive military support and aid from Russia.

# My War Begins

I was born in Chicago, Illinois January 2, 1947 on a cold winter morning into a struggling middle class family. I say struggling because we lived in my grandparent's home with my parents Alfred and Alice, two sisters Joan and Joyce, three brothers Guy, Ronald, and Steve and my aunt Eleanor. Sounds cozy, right? My grandparents Franz Oscar and Sophia Antti had immigrated to the USA (the legal way) from Sweden. They were born and lived about 50 miles from the Arctic Circle. My grandmother Sophia came to this country alone at age 17 by ship via Ellis Island, New York in 1908 to marry Franz Oscar, then living in Chicago. My mother's parents Jacob and Mary were born in this country. So you see I come from "sturdy stock"!

The house was a two-story building with a basement, but it wasn't really very big. Maybe we weren't middle class after all, but we were and are today very classy people. At least my three brothers and my sister Joyce (the family gem) are. My lovely sister Joan is no longer with us, a victim of cancer.

Chicago is a very big city set on the shores of Lake Michigan.

The winters can be very nasty with the biting winds howling from the lake. The summers were hot and sticky, and sometimes stifling. Growing up there was good training for Vietnam! My family moved several times when I was young, but I found where they were every time. Just kidding!

I grew up during the time when families were just buying their first television sets. The television in our house belonged to my grandparents. The early 1950's broadcasts except for movies were live shows like "That's My Boy", "You Bet Your Life" with Groucho Marx (one of the first game shows), "The Life of Riley" starring William Bendix, "The Honeymooners" starring Jackie Gleason, "I Love Lucy" with Lucille Ball and Desi Arnaz to name a few. The programming included lots of World War II movies, westerns, horror films like "Dracula" and other classics, all in glorious black and white! We never thought we were deprived because we didn't know anything different. Then someone got a new color television and all the other neighborhood kids wanted to go to their house to watch Disney! Then we all felt deprived not owning a color set.

We weren't couch potatoes because we had an empty lot on the corner and we used it to stay amused. During the day we would re-enact the Knights of the Round Table with swords and shields, Cowboys and Indians, Davey Crockett at the Alamo. We re-fought World War II many times, lived in the "Wild West" with Marshall Dillon of "Gunsmoke", "Maverick" with James Garner, "Hop-Along Cassidy" starring William Boyd and every gunslinger on the "tube". These were just a few of the many interesting programs of my childhood.   Sorry if I forgot one of your favorite shows.

The boys were programmed for war and shooting. We were taught that if there was a war it was our honor and duty to go. We were also programmed with the idea of destruction of our evil enemies.

The summers were hot and sticky even in the evenings. Chicago has a good amount of rain in the summer. We never let weather stop our play. The empty lot served many purposes for our entertainment and sometimes income. We lived in a time when kids could be outdoors in the evenings without fear. That empty lot was our evening entertainment (I think it gave our parents some peace and quiet), and we were running around the empty lot area

## My War Begins 7

until 10:30pm to 11:30pm. Someone in the neighborhood would dig a hole and we'd find wood to burn. We had a big bonfire. That fire served two purposes, to act as a campfire and to be a place to cook food.

Each person was responsible for bringing his or her own food. The favorite choices were baking potatoes and ears of corn wrapped in aluminum foil, drinks, and for desert marshmallows for roasting on a stick. Cooking didn't take any effort because we'd throw the wrapped potato or ear of corn into the fire. Somehow we always had enough butter and salt to go around.

The group would sit around the fire and talk or tell scary stories. (I wonder if any kids do that today.) The more experienced kids knew when the food would be done, the less experienced ones would check their food about five times. When the food was done each person would get their food out of the fire with a stick, unwrap it, and stab the potatoes with a knife to make sure it was done to their liking.

Both the potatoes and the corn tasted wonderful with butter! When the food was gone, it was marshmallow time, yeah! Each kid had their favorite way of roasting marshmallows. I preferred mine to be black. I guess that you could call me a burner. Writing this part is making me hungry.

Let the games begin! This was the cry for "kick the can", the perfect game to play in the dark. The whole neighborhood of kids would keep busy for hours playing games. I remember parents having to threaten their children, just to get them to come home. Sometimes they would come and drag them home.

During the day we also did constructive things to raise money for ourselves. One day my friend from across the street, Ricky Holmes, and I decided to dig a deep elongated hole with a L-turn into a big room, then covered them with wood pallets and covered the pallets with dirt. This was at the empty lot. The next stage was to seed our "Coal Mine" with lumps of coal from Ricky's basement, and then stick candles into the walls for light. We were almost ready for the opening of our main attraction. We made signs "Coal Mine Tours 5 Cents" and placed them along the two open sides of the lot. We sold souvenirs 5 cents for a lump of coal. I believe we made $2.35 on the "Anthracite Venture".

The empty lot on the corner was the source of another childhood business venture. I came up with the idea to use the dirt from the lot for another sellable product "potting soil". I took a bucket and some screening and went to the empty lot. Then I placed the screen over the bucket, shoveled the dirt on the screen and picket out the stones, sticks, glass etc. while the "clean dirt" fell into the bucket. Then I combined that dirt with some rich dark dirt from our home garden. This product was mixed until the color was even; the next step was to bag up the product in one pound bags. My marketing plan was to put up a small table on the sidewalk to sell the potting soil to the people who came from the train station on their way home. Being an astute businessman I enlisted the help of the cute girl next door to garner interest (like a junior miss Vanna White). We split the profits 60-40. The bags were sold for 20 cents each; our sales amounted to $6.00. Oh, by the way, it was spring time and the product was a seasonal hit.

To raise money for March of Dimes (my mother's favorite charity) we put on a complete "circus" with clowns, wild animals and acrobats. Ross Vecky and I were hobo clowns who came down from the railroad tracks after a freight train passed. We disrupted the whole circus on purpose. We had fun and made money for a worthy cause!

My brother Guy got married to Gail Hukkala, a model and high school girl friend, in the mid 1950's. Her father was an artist for the Chicago Tribune newspaper. When I visited her father's apartment I became enthralled with his paintings and became inspired to become an artist. I have since then been highly interested in art. This time was during the Beatnik era, so I had my "pad" (room) down in the basement. I bought a set of Bongo drums and set out to become a "Beatnik" painter and musician.

We grew into our teen years and the manly art of war was replaced by something more interesting, the feminine sex. This was a most awkward time in our lives and like most young men we learned about sex from magazines (instead of our parents).

The most comical part was the misinformation from our peers and our own suppositions. One thing was certain <u>killing</u> was replaced by <u>kissing</u> at least until war reared its ugly head.

My mother died when I was almost thirteen, and that was a very trying time for the family. My father eventually remarried, and the two youngest ones, Steve and I, moved to Elk Grove Village, a northwest suburb of Chicago. My father left me with my stepmother Bernie and went to Sweden with my grandmother and my younger brother Steve. My father was seeking a cure for his battle with cancer, which I knew nothing about.

I had chosen not to accompany my father to Sweden because I was in high school and had friends, and it was too much of a change for me. I was a member of the school gymnastics team, and seemed to have a future in that sport. My stepmother was good to me, and my stepbrother Roy and stepsister Debbie Landstrom were great also. I went to school, competed in gymnastics, and worked in a snack shop at the Elk Grove Bowling Alley. I was a bit shy and reserved in my demeanor, so I kept busy. Summer vacation I would work in the snack shop during the busy lunch time. The owner of the restaurant, Fred Wulf, would bet construction workers who frequented there, that they couldn't beat me in arm wrestling. That didn't mean I could beat them, but I never lost during the two years I worked during the day!

My sophomore year I was conference Parallel Bars, Still Rings and All-Around Champion. When you consider the number of medals given out, I was the third place team by myself. Unfortunately other things got in the way of my gymnastics career and it didn't progress any further. No excuses. I remained in school and graduated from Forest View High School, Arlington Heights in June 1965.

I was drafted and began my brief military career in the U.S. Army February 14, 1966. My Basic Training and Advanced Individual Training took place at Fort Hood, Texas. Happy Valentine's Day to me! I actually received my infantry training playing war in the empty lot near our house. The training format was watching war movies-observe and don't do what they do in the movies. About June or July 1966 I got deployment orders for Vietnam. After a month's leave I was to report to Oakland Army TERMINAL (I don't like that word!).

I left Chicago two weeks before I had to report, to visit my brother Guy in California. My father had returned from Sweden after his unsuccessful three year medical stay. I didn't know the extent of his condition and how the cancer had progressed. I said my good-byes, and was driven to Chicago's O'Hare airport.

Little did I know that it was the last time I'd ever see him!

The plane left about 8:00pm bound for Oakland airport. I don't remember much about the flight except that it arrived around 12:15 in the morning. (For you younger readers the flight cost around $52.00.) My brother Guy and his second wife Fern were there to meet me. It was the first time I had met her and my first time in California. We departed Oakland heading northeast to the Napa Valley. As we drove along Interstate 80 I was enthralled with the dark hills with tiny specks of little shiny lights. The farther we drove, the less frequent the lights became and the darker the hills became. It was late when we arrived at their really nice home off Silverado Trail in northeast Napa. The visit was one of the nicest times I had experienced in my life up to that time.

This little slice of Heaven in Napa was the end of my "pre-Vietnam" life. I was on the threshold of a year that would consume the rest of my life.

# October 1966

My last taste of normal life was staying with my brother Guy and Fern in Napa. He drove me to the Oakland Army TERMINAL (I still don't like that word). When the Army was ready after one day, they herded us on a bus bound for Travis Air Force Base in Fairfield, California where we began our luxury flight to oblivion.

As we left Travis Air Force Base, the sun was shining; it was a beautiful day. The airplane was an old 4-engine propjet. The first stop was Hawaii, Guam, then to Japan and finally Vietnam; the flight was about 38 hours. It would have been nice to be able to stop and visit all those other places and skip Vietnam, but the U.S. Army wasn't very accommodating.

We landed about 3:00 in the morning October 13, 1966. After we got off the plane, I felt like I was in a surreal movie.

Dull, dirty, yellow lighting broke the morning darkness. It wasn't just dark-it was depressing and hot as hell, and so humid you could cut it with a knife. We had difficulty breathing and it smelled like shit at the Elephant Compound at Lincoln Park Zoo in

Chicago! The whole situation was made worse when we were herded into a small room and greeted by a veteran in the typical military fashion, giving us the usual lecture about what to do and not do. We were too tired to do much of anything wrong. It seemed like they didn't know what to have us do so early in the morning, and so we did the traditional military activity-we waited! We waited around the airport, and the longer we waited the more we realized that we were in Hell. No words could paint as vivid a picture of my first impressions of Vietnam and how I felt about being there.

Let me try. It was hot as Hell, it smelled like Hell, I felt like Hell, I looked like Hell, it was as depressing as Hell, and it was Hell. And those were the good points. Get the picture?

We waited until it was almost light outside, and the view of our surroundings didn't improve as time went ticking by. There were women wearing dark pajamas, sweeping at the Tan Son Nhut Airport with brooms that looked like fans. We wandered around the airport for about an hour or two more wondering when we would get going.

We waited a long time and then damned if they didn't hurry us out, as if we were dragging our feet. We were loaded onto some beat up old buses like you'd see in an old movie, only these buses had wire covers over the windows for our protection-or was it to keep us from escaping? The buses drove us to a processing center I didn't know where, I think it was Long Binh. They processed us in, gave us our gear (clothes), we changed and then...we waited (sound familiar eh?). By now it must have been about 12:00 noon. Anyway, we left before chow and they herded us onto the back of an open troop transport truck and told us we were going to Cu Chi. Where the hell is that? AND THEY DIDN'T EVEN FEED US ANYTHING!

I felt like the cattle look. You know the ones who are on a transport trailer on the way to a meat processing plant. Little did I know how accurate the similarity was? The trip was a distance of about 25 miles northwest of Saigon. I didn't know where we were going, but I did know it wasn't home! The good thing was, I had never heard of Cu Chi, so it really didn't matter where we were going.

In society, at least in the USA, it may be difficult to determine what

Northwest Saigon

position in life someone embraces. An attorney and a factory worker might be at the same place on a weekend outing, and you couldn't tell who did what for a living.

My first impression while riding to my new home away from home was that there were two basic classes, the rich and the poor. You could notice in how the women dressed, the poor wore a pajama style shirt and pants and a pointed round hat called Nung la's made from coconut palm leaves.

Notice the two women, one with the umbrella and the other with the hat. They are probably not of the same class.

This contrasted with the more affluent, who wore long flowing skirts over silk-looking pants and tops with fancier hats and umbrellas for shade. The farther we went out of Saigon, the more apparent it became.

The Saigon area was green, but the houses sure didn't look like home. The streets were busy like most cities in the world, but the areas we went through didn't look like the Paris of the Orient to me.

The houses were quite different, all with roofs of corrugated steel. Mostly there were areas of what we would call shantytowns with an occasional, almost regular house by our standards. It almost seemed that the people didn't believe life was supposed to last long.

Very few of the structures looked like what you would think this city should. Perhaps we weren't in the elite area, and I know that we didn't see the river area.

The odors from the first minutes in Vietnam around the airport were thick with the heat and the humidity, all part of the constant decay. This heightened our depressed feelings.

We've probably all driven by a dairy farm and caught the pungent aroma of cow manure wafting on the air. Keep that memory alive in your nasal memory as you read this book, because that smell is what we endured. I will from time to time remind you so your experience will stay elevated.

The clothing sure looked different. Didn't these people wear anything but pajamas?

We had begun our journey to Cu Chi, and while riding in the back of an open truck, I was taking in the sights. The area we were going through had many shops that looked like Tijuana or Nuevo Laredo, Mexico, resembling tourist traps. One of the corrugated roofed structures on my left had a sign "Seventh Day Adventist Church". I remembered that my brother Guy was a member of the

Seventh Day Adventist Church. Since I had attended his church 4 days earlier, the sign reminded me of home.

Typical suburban area

The closer we got to our destination, the farther apart the dwellings became and the worse the roads became. The farther we went the less it looked like a city. As the number of farms increased, it was obvious we were heading into the country. Guess what? I wasn't getting light duty. I was going close to the action! My perspective on life was changing rapidly.

We finally arrived at Cu Chi about 1:30pm, just in time for NO CHOW! The base seemed pretty big. As we rode in, there was a long area with barbed wire lanes like you see today at different events, only they are not made of barbed wire. The base roads were reddish dirt with diesel sprayed on them to keep the dust down, but very slippery during the rainy season.

We stopped at the 25th Infantry Division Headquarters area, which was an area with rows of Quonset huts all looking so nice and orderly. We unloaded and guess what, we waited! Who developed the military system of hurry up and wait anyhow? By that afternoon it was maybe 20 to 25 degrees hotter than in the early morning when we arrived, imagine that!

They came out and told us which trucks to get on, and then they shipped us off to our new home away from home. This may sound sketchy but it was 41 years ago and just how long we waited and who told us what to do escapes my memory. We rode for a while. There were areas with rows and rows of tropical tents over a wooden skeletal frame attached to a wooden base. Each had a front and back door. These were similar to the barrack (Hooches), structures seen on the television series MASH.

The Company Area

Each unit had a sign with their unit logo denoting their area. We stopped at the 1st Battalion 5th Mechanized Infantry Headquarters, I showed someone my orders. They pointed me towards Company B. I was home! BUT NO FOOD! The US Army sure got its money that day for my services! I was hoping for evening chow. It was even 4:30pm so unless I was really unlucky the chances that would be able to eat were pretty good. I hadn't eaten anything for quite a while and this would be my first meal in Vietnam so I had no idea what the food was available. I hope it's OK.

The First Sergeant greeted me and then what do you think happened? Right...I waited! He probably was shocked that he had gotten replacements and had to go lay down until the shock

Standard of the 1st Battalion 5th Mechanized Infantry, B Company

subsided. He returned and told me I was to be in the 3rd Squad-the "PRETTY BOY SQUAD". A squad consisted of 11 men when at full strength, I soon learned we rarely had that many. A platoon consisted of 44 men when at full strength.

I ended up at the 1st Battalion, 5th Mechanized Infantry, Company B, 1st Platoon, 3rd Squad, 25th Infantry Division. Now isn't that a mouth full. It was like a country club compared to where I was going to spend the rest of my youth! The company consists of about 220 men when at full strength. Battalions or at least ours consisted of 4 companies plus other support soldiers.

The 3rd Squad's hooch was the first one down from the First Sergeant's hooch. The perfect place for our First Sergeants hooch was on the way to the latrine area, or should I say OUTHOUSE. Ah, the latrines. Now that's another story.

Those who have served in the military know how fanatical they are about neatness and cleanliness. Well, forget it! This was not the cleanest place to live, plus we were hardly ever there. The hooches had drainage ditches all around for the rainy season.
The ditches were dangerous if you were walking around outside after consuming a couple of canteen cups half filled with rum and

coke. You could trip and break you leg, which would look a little suspicious.

1st Platoon, 3rd Squad Hooch with Clyde Macon

Come to think about it except for the few snacks at the airport terminal I hadn't eaten since the meal we had the night before on the airplane. That was almost 24 hours ago, I could have eaten the leg of an elephant!

Now after all that you're wondering, did I ever GET ANYTHING TO EAT? I ate at the mess hall that evening meal. I did get to eat on a more regular schedule after that time.

I was shown to my new home. I don't remember by whom or exactly when or even where my cot resided. The hooch was a tent with mosquito netting on the sides. There was netting for individual areas to keep out the insects, cots for beds, and the traditional metal footlockers. Not much of a décor. MARTHA STEWART, WHERE ARE YOU?

The next day, October 14th they sent me to school, no not Algebra but "Jungle Warfare School"! It was a week's course. We started about 9:00am but I don't know when it ended. It was interesting,

"Home Sweet Home"

because they had examples of what to expect out in the boonies. The instructors had first-hand experience in the bush and knew that too much OJT (on the job training) was not the best way to learn because if you flunked...well, let's not talk about that.

The company was in and out of the Cu Chi base camp during this period. When I arrived, the company was out in the field. It worked out okay, because I had to go to school. The company arrived my third day at base camp on October 15th and that's when I first met the guys.

Well, my first recollection of meeting anyone was Sgt. Norman "Butch" Petit, the 3rd Squad leader, when I got back from school. The squad was nicknamed the "PRETTY BOY SQUAD". He was as friendly as most are to someone who's new. This is probably because you replaced someone who went back home or someone who didn't make it. He was considerably shorter than me but well tanned. He was a New Yorker. You know how they are, don't you? I appreciated his directness and toughness. I could tell that he knew how to stay alive and that was my aim, so I listened. He always wanted to show new guys the ropes, because he felt it was his responsibility. Those who listened and didn't think that they knew everything received the benefit.

Sgt. Norman "Butch" Petit

I remember meeting the rest of the squad. They were: Roy Love, Thomas Sullivan, Melvin Sherrell, Vince Crone and Clyde Macon. I don't remember their faces or my first impressions of them. I can now associate their faces and names due to their pictures on our web site. The guys who are alive today probably don't remember me either.

It was a little dark in the hooch with the flaps rolled down on the sides. I felt lucky that the bunk I had taken didn't already belong to one of the guys, and I didn't want to know who the previous owner had been. The new guy wasn't exactly shunned, but maybe they just had to get to know you. I really regret not remembering much about them, especially those who aren't with us any longer.

That evening was a little less tense for me as I became more used to my new surroundings. I still felt alienated because I was the new "Green Horn". Everything seemed to be a little better after chow. Most of the time the food was typical military chow, and military food is usually good quality, but nothing like "Mom's" unless she was just an average cook.

*October 1966*

We had several "Do-Wop" music aficionados', especially Butch Petit, who was an avid listener of "Do-Wop" music.

"Do-Wop" is okay, but after 8 or 10 songs it all starts to sound the same. I guess it was better than listening to the grass grow or just dead silence. Even though they had not gotten a lot of sleep out in the field, it was still difficult for them to go to bed early. Maybe it's because they could stay up and visit and not worry about the Viet Cong. I believe it was because they had been out in the field so many days that the lack of sleep along with stress had become a bad habit for them.

The next day, the 15th, and the remainder of a week, the company was out in the field on an operation and I was still in school. The company came back in for their one day of preparation for another mission on the 21st of October.

The 22nd of October was a nice enough day, in the morning at least. We were awakened early (I could have slept all day). The first couple of days when you wake up in a strange environment can be a bit un-nerving, like a bad dream for two or three seconds then it feels okay. But I don't know if it was ever really okay. It's kind of like a bad dream, but when you wake up it isn't a dream.

We got ready to go, dressed in our latest Paris fashion designer fatigues, packed up our gear: ammo, weapons and extra clothes, HA, HA, HA. Then our usual breakfast of powdered eggs, toast potatoes, and washed down with reconstituted Foremost Milk.

When it was time, we fell out, lined up in front of the hooch. We then moved out to the motor pool to get loaded onto B13, the "PRETTY BOY SQUAD'S" Armored Personnel Carrier. The drivers started the engines, revved them up, brought them down to an idle, and then...we did like good little soldiers usually did. We waited which doesn't make any sense to me. How much sense does it make to you?

This was going to be my first big adventure, just like all the old war movies we'd seen as kids. To be truthful a lot of us were still kids, including some of our leaders!

B Company in formation ready for another long operation

What an impression the old war movies had on our generation. We were Americans and we were ready for war should our country call. I believe this was the impression most of us had while we were growing up during the forties and fifties. We had spent countless hours watching American soldiers, our heroes, facing the evil enemy. At the age of 19, I was about to become one of them.

Finally, after a seemingly long, nervous (for me) period of time, we were underway. The Company moved to the west end of the base and exited through the gate and turned to the right. As the morning sun was on our right side, we must have been heading north.

The long line of Armored Personnel Carriers was stretched out along Highway 1. This road wasn't like our freeways it resembled a gravel road as you would find in rural farming areas in the United States, but it was a major road in Vietnam.

This was my first day in a combat zone outside of my time at the base camp. Those times growing up fighting WWII over and over again seemed to be starting for me as I looked down the road.

The town of Cu Chi that I saw as we were leaving was some tin sheds that served as shops, and like any good military base town

The "Pretty Boy Squad" Butch Petit and the 3rd Squad

had all sorts of diversions and services including laundry. Like we had dress clothes to wear and some place or event to attend!

The long train of combat vehicles continued north for quite a while and the farther we went, the area became more remote with fewer houses. We were out in the sticks.

Whenever we were traveling along a road, children in Vietnam, like children just about everywhere in every war since the beginning of war, would hang out along the road, seemingly enthralled with the military. We stopped one time for a little while, and an 8-year-old lad alongside the road was trying to sell the services of his sister!

Something about boom-boom, and she love you long time. Hmm... very enterprising! I thought that the boy was being funny, but soon I learned that he was serious. This action was highly inappropriate by our standards, but very common during this time. It was their survival method, anything to put food on the table. Poor people sometimes resort to prostitution for survival.

Who are we to judge, we who live an easier life, and never have experienced true hunger?

Children watching the GI's going on a Mission.

I can remember riding (or should I say gliding) by a "small village" and seeing children standing and waving, most of them rather short. And then, a not-so-little black-skinned girl was waving to us in the midst of them. She looked out of place, but not unlikely in this type of environment and human beings, doing human things.

Men being men and the abject poverty that existed in Vietnam, guess what? The "Oldest Profession" was alive and well, a matter of supply and demand. This is not a moral statement, this is a statement of fact. I've wondered how much money was collected from prostitution and how much of it fell into the hands of the Viet Cong. It would be interesting to be able to learn how much money prostitution accounted for in a percentage of the total income of Cu Chi.

War creates especially different circumstances that move men and boys to seek activities that they would not partake of at home, at least not commercially. The possibility of dying a virgin was greatly increased in wartime. It would be a shame to die that way! It's strange that a country that sends its young men as soldiers into a crazy set of circumstances is the quickest to judge the actions of its healthy male fighting force, and then expects them to behave as if they were going to a church social.

Armored Personnel Carrier (Track) beside "Death Taxi"

We traveled for quite a while, and this was my first time riding on an Armored Personnel Carrier.

Sorry, I forgot to explain about the Armored Personnel Carrier. It's an aluminum armored vehicle like a big rectangle box about 8'X7'X15' with an aluminum turret on the top front called the Track Commander's Hatch that rotates. It had a 50-caliber machine gun mounted on the front top. The driver sat down into the body of the vehicle with his head sticking out. The driver didn't have a steering wheel like a car. He had a right and left lever that was pushed or pulled to turn the vehicle. The section behind the hatch was flat, with a big rectangular hole cut out where soldiers could stand and fire their weapons at the enemy. The back was a ramp that could be raised or lowered for access or with a "man" door when the ramp was raised.

The Armored Personnel Carrier didn't have wheels like a truck; rather it had tracks like you would see on a farm tractor.

This was quite a different feel to ride in, as they didn't roll like a wheeled vehicle; it seemed more to slide along. When they glided forward fast, it did so with a rhythm and sort of lunging-forward and jerking-backwards. This was accomplished with a rumbling sound in time with the lunging-forward rhythm. These vehicles were fun to drive (or should I say slide) especially on the base camp roads during the rainy season when the roads were wet.

This was October, and you could tell that there had been a recent rain. The area was green, but not like you would picture a verdant jungle environment. I noticed that it looked kind of an olive drab color, which puzzled me. It didn't seem right.

Later on, I found out that spraying the jungle from airplanes with a chemical called "Agent Orange" had killed the vegetation in this area! Hmm.... what else could it kill or harm????

The terrain began to change and we slowed down and moved into the wooded area around 10:00am. It took us over two hours to get to the area of the Ho Bo Woods. We entered the woods, and it felt to me like I was entering the not so enchanted forest. The Ho Bo Woods took on an eerie sense of mysterious foreboding, and I felt very alone and disconnected like in a bad dream.

Moving off the road into the wooded area the terrain then became rougher and more uneven, with more and more thick underbrush and trees. The Armored Personnel Carriers moved more slow & laboriously with a churning and grinding sound through the area. As I looked back I could see a trench along the previous wood line. There was something in the air. It didn't smell good, it didn't feel good, a kind of sick electrical aura. It just felt damn creepy!

My feelings weren't unfounded. We weren't there long when we got some action!

```
Still October 22, 1966 at 10:58am at XT596255
(this XT number is a map coordinate, the Army kept
a record of activity by coordinates of latitude
and longitude location as accurately as possible).
B Company located and the destroyed 2 Viet Cong
structures. Around 11:15am Viet Cong fired two
```

B Company 1st Platoon, 3rd Squad in the Ho Bo Woods

rifle grenades at XT596255, one Wounded-in-Action. At 11:28am one track hit an anti-tank mine at XT96255 the result light damage. Five booby traps were destroyed at 11:35am. After 12:15pm B Company was engaged by an estimated Viet Cong Squad resulting in one Wounded-in-Action and one Viet Cong Killed-in-Action at XT599274 (See Map A #1 Page 314). Recon Platoon sustained two Wounded-in-Action at 11:38am when the Armored Personnel Carrier was hit by an AP round XT588281.

We were riding up and down, and then turned left along a creek or a trench. The Armored Personnel Carrier went down a little hill and then turned uphill slightly as the Track Commanders hatch swung to the right then left, and the Armored Personnel Carrier turned right a little. From my side on the left behind the hatch, which was tilted, I couldn't see to fire. The Armored Personnel Carrier was swerving and jerking as it navigated the rugged terrain and bullets were zinging all around the track. By this time the 50-caliber machine gun was blazing away. Like most weapons they have their own signature sound: the 50-caliber sounds like a loud hard rapid Bang, Bang, Bang---Bang, Bang, Bang---Bang, Bang, Bang---with a jerking and shaking noise coupled with the tinkling sound

50-caliber machine gun in front of the cupola

of the metal ammo belt advancing and brass casings falling and tinkling onto the surface of the Armored Personnel Carrier. The 50-caliber was the sound of death to the enemy! Since I couldn't see to fire, I was waiting for my opportunity. There was a brief stop in the shooting, then the 50-caliber fired again: Bang, Bang, Bang---Bang, Bang, Bang---Bang, Bang, Bang---now I could see forward.

The Armored Personnel Carrier turned to the left about a quarter turn and started to tilt downhill. Then B13 went downward again with the machine gun blazing Bang, Bang and BOOOM! Flying up into the air at the same time a bloody half clothed lower human torso and leg to the right, and an upper torso and arm to the left, in the middle more pieces of bloody, raw human flesh!

That poor Viet Cong bastard never knew what hit him!

We were still in the throes of battle! We moved on down to the left, the 50-caliber machine gun still firing away. Bullets were zinging all around the track and past the left side of my head! Now, I had an opportunity to fire, so I fired my newly obtained M-16 Rifle and it jammed! It fucking jammed!

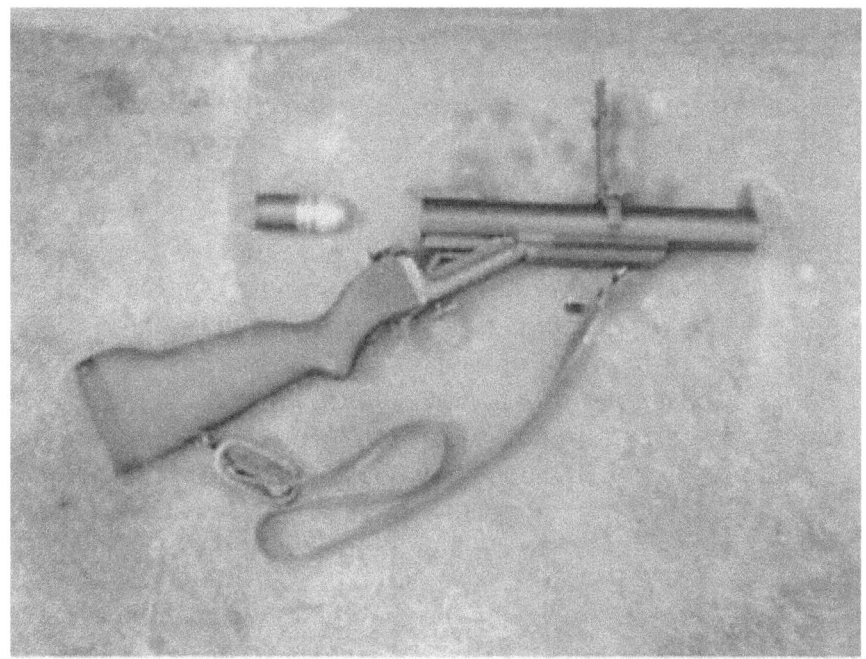

The M-79 Grenade Launcher (40 mm) my new weapon

My next reaction was to try to clear the weapon. Nope. Then I tossed that damn M-16 onto the seat below! Then I yelled out, "I could have been killed, this damn thing is a worthless piece of SHIT!" "I don't ever want to see this damn piece of BULL SHIT again! Get me a fucking weapon that works!" Boy was I pissed! By the way I did get my way an M-79 Grenade Launcher.

It didn't occur to me until later what I had experienced and what situations I could expect in the future. My baptism of fire was a strange mixture of acceptance and resignation for my fate! In the heat of battle (and I mean heat), you do what you have to. You lose your humanity in the twinkling of an eye, and do what you need for survival and still do your job. Thinking or feelings are luxuries you cannot afford! There is no time for thinking and these were young men who a little over one to two years ago had graduated from high school. Young men full of hope and promise for a better future, functioning on the lowest level of human activity. What a price to pay, and what a country, to ask us to pay that price.

It's difficult to portray the importance of this experience. Please consider yourself under the same extreme human experiences and ask "How would I react, and how would this affect my life, my family and me?" Come cry with us and help heal old wounds!

It was our job, no our duty to make sure that the poor Viet Cong bastard in this experience of mine died for his cause and so much the better. Yes, killing isn't a good thing, but given one of them or one of us, only a fool and a traitor would choose one of us. Have you ever considered how those choices are made in combat? You must understand a soldier isn't just thinking of himself. You're part of a team where you watch each other's back; the survival odds are greatly increased when we stuck together.

In my mind's eye I can still see that soldier's bloody raw flesh pieces flying into the air. This was the end of one more of the enemy, paying the supreme sacrifice for his misguided beliefs.
All the past war movies and their bloody examples took on a new personal meaning to me. All-in-all, it was quite a shocking and profound experience!

WELCOME TO MY VIETNAM!

When we set up camp, the location of our perimeter (the outside edge of a base camp, an evening circle of defense) was every day determined either in the air by the Colonel in the small bubble helicopter, or by a predetermined target location. It didn't matter to us. We were just glad to stop traveling for the day (unless we were heading back to base camp Cu Chi). This was my first of many jungle sleepovers.

The powers (brass) decided to call it a day at 4:30pm, except for Listening Posts (a nightly human early warning device of three

The Colonel's Helicopter

men in front of the perimeter) and Ambushes (ten to fifteen men away from the base camp set up and waiting to surprise, attack and kill the enemy). I didn't participate in either at that time. Whew! We were to set up a battalion-size perimeter for the evening. Setting up the perimeter was tantamount to circling the wagons as was done in the Pioneer Days of the old Wild West.

The Armored Personnel Carriers would come into the designated area. They would follow by company, platoon, and squad order to set up this perimeter. A squad manned an Armored Personnel Carrier. The drivers kept the track about forty feet from the next one along the perimeter. Then they would turn to the left and stop. The Armored Personnel Carrier was facing out toward the line of fire. The 50-caliber machine gun mounted on the front was facing the jungle, and the back ramp was lowered to the ground on the perimeter inside. Each company had support units that would be located inside the perimeter. The Captain's, Executive Officer and First Sergeant's track was inside. The Weapons Platoon-Mortars, the "Angel Track" of the Medics, Mechanics track and the maybe the cooks were all inside. Since this was a Battalion Perimeter, with Recon Platoon guarding Headquarters Company in the middle. The companies were linked together in one big family circle. When it a company or a platoon perimeter they would link that size.

Notice the spacing between the three Armored Personnel Carriers. They are the beginning of a perimeter. Imagine 30 to 40 tracks like those in a circle, and that's what a perimeter would be like.

A foxhole was dug about twenty feet to the left of the Armored Personnel Carrier. An M-60 a 7.62 X 52 mm fully automatic air-cooled machine gun was placed in the foxhole. This same configuration of Armored Personnel Carrier and M-60 foxhole, was then repeated to the left all around the area until they were linked in a circle. Then the men set up trip flares about fifteen to twenty feet in front of the perimeter covering the entire perimeter. Once it was darker Listening Posts were sent out as an early warning device 65 meters and Ambushes about 1700 to 2000 meters out as an offensive device. (See Battalion Base Camp Page 316)

This practice was repeated every night in the field. I must add that everyone on the perimeter took turns at watch but not Listening Post. The perimeter rotation was two-hours-on watch & two-hours-off (sleep time for two hours). We were set up, and it was my first time for watch at 12:00am. I was on watch in the foxhole fifteen feet from the Armored Personnel Carrier B13, not really far. It seemed like a hundred miles! We would have been on the foxhole perimeter earlier, but once we were settled we didn't or couldn't go to sleep. This was to become a bad habit even though we were tired. We would get a second wind after the stress of the day was initially gone and the night set in.

My first watch was to be a life altering experience. There were two of us at this foxhole, and now I was the one awake. There should have been three, but our unit was always under-strength and the others were on Listening Post or Ambush. The position that I was responsible for watching could be the open door to the Battalion, so a lot was riding on me. Consider I was nineteen and this duty was thrust upon me. Consider the nineteen year olds you know, and ask how would they handle this circumstance? Better still think back to you at that same impressionable age.

This particular night was cloudy. The moon wasn't providing any light. Here I was sitting up staring into this shrouded veil of black fear seeing nothing. I have to admit that I was scared and nervous. Every little noise (and there were a lot of them) sounded to me like a platoon of Viet Cong trying to sneak into the perimeter. Boy was I scared and I admit it! This was similar to going on a camping trip in the woods. It is pitch black out there and you have to walk to the outhouse and you don't have a flashlight. As you are stumbling along you hear noises and they startle you. Multiply that first time experience by one hundred and you come close to how scared I was. Those two hours seemed like an eternity to me and were an exercise in terror!

While on this watch I pondered the experience of my first day in the jungle. Two hours of reflection didn't take away the fear, it added to it. I had learned that life hangs from a thread and that I was dangling on a thin one at best. I saw life blown up in an instant. I learned by my experience that the M-16 automatic rifle was a piece of crap and a danger for our soldiers. How many times was that problem taking place in combat and how many lives were lost due to the M-16 jamming? This was my first day of combat, and wasn't to be the last terror in the night. The first two hours finally passed and it was someone else's turn. I awakened him and turned my responsibility over to him. I laid my head down on the grass or dirt and went to sleep after 2:00am....At 4:00am, I was awakened from what felt like a flash. It was my turn again for watch. The night was still dark and scary and I sat up with my eyes peeled for the enemy. I heard someone inside the perimeter make some noise at about 5:30am. Then there was more stirring. It was time for us to begin a new day in Vietnam. I was armed with two hours sleep to face a new day. What had I gotten myself into? (By the way, this meant that my second day would last from 4:00am to probably 12:00 in the next morning!) The sun began to rise and the dark veil of terror was pierced by its rising rays. As I was soon to find out, we seldom quit operations as early as 4:30pm. Usually it was around 8:00pm to 10:00pm. This first night in the jungle was an enlightening experience for me, and with my first day of combat encounter with death was a day I'll never forget.

October 23, 1966 the Battalion conducted Search Destroy operations. The morning was without enemy contact. Around 2:00pm at XT587306 things heated up for B Company engaged four Viet Cong with mortars and artillery, with two Viet Cong Killed-in-Action (possible). At 2:30pm an Armored Personnel Carrier from B Company was hit with recoilless rifle fire, resulting in one Wounded-in-Action at XT596312. One Armored Personnel Carrier hit an anti-tank mine at 2:40pm result two Bobcats Killed-in-Action and two Wounded-in-Action at XT596312. B Company located and destroyed 4 structures, 2 tunnels, 8 bunkers, 400 lbs of rice, 500 piastres (money) and Documents. Company C destroyed 38 bunkers and 5 bicycles at 1:00pm at XT583309. Company C closed base XT598828 and engaged 9 Viet Cong resulting in two VC Killed-in-Action and one with more possible. Company A continued operations in Tan Phu Trung. A Company had two platoons conduct 2 airmobile assaults at XT00132, 00135 with one old VC body count, and destroyed 2 structures, 3 bunkers, and 3 sampans.

We had good hunting that day; B Company located and destroyed 4 Viet Cong structures, 2 tunnels, 8 bunkers, 400 Lbs of rice, 500 Piastres (money), and some documents. We lost two men, with two wounded. I wonder if it was worth the cost.

October 24th, 1966 Battalion conducted operations in the Ho Bo Woods and continued Search and

Destroy missions. At 9:40am C Company sustained one Wounded-in-Action from a sniper. At12:30pm Company C destroyed 3 bunkers at XT579266. Around 1:30pm Company B located a Viet Cong base camp consisting of 20 bunkers & 2 trenches at XT597266. At 4:50pm Company C destroyed a Booby Trap factory, 20 booby traps, 600 lbs of TNT, and 1 Claymore. Recon Platoon engaged two Viet Cong VC at 11:00am resulting in two VC Killed-in-Action possible. All closed Cu Chi base camp at 6:00pm.

(I know we weren't invited, but why was "Charlie" so rude by not being there to greet us of B Company? It must have been his lucky day!)

We were so lonesome for our cozy home at Cu Chi. So by 6:00pm all elements of the Battalion arrived home. If I remember rightly, it was an evening at the movies and the Enlisted Men's Club. The next day October 25, 1966 was a day to stay home at Cu Chi. We spent the day cleaning our weapons and us. I can't remember, but I am sure the army had some activities planned for us that day. I guess there must be some un-written law in the Army that states, "We must not allow our soldiers (no matter how over worked and sleep deprived they may be) to rest more than one day!"

October 26$^{th}$, 1966 B Company was conducting Ambush Patrols in Bao Cap XT633178. No enemy contact was made (except for ANTS!). Company A departed forward base and returned to Cu Chi base camp.

Towards evening a large formation of menacing clouds full of liquid joy was gradually hiding the sky. We had stopped to set up our usual evening base camp. We dug out our position for the M-60 machine gun and had the honor to man the position better known as a Foxhole.

It became darker and darker, even though it was only 7:00pm. We felt a drop, plop-plop, plop-plop, plop, plop- plop- plop, and plop-plop-plop-plop-plop! Then all bloody hell broke loose and it rained and rained, harder than a Wisconsin deluge in summer. It wasn't raining cats and dogs; it was raining elephants and hippos!!!

The worst part was, we were not prepared for heavy rain. Hell, we weren't prepared for morning dew. So here we lay all night in a puddle of water, soaked to the gills and freezing our butts off. We didn't even have a poncho. Foxhole, not on your life, it was more like a swimming hole!

Close your eyes and pour a pitcher of cold water all over yourself. Sit in front of an electric fan for two hours, turn the switch on high. Now imagine how it feels to be there. You're halfway to feeling how we felt!

The day had been very hot and the rain should have been refreshing. However, when you go from 105 to 69 degrees and wet, well, I think you get the picture. Does chilled to the bone mean anything to you? It gives me the shivers writing this.

October 27th, 1966 B Company was still at Bao Cap conducting Ambush Patrols. Company A captured one Viet Cong XT498154 with a pistol belt, 1 grenade, 25,000 piastres, and misc. documents.

We were soaking wet in the morning. We got some breakfast, and then plotted to get ourselves some rain gear.

Before it was time to begin our daily grind, someone decided we needed to do some target practice with a weapon known to us as a "LAW", which was like an old bazooka used on enemy tanks in previous wars. Actually, the LAW was an M-72 Light Anti-tank Weapon. It was a light tube about 3.5 feet long to 4 feet long, and about 5 inches around. It was like a tube you would use to store or ship rolled-up posters; it was self-contained with a built-in trigger mechanism and gun-sight that you pull out. The explosive portion was preloaded and was ready when you took off the cover. It was imperative that no one, except the enemy, was standing in front or back of you. Safety first was our motto while handling firearms. I was game to try it, so we got it set up, and I aimed it at a 8" round tree about 80 feet away and fired. It struck that tree and boom cut it in half. Cool! That was my first and last usage of the "LAW".

October 28, 1966 B Company was providing Security and conducting Ambushes in support of the civil affairs and security operations in Tan Phu Trung map coordinates XT5910. At 8:30am Company A captured one Viet Cong XT552155. At 3:10pm A Company destroyed 2 bunkers at XT509158. Company C found and destroyed 2 Grenade booby traps and 1 Punji Pit XT515413 at 12:25pm. All elements returned to Forward base camp 3:20pm.

October 29, 1966 a platoon of B Company escorted C Company 2nd/13$^{th}$ Artillery to Trang Bang. The rest of B Company continued providing Security and running Ambushes. C Company found and destroyed 1 Chicom anti-tank mine at 12:24pm area of XT535150. At 3:55pm a track detonated an anti-tank mine resulting in minor damage. Company A established a Forward base at XT525141.

October 30, 1966 B Company was at Tan Phu Trung doing Security for civilian Medcap's and running Ambushes. Company A conducted operations with negative results and remained at current base.

I had spent my first eighteen days in Vietnam and had seen the elephant (so to speak) as far as combat goes. I had experienced first-hand the horrors and realities of war in the jungle; I found no glamour in it.

I became a hardened, detached and callus-minded young man in the twinkling of an eye. I have felt those effects my entire life. I would say adult life but I am still a teenager wandering around the Ho Bo Woods, trying to get out but hopelessly trapped in time and space.

When we received information of the outside world through radio and the Tropic Lightening Division Newspaper, we just couldn't understand the "Peace Movement". Actually it was just an "Anti-War Movement" because it had nothing to do with peace. It was effective in one manner, it made us feel abandoned and undermined. The United States of America didn't support us.

## The Good Works of the US Army Medical Personnel

The Viet Cong beginning in 1957 embarked on a campaign to terrorize unarmed villagers in South Vietnam. The program was designed to subdue their spirit and make them conform. The Viet Cong's cruelty contrasted with the humane efforts of the US Army Medical personnel as described below.

The Battalion was involved in Operation Kailua in the Province of Hau Nghia starting on October 12, 1966. The operation was very successful from a civil affairs standpoint. The operation included many selfless acts, including those described below.

The next picture shows Medics treating a Viet Cong who had tried to kill us. If the Viet Cong had captured one of us we'd have been beaten and…. Next section is about Medics helping citizens.

Division Surgeons, treating 2,511 Vietnamese Nationals, conducted a total of 19 Medcaps (Civilian Treatment Clinics). Those helped were civilians who would have gone without medical care if our surgeons had decided it was too dangerous, but I think that their sacrifice was brave and very admirable.

The 1st Battalion 5th Mechanized Infantry and the 2nd of the 27th Infantry provided assistance in work details and security.

Our Battalion provided special work services to the Vietnamese communities in the area during this time. I never heard of the Viet Cong providing anything but terror and brutality for villagers.

I wonder why our country never heard about the Viet Cong's activities. I can only guess the people were spoon fed the wrong information and it didn't necessarily include truth. We wondered how or why the wrong information was getting broadcast to the American people. We felt that the country we loved hated us and considered to be something less than human.

The following two pages shows the type of activities that you'd expect to see American soldiers doing and actually did! The picture on the next page is in blaring contrast to the Viet Cong's activities towards their own people.

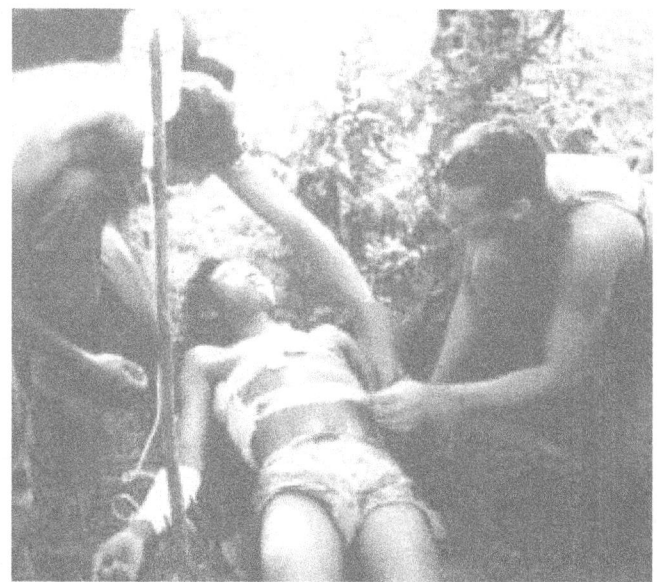
A wounded Viet Cong

The following "helping hands" materials were provided to the local civilians:

| | |
|---|---|
| Clothing | 5,760 pounds |
| Food | 2,350 pounds |
| Candy | 127 pounds |
| Soap | 169 bars |
| Shoes | 123 pairs |
| Women's Purses | 55 each |
| Raincoats | 15 each |
| School Tablets | 150 each |

S-2 personnel flying 14 airdrops dropped approximately 156,000 leaflets. In addition, other battalions in the area of operation handed out 14,400 leaflets about activities in the area.

The brigade S-5 personnel transported 3 Vietnamese amputees from Phuoc Hiep to the Amputee Hospital in Saigon to be fitted with artificial limbs. The brigade presented a gift to the family of the amputees, 500 Vietnamese dollars, to enable them to pay for transportation to visit the hospitalized members of their families.

In Duc Hanh at XT5707 the 2$^{nd}$ of the 27$^{th}$ Infantry continued to work on road repair, outposts, and a playground. The 1$^{st}$ of the 5$^{th}$ Infantry strung 500 meters of barbed wire around the school at Tan Trung at XT6810.

The School at Tan Phu Trung

These are some of the good things we did while protecting the villagers from the terrors of the Viet Cong. When we were in the jungle keeping the Viet Cong busy, it helped to maintain a more peaceful life style for the villages. The men of the 25$^{th}$ Infantry Division were dedicated to these types of programs that aided the oppressed Vietnamese civilians.

I just thought you'd appreciate hearing about some of the good things the American GI's had done. I hope you will understand more fully some of the real reasons we were there.

October 31 started out just like the previous days, except it was Halloween. We never really got used to being out in the jungle.

Brave men feel fear and doubt every day out in the jungle, but they go on and do their duty. There are few who compare to my combat Brothers -in-Arms who served with the Cu Chi Reaction Force-the 1st of the 5th Mechanized Infantry.

October 31, 1966 the Battalion spent the day doing Search and Destroy operations all day, and then that evening we were on Ambush or Listening Post. (See Map A #2 Page 314.)

Yeah, we didn't enjoy Ambushes, but we resigned ourselves to our duty. Then someone had to open his big mouth and mention that it was Halloween. This was my first Ambush and I was already scared!

Darkness fell and transformed the day into night. But something was wrong. There was a full moon beaming down reflecting light. This produced an eerie spooky aura. We prepared for the usual Ambush, and when we were ready, we weren't ready.

The trusty band of followers was assembled, and Butch Petit was going over the details because we had some Ambush Virgins in the party. One guy named Woods started to kick up a fuss and refused to go out on Ambush. He was ranting about getting killed, and he wasn't going out and on and on. Then he went berserk and started yelling, threw down his rifle, and continued to refuse. He didn't go out on Ambush, and I think he went back to the base camp and...?

The outburst didn't set the stage for a good Ambush, but like good soldiers we did it anyway. We left the perimeter and took about an hour to get to our location and another 15 minutes to set up. It was still dark enough to conjure up all kinds of spooky sounds and movements. There were three sets of lunatics (Luna as in lunar, as in moon, and it is well known that the full moon exerts a gravitational pull on the earth and affects peoples' moods.); the three sets of lunatics were Charlie, us, and the animals.

We weren't crazy, we just had overactive imaginations, and we were just spooked! I don't think anyone would sleep during this Ambush even if it weren't against regulations. This was a recipe for a disaster, but nothing happened, which is probably a miracle! Once we had returned to the perimeter, it was a big relief that this ambush was finally over!

* * * * *

There were fifty-six men wounded-in-action during October.

Those five valiant men who died in the service of Liberty during October were:

    George W. Alexander    Gerald J. Collier

    John C. Ardis    William Thomas London

    Jimmy Doyle Phipps

I didn't know these men personally but mourn them as brothers.

## November 1966

November 1, 1966 the Battalion continued operations in the same general area. Company C continued to exploit the tunnel complex. A large ammo cache which included 1 US 45 caliber SMG was found in the tunnel at 10:10am. At 5:45pm, C Company destroyed the tunnel complex. The Battalion finished the day conducting maintenance of vehicles and equipment.

November 2, 1966 the Battalion continued Search and Destroy operations in the same general area.

November 3, 1966 the Battalion commenced an attack at 6:15am at XT6322. B Company engaged an unknown number of Viet Cong at XT614227. Three Viet Cong's were Killed-in-Action confirmed by body count; two Chicom assault rifles, 2 claymore mines and 2 grenades were captured. At 4:05pm, one Armored Personnel Carrier detonated an anti tank mine at XT646237, some minor damage and one Wounded-in-Action. Two bunkers & one CBU bomb were destroyed at 4:45pm. Company B established a base XT647241 at 5:25pm.

November 4, 1966 the Battalion conducted a Reconnaissance in Force. C Company located a Viet Cong base camp at XT646245 and a bunker XT641235, finding four M-79 rounds and a pistol belt.

An unpleasant thought just came over me. Where and how did the Viet Cong get those rounds and the pistol belt? Did someone leave it? Or a worse alternative would be that they got it with the owner attached to it. I hope that it was lost is all I can say!

At 10:00am B Company found a weapons cache at XT644237 which included: one US M-1 rifle, one 30 caliber machine gun, one US browning automatic rifle, six Chicom carbines, SA ammo, two claymore mines, explosives and two 155 duds (no, not milk duds)! B Company at 9:23pm was fired upon by small arms at XT579189. They immediately returned fire and killed one Viet Cong.

We finished the day's operation at 11:50pm. A long hard day! That evening and into the morning we did our usual sleep, or the non-sleep seesaw. As you can imagine, it was a very exhausting time.

November 5, 1966 B Company moved to Go Dau Ha. The company arrived at 5:30pm, no activity occurred. An Aerial observer reported a 50-to-60 vehicle convoy crossing the Vietnam and Cambodian border at 10:15pm at XT2824. At 10:30pm B Company was called upon to intercept the convoy XT301250 and occupy positions there. B Company was alerted and moved to an assembly area XT416238 at 1:55am. (See Map B #1 Page 315)

There were always rumors flying around about North Vietnamese Army (NVA) regulars coming into our area in mass. Rumors have an element of truth but more often than not it's only a GI rumor.

There was some North Vietnamese Army regular army soldiers scattered in with other local Viet Cong units.

We stopped somewhere around 5:00pm and at that point we set up a perimeter and waited for darkness. We laid out our usual positions about 20 feet between Armored Personnel Carriers and got to dig our foxholes in the volcanic soil, which was like cement layers. We had laid out trip flares just in case and settled down for the evening.

It's strange that, even though we were tired, if we didn't go to sleep right away we'd get a second wind and then we couldn't get to sleep until later. At this time we were awake at our positions and as usual the "bullshit" was flowing because we had passed that sleep threshold.

(That same thing happens to me almost every day today, and it gets pretty frustrating. It's amazing that habits developed 40 years ago can affect everything you do today.)

It was still early by our standards, almost 10:00pm. We were enjoying the end of a short day. We had been at the base camp since 5:30pm, quite an unusual day.

```
After 10:15pm B Company was ready to move out and
moved out shortly.
```

Now given the previous rumors in the last couple of days, our "grunt rumor mill" was churning out all kinds of possibilities. Some were even exotic, I don't remember any but one. We got the idea that a division or a battalion of North Vietnam Army troops was operating in the area and we were going up against them. We were nervous and excited at the same time, because in face-to-face and toe-to-toe battle we'd kick their ass well! Remember, we knew nothing of the convoy!

We were told to strike our position and get ready to move out.
The call came and we fired up the Armored Personnel Carriers
and began our journey to wherever we were going. They didn't give us any coordinates!

Traveling during the day was dangerous enough, as it was difficult to spot mines, and the Viet Cong were famous for hit and run ambushes. At night the element of surprise was heightened. Our superior firepower and speed were our main strengths; the night gave them the advantage of camouflage because they were hard to spot especially in black pajamas!

It was our job and duty to move as the circumstances dictated, so we were off on another adventure. We traveled a short distance to the highway and then we really began to move. I guess the Viet Cong were sleeping and didn't know we were coming. We weren't ambushed and we didn't hit any mines along the way!

The B Company arrived at coordinates XT301250 at 10:30pm and set up a defensive perimeter. The company was supposed to intercept the convoy.

We waited here for further orders or something to happen like enemy contact. We waited for over three hours on pins and needles, and tension was mounting as the clock ticked and ticked and ticked.

At 1:55am B Company was ordered to move out and assemble with the rest of the Battalion at XT416238.

I don't remember if we ever got any word as to a convoy or not, but we never saw any other vehicles than our own. How could a convoy of 50 to 60 vehicles have just vanished into thin air? The aerial observer couldn't have seen a mirage---could he??  All I know is, they got us all worked up, hot and bothered, and burned up a lot of adrenalin, and we had little to spare!  We had spent the better part of the late evening on a wild goose chase and without results except to set us up for another long grueling day. If we'd been involved in one hell of a fight losing sleep would have been a small price to pay.  Who can remember loss of sleep on this day? We had so, so many days with little or no sleep.

My analysis of the after action reports shows that many times our Battalion finished an operation in the field and stayed from one to two weeks in the field without rest. We often began an operation one to two weeks before the official date. Was it because we had Armored Personnel Carriers, and the Army Officers thought we didn't need any time to prepare for those operations? What was the great necessity of depriving us of mental restoration? Should anyone know that reason, please enlighten this bewildered soul.

November 6, 1966 at 7:00am, the Battalion was attached to the 1st Infantry Division. The After-Action-Report from Attleboro had the Battalion 1st of the 5th (Mech) Infantry leaving Go Da Ha at 10:05am for Soui DA XT3458, and attaching to the 3rd Brigade, 1st Infantry Division. The Battalion established a base camp and provided perimeter defense for the 3rd B Headquarters, forward supply air head, two Artillery Batteries, a Special Forces compound and a Popular Forces compound. A Company supported two artillery units.

November 7, 1966, the Battalion continued perimeter duty for the Light Infantry Division 3rd Brigade Head Quarters.

November 8, 1966 B Company left Fire Support Base that we had been on watch at XT340583, and moved to another Fire Support Base at XT394622 to relieve the Scout Platoon. Extensive patrolling was conducted throughout the area, but no specific results recorded. Another Fire Support Base was established at XT305535, and the 4th Battalion, 31st Infantry was placed under OPCON (connect by an operation as a temporary part of a unit) 1/5th Mechanized Infantry to secure the base. Night Ambushes made no contact and returned at first light. (See Map B #2 Page 315)

## Ambush
This was an area where we suspected a large enemy force, so of course we were scared shitless. But you could never show it. After all Butch and the other guys had gone many times and survived,

so what was the big deal? Or so I told myself. Outwardly I was calm getting my stuff together, as I didn't want to have something missing when I needed it. All these what-ifs ran through my mind. What if I separated from the rest of the Ambush if we encounter the Viet Cong? What if I can't find my way back to the company? What if I fall asleep?   What if my gun jams? What if...What if... so what?  What will be, will be.

I remember the mystique of everyone getting together at the back of good ole B13. Butch Petit was always good about explaining everything, which was great because nowhere in my training before did we talk about the thing to do on an Ambush. After all, my Advanced Individual Training was as a parts clerk in the motor pool.

The best advice Butch gave us, because we had Ambush Virgins with us, was to make a mental record of the landmarks (hell, the whole country looked the same to us). As you go along, watch where you step and how much pressure you use when walking. Try to follow in the footsteps of the person in front of you. Then he gave us the best words of wisdom his 9-10 months of experience could give. "Don't Fuck Up!"  He also said, "If they start shooting, don't panic and run.  Just hug the ground as close as possible. Then instantly choose where to fire so you don't waste ammo or shoot your buddy. Having a cool head will save you in the long run."  "Sleep if you don't mind being dead!!"

There were about 8 or 10 of us going out on one Ambush. I think Butch was the point man, but I am not really sure. We took off from the company perimeter, heading east through the trip flares and claymore mines. We went past the Listening Post location. We were spaced about 6-8 feet apart. Moving under circumstances like these seemed to take forever because caution is always better than being careless. There were a few landmarks to note, such as a wooded area on my left, which would be on my right returning back. Then there was a clearing to the right, leading to a creek bed. We turned left along the creek and then across a field to a hedge row. As we walked, it was dark, especially in wooded areas.

The hedge seemed to be a bit of a problem getting through. I think a good part of it was bamboo. We waited while the point man tried several times to find a way through the thick vegetation. Finally he found a way through about 20 meters down the row of hedges to the left.

We each took our turn getting through the barrier, one by one. Now was the time to get your bearings on how to get through this on the way back, especially if we were in a hurry. Once we were through, we all marked the spot in the best way we could in the dark. Once we were all through the barrier, the point man went right for about 100 meters. There was a clearing about 60 meters in front of us. There was a trail that ran parallel along the wooded area we had just arrived at. This is where we set up the ambush.

We had some coverage since we were a little into the brush in front of the wood line with a clear shot at the trail. That's where we set up our offensive and defensive positions. We set up Claymore mines, two directed straight at the trail, and two more on either side of the trail. We got in position to man the Claymores and to protect our rear.

We were now ready for the Viet Cong rats to enter our trap. By this time it was 1:00am. Ambush duty was an all night responsibility, and we began our Ambush. Since there were 3 "greenies" on this Ambush, we were next to someone with more experience. Like I said before, it was dark and scary! Every noise was Charlie coming to cut our throats. At night all kinds of creatures move around and make noise. Some animals like water buffalo, wild boars and smaller animals even sound like humans when they're moving about, which makes for an eerie evening.

The first 2 hours was nerve racking, but it passed without incident. At 3:00am I was really tired and wanted to lay down my sleepy little head but I didn't. My eyes closed, and exhaustion overtook my fear and strangled it but I nodded and kept awake. We were able to get through the night without incident.

We were called back at 5:00am; the morning light had changed the darkness and gave us better visibility. It was time to pick up our presents for the Viet Cong. How rude of them, we invited them to a party and they didn't even show up! No presents today for you Charlie! Going out and coming back in were dangerous times! We had quite a hike back to make it in time for chow, that's if there was anything left. We retraced our steps back to the base camp.

This time we were able to easily navigate through the bamboo hedge with the assistance of daylight. As we neared the camp, we radioed in to alert them of our presence. We did not want to be greeted with open fire. We were back, safe and sound.

This Ambush was a success and a failure all in one. It was a failure because we really wanted to get those Viet Cong and pay them back for our lost comrades. It was a success because no one was hurt or killed. I felt relieved at being alive after this Ambush experience, and tired because of the lack of sleep. Today would be another day with more of the same, just another day in paradise!

```
November 9, 1966 the Battalion sent on local
patrols North and Southeast of the destroyed
bridge at XT393628 to locate a crossing point for
the Armored Personnel Carriers. (See Map B #3 PAGE
315)
```

I hadn't been out in the field long, and we were patrolling an area that was wooded with hedge lines. The interesting part about Vietnam was that in the hostile areas where we spent most of our time, when you saw bushes in a line there was usually a trench the enemy had dug and would use to hide, shoot and kill you. Try walking in the woods and imagine you have to be on a constant vigil for the enemy who is dedicated to killing you!

On one daytime mission I remember being with Butch Petit and Roy Love. We were walking down a path where the trees weren't very dense, but there was a lot of dense vegetation like bushes.
Butch was in the lead, carrying his girl friend. Well, maybe not his girl friend but they were close. A different type of pumping was required. He loved that weapon because of two reasons. The first was that it worked! Secondly, it could accomplish a scattered
spray without diluting its effectiveness. In the thick underbrush or straight on shooting, it would be a surprise to those on the receiver end. It was a 12-gauge shotgun pump action. The beauty of the 12-gauge shotgun was it could be effective when you couldn't see your enemy in the dark canopy of the jungle, but you could only hear them.

*November 1966*

This is what our patrol looked like

As I was soon to be made aware, the everyday things you do in normal life became life or death situations such as; eating, sleeping, day dreaming, talking, smoking, walking, wearing after shave lotion and even breathing.

Imagine you are out in the jungle on a Listening Post, and the three were awake at watch and after a couple hours one falls asleep and a couple hours later all are asleep and one's snoring like a buzz saw! The Viet Cong sneak up, and before you know it, kills you and the others of the Listening Post members; you could say the snoring killed them! Today I cannot fall asleep if I hear snoring!

How would you like to live under the stress of walking to work every day and worrying about stepping on a land mine? Compound that with the constant threat, a totally hostile environment: the life-ending Bamboo Viper, that little green snake where there is no cure or a hundred others just like him; critters like wild Boars; nasty viscous Monkeys; Baboons, even Water Buffalos; and Tigers.

Forget ants at a picnic; try the Red Fire Ants and Jumbo

Black Ants that would eat you alive if they were given the opportunity. There is a huge gap between reading about it and living it!

When we went on patrol, I had to learn how to walk. That's right, walk! I had to learn how to walk in an area laden with traps to kill and maim us. Stomping around on the ground could result in your foot and leg falling into a Punji Pit! Punji Pits were holes in the ground of varying size, about 2 feet or deeper. The Viet Cong, being resourceful, would take stakes of bamboo, sharpen them at one end, and force about 4 or 5 of them into the ground at the bottom of the pit. Before they covered the pit they would cover the stakes with shit. That's right shit!

Imagine the infection you would receive and the effects on your health maybe lose a foot or a leg! Charlie's taken one more GI out of the field and into the hospital.

We hadn't walked long when I ran across one of the punji pits a little way from the middle of the trail. Somehow they didn't do a great job of disguising it, so we caved it in, and smashed the stakes so no one would accidentally step in it. The punji pit was very sinister looking.

They were usually quite good at covering the pits in such a way so you wouldn't know they were there. Think of the stress. You can't even walk without worrying where you step and how much pressure to put on the ground with your foot!

At one point we had found a crossing site about 100 meters or so from the position of our Armored Personnel Carriers. We were walking down the trail when, wafting on the breeze, came a light mist of chlorine gas. The gas wasn't thick and didn't have the desired effect. It was only mildly irritating to the eyes and throat. Passing through the gas was a relief.

Around 11:10am, 8 Viet Cong were spotted near the hedge line to the left side of our position as we were going back to the Armored Personnel Carriers.

The squad engaged the enemy but contact was broken with small arms fire and from mortar support from B Company Weapons Squad.

Punji pit being constructed in the bush

The first thing was fire towards the enemy as you drop to the earth or a protected area, i.e. "hit the dirt"! We engaged them with small arms fire, and quickly the Viet Cong broke contact and fled the area with their tails between their legs!

We cautiously headed to where they had been spotted and made a thorough search of that area led by our squad leader Butch Petit.

B Company Weapons Squad, Thanks Guys!

The fox had jumped into his hole and run away to fight another day. Their attack lasted a very short time, and we were the only battalion unit to engage the Viet Cong that day.

As usual, as I was to find out, Charlie split the area when it got too hot! We returned to the location of the Armored Personnel Carriers, mounted up and returned to the company perimeter that afternoon. The company established one Ambush and two Listening Posts known as "bait" during the evening darkness. Later at 8:37pm two Viet Cong were seen sneaking up on the company perimeter. They were greeted with mortars and 50-caliber machine gun fire. Oh, the lovely site of tracer rounds in the evening, alas. A check revealed inconclusive results.

```
November 10, 1966 the Battalion conducted Search
and Destroy operations, no enemy activity was
encountered. The Battalion destroyed 4 Hooches, 3
Viet Cong bunkers, a company sized overnight base
camp, and numerous foxholes. The best estimate
from the things found indicated that a Viet Cong
company had been there about 3 days prior.
```

*November 1966*

A bunker set up in base camp as a defensive position and foxholes strategically placed all around possibly an escape tunnel for good measure

That night 3 Listening Posts were set for the evening's "bait". While this was common practice in our everyday life in Nam, this happened to be my first Listening Post. My mental record of my first month in Vietnam is fairly well imprinted on my brain. Remember, I was 19 years of age, and before Nam, pretty well wet behind my ears. But I wasn't a sissy, and up to this point it seemed to be an adventure.

Lonely could only begin to describe how I felt, and I was with two other non-sleeping GI's. It was lonelier than on Ambush. We went about 60 to 80 meters from the bosom of the company's perimeter. It was so dark! We set up our position as best we could and settled in for the evening. It was scary, so scary that we even overlooked the fact that we were "BAIT"! Every noise, a rustling of the underbrush, an animal noise, almost anything, sounded like a regiment of the enemy breathing down our necks. We were the ones on watch and the others were sleeping, if they could sleep. It was dark, scary and lonely, and anyone who says they weren't scared is either a fool or a liar, especially their first time. I am not a fool or a liar, I was scared! Morning couldn't come quick enough, and dawn was a reason to celebrate. We were still alive! When we got the call, picked up our gear and policed the area. We couldn't run into the perimeter, because we would startle someone on watch and reap the bitter consequences. We casually walked back in, one more unpleasant thing to get used to.

---

This might sound crazy, but by this time I felt like I was never going to get out of this bad dream. To think of it, one day in combat seems like weeks. I felt like half of my life had been spent in Vietnam. I had just been out in the field from October 22 to November 11, 1966, which amounts to 19 days in the field without much of a break. Time is a funny thing. When it could be your end, it seems very precious, but when the pressure is off, its importance diminishes. Human beings are sure funny, with me being a chief clown! We managed to struggle on day after day, without the full weight of the possibilities speaking to our minds. The subconscious mind files it away for a later day, but there it is! To live in spite of apparent danger is the trick we play on ourselves, because the trauma is just waiting to express itself. Sometimes it appears in ugly ways.

---

Breakfast was a welcome sight (I can't believe I said that), and we ate like hungry wolves! We had no choice but to embrace another day in the Republic of South Vietnam.

November 11, 1966 Company A found a small Viet Cong base camp at XT269753 loaded with supplies, weapons and 150 gallons of acid-like fluid buried in the ground. Three Bobcats were wounded by the acid. The VC base camp was destroyed at 1:59pm. B Company was following A Company to explore some trails leading north, while at XT274729 at 10:06am we found 2 live pigs, a hut, and several signs of recent activity. There were two other trails found so B Company established Blocking Positions with two platoons in conjunction with C Company's operation on the west. The Blocking Positions had negative results and at 4:30pm the companies two

Platoons departed and returned to the Battalion field base camp. (See Map B #4 Page 315)

A large Viet Cong Complex was around this Hooch in the center.

Early that evening we were in an area that was thick with clumps of bushes. The day had ended sooner than usual and we actually had some time to relax and reflect. Our Armored Personnel Carriers were circled in the traditional pioneer defensive position as in the early western United States expansion of the 1800's.

I had some "comic book" I was reading. Actually it was a dirty comic book written in an Asian style. It was about sex in the most crude form and subject matter, but it was entertaining. I got bored reading the book and just decided to relax.

We had hot chow for supper, so when we got the call we sent the usual 50% of our men from the perimeter to chow. The other 50% continued to watch at the perimeter in case the Viet Cong decided to attack. What did we have to eat? Who can remember?
Who cared? It was hot chow we didn't have to cook ourselves.

## The Letter

This is an unforgettable memory. Mail call was a favorite event for all combat and non-combat veterans. Out of the smelly cruel jungle, with the night (the loneliness time) knocking at the door, a letter from home was like a little bit of *HEAVEN!* A package from home was *HEAVEN!* We didn't always get mail.

That night I received a letter from home. It was from my sister Joyce! It's funny when you get a letter. You first look at the envelope. Mesmerized, you continue to look at it in a brief trance-like stare. Once the brief moment is gone, you tear at it in a hurry. I don't have the letter now. It's gone to where all letters go, but its memory still lingers.

> Dear Rich,
> I have some bad news to report. Our father died on October 25, 1966 from cancer. We tried to locate you through the Red Cross. The Army said they couldn't find where you were, etc., etc., etc.

Well, that wasn't exactly what I had anticipated, and I was in extreme shock. I can't tell you how I felt. The words escape me. I was devastated. I didn't know how sick he was or I probably could have delayed my coming to Vietnam. I have felt guilty all my adult life because I couldn't be there to say good bye when my Father died and to have missed his funeral.

As I am typing this into my computer, the tears are dropping from my eyes and onto the desk below. It's so hard to find the words to reflect my true feelings.

I showed the letter to Butch Petit so they wouldn't think I'd cracked up. He read it and said, "You're going home." He took the letter on up the line and then came back. He told me to pack and be ready to leave. I don't remember when, but I was getting out of there and back to the "World"! This was my first month in Vietnam but not my last. I turned in my M-79 and waited, but sure felt naked without it.

## November 1966

Following is a record of my unit's experiences in the field and my experiences during my bereavement leave in the USA. Note the difference between Vietnam and the United States is one day. The daily activity noted with NAM indicates the activity in Vietnam; it is followed by my daily activity in the United States as noted by USA. Sometimes the activities are happening at the same time, but usually it is dark in Vietnam in the early morning, it is light in the United States and it is mid-afternoon. My main purpose is for you the reader to grasp the contrast of my life in the States and what I was experiencing in Vietnam.

```
NAM-November 12, 1966 a Saturday I said good-bye
and good luck to the guys as B Company left
Battalion base at 6:00am on Search and Destroy
operations.
```

I stayed behind waiting for a helicopter back to Cu Chi. I was taking very little with me, some Army fatigues and personal gear. I would probably not use any of these things again.

I was still in shock about losing my father. I had missed the funeral, but I was still going home. When I was 12, my mom passed away, and now at 19 my dad was gone. Now I was really on my own.

While waiting for that chopper I was churning over and over in my mind how strange life can be. Some of us young people were allowed to graduate high school and go on to college or maybe get a job, learning how to grow up while being within the protected emotional bosom of their family. When you think of my comrades in Vietnam, adulthood was thrust upon us. My conscious mind was numb and my subconscious mind had these and many other things flip flopping around.

The helicopter came in quickly, someone said goodbye, good luck. I ran to the door and climbed in. The pilot got out of there a lot quicker than he came in. I arrived at Cu Chi at the helipad at the southeast part of the Cu Chi base camp. I had about a 5 city blocks walk back to B Company, but to my surprise someone knew I was coming and they had a jeep to take me to B Company. I went to the third squad hooch to get my stuff, which wasn't much.

I had some civilian clothes that I packed in a bag, and a dress uniform to wear home. I actually had time to take a shower. That shower was an exhilarating experience and I felt like a human being as I got dressed. By the time I got to the hooch, and was alone and sat down, it hit me what had happened and I had a good cry. Tough men aren't supposed to cry, are they?

Before I left, I was processed out. There was a wait because my flight wasn't until later. They came for me at the hooch and then drove me to the helipad, and then I did what all-good little GI's did, I waited. The helicopter finally came. I got on, and took off for the airport. I arrived at around 1:00pm and continued to wait for my flight that would take me back home to grieve with my family.

```
NAM-November 12, 1966 B Company left to conduct a
Reconnaissance in Force in the area of XT279790.
Heavy footprints were found on an East-to-West
trail around XT265784. A North-to-South trail,
with heavy grass beaten down, was found XT257784,
which indicated a probable force had been there,
or supply activity. A Viet Cong base camp, which
could accommodate several Viet Cong, was found 15
minutes later at XT253782. A search of the area
revealed nothing of importance. However, the camp-
site had been used in the last 3 or 4 days. The
company then found and destroyed seven two man
shelters around 12:02pm. About 1:00pm further down
the trail found and destroyed 10 foxholes. 1 CBU
bomblet was destroyed at 2:20pm. B Company then
departed the area and closed base at 2:35pm.
```

(Hey, they were done with their mission before I had taken off!)
I waited almost two hours before being able to board the plane; it was 3:15pm when I was able to get settled in my seat. Tan Son Nhut was the world's busiest airport in the world at this time. The plane was a welcome piece of civilization and pretty comfortable. As I sat there waiting for the plane to take off, I thought to myself whether I was a "chicken shit" for deserting the rest of the guys.
On one hand I was glad to be leaving Vietnam, but was feeling guilty for leaving my unit. In case you haven't figured this out yet,

## November 1966

we GI's can collect and store more guilt than anyone.

The plane finally started to move at 4:00pm. The plane began to taxi, moved into position on the runway, and then whoosh! We were going lickety-split down the runway and lifted off. Everyone on board yelled out "Hurrah"! I was "Leaving on a jet plane" to quote a song, and "Don't know when I'll be back again"!

NAM-November 13, 1966 Companies A & B exploited a B52 airstrike at 8:20am. Company A had finished by 1:30pm and returned to base at 3:20pm received automatic weapons fire at XT230772, fire was returned with negative results. At 3:27pm one Armored Personnel Carrier hit a mine at XT239773, it received extensive damage and four Bobcats received minor wounds. The vehicle was towed away. B Company found ox cart tracks and two sets of fresh foot prints made since the rain the evening of the 12th. Upon reaching a road block they received a blast from a Claymore mine, no damages but one minor injury. Artillery and air strikes were placed on the area. The Company left the area in route to base at XT175764 a track hit a mine no casualties sustained. Air strikes were called and destroyed 15 houses with 15 more by B Company. The enemy way station was destroyed, Company then returned to base. C Company was base security.

USA-The flight was long, about 32 hours. I only knew that I was going home. We stopped in Alaska. It was cold in November and I had become used to hotter weather. I was wearing a short-sleeve khaki uniform shirt. The walk from the plane to the terminal was quite exhilarating! We took off after refueling, heading toward San Francisco. We landed at 7:00pm on Saturday November 12, 1966.

(Our Freedom is precious and no one knows that better than a Combat Veteran. Thank you if you are a veteran reading this.)

I called my brother Guy around 7:30pm while I was waiting for my luggage. Since my brother had moved to Napa, he was the lucky one to pick me up. The trip from San Francisco to Napa took about an hour and 20 minutes, more waiting to see my family. It seemed to me that I'd been waiting all my life. Why wait, go get it!

My brother was glad to see me, and I to see him. We left the airport for Napa. We talked very little, because I had learned to be pretty quiet and closed-mouth. I just couldn't tell him what was really happening because I didn't want any of my family to know what I had experienced. I had no concrete reason to stay in the States, so after my leave I was probably to return to Vietnam. If I told them too much, they would have been scared to death! We arrived in Napa about 11:30pm on Saturday November 12, 1966.
I remember waking up around 11:00am the next morning a sunny Sunday. I was safe and sound and living in the lap of luxury compared to the day before!

NAM-It was 1:00am in the morning in Vietnam, Monday, November 14, 1966. The morning in the field began at 6:30am for B Company. At 8:28am B Company made a search of the area north of the Battalion Base Camp at XT265810, XT266815 and XT273817. They found and destroyed in the area of XT270817 at 10:35am, 1900 pounds of bagged rice. At 12:01pm a Viet Cong base, which was designed for three hundred soldiers, was found at XT261809. The camp was completely ringed with foxholes and early warning positions on a trail leading into the area. The base camp appeared to have been used a week earlier. A small way station of thirty Viet Cong capacity was found at 3:00pm at XT278828. There were 5 foxholes at this camp. One platoon was left behind to provide additional security until the re-supply was complete.

USA-It was Sunday November 13 in Napa, California. That morning I woke up about 11:00am. I decided I needed a shower, ah, what luxury. When I went to get dressed then I opened my small bag to get some clothes out, it hit me. Whew! The smell of Vietnam had permeated my clothes after only one month. I felt I was back in "Nam". This is a true reminder of the signature odor that we breathed daily in Vietnam. The following will amaze you. We had to wash those clothes three times in hot water and still couldn't get the smell out all of them, and we had to toss out about half of the clothes!

I am sitting here writing and feeling mortified to think that maybe it got into my skin so bad that I, too, smelled and could have been causing nasal nausea. Now that's powerful! I spent the afternoon relaxing with my brother and watching a football game on TV. Later that day I was enjoying a great home cooked meal and visiting with friends and family. I went to bed around midnight. I was safe and comfortable, but my mind was comparing my current living conditions with what I imagined my company was doing back in Vietnam. We have no idea how great our country is!!!

NAM-November 15, 1966 was a Tuesday morning in Vietnam. Around 6:00am B Company conducted a Reconnaissance in Force of objective 1 at XT2786 that is southwest of Katum. They secured a Landing Zone for an Artillery Battery to complete the establishment of Fire Support Base #2 without incident. A Company conducted a Reconnaissance in force of objective 2, XT2585 with negative results-closed new Battalion base at 2:16pm. C Company displaced and moved to new Battalion base, in route five tracks were mired and remained at XT266852 the evening without incident.

USA-While the above was occurring in Vietnam, it was Monday, November 14, 1966. I was with my brother. He had to go to work that morning, and I was able to relax and goof off. It's strange and unfortunate how quickly someone can forget where he was 5 days earlier. Not that I didn't think about Nam, but it started to become a bad dream. I was a boy from Chicago and November wasn't a nice month there. It usually starts to get cold and dreary with bare trees everywhere, a stark comparison to Napa in warm and sunny California.

NAM-November 16, 1966 a Wednesday and as usual the

day began around 6:00am. The Battalion conducted Search and Destroy operations in Zone. Each company was conducting a different section around the area of the Battalion Base Camp. There were basically no incidents except the Recon Platoon encountered two Viet Cong dressed in black uniforms and engaged. The VC escaped the east.

USA-It was Tuesday November 15th. Part of the day I spent asleep and then I spent the rest of day with my brother. We had lunch at a fast food stand, and then took a pleasant drive up the Napa valley. The hills were green and golden with rows and rows of grape vines surrounding us on both sides of the road. Throughout the valley were hills, many with houses on the tops. What a view. I didn't know it, but my brother was planting a seed in my mind. This was quite a contrast with life in Nam!

NAM-November 17, 1966 was a Thursday morning in Vietnam. The Battalion conducted Patrols in Zone. Company A dispatched elements to the south, south-west with negative results. C Company conducted Patrols in Zone at 11:45am destroyed 29 positions with aiming stakes for sectors of fire XT285841. Recon Platoon discovered and destroyed 3 huts, 3 bunkers, 1 khaki uniform, 1 large Viet Cong class room and several documents. The platoon on return was mortared resulting in four Wounded-in-Action and closed at 11:24am. The Battalion had three Ambushes and six Listening Posts that evening. No enemy contact was made throughout the night.

USA-November 16, 1966 Wednesday was a quiet day and calm. My day in Napa was fairly uneventful as with my friends in B Company. I bought some civilian clothes, as my wardrobe lacked substance. I wish all of my days were as slow and un-eventful, especially back in the battalion. Our lives were so much more peaceful living in safety of our country that we forget what's taking place in other lands. What a precious gift.

NAM-November 18, 1966 was a Friday in Vietnam. B &

C Companies departed at 7:00am. At 9:10am Company C located a VC base camp at XT286896 consisting of a mess hall for 40, 2 showers, 300 meters of wire for electrical, 6 bicycles, documents, a radio station, hospital, a political training center, and several outposts with telephones. B Company while in route engaged two of the enemy at XT312908 around 9:56am. In the firefight, one Viet Cong was killed, by body count. A search of the area disclosed a command-detonated Claymore, 2 fresh dug firing positions, 1 gas mask, a first aid pack, and one dozen dry cell 1.5-volt batteries. The Cambodian Battery Company made the batteries. C Company at 11:06am located another VC base camp XT283895 with a 40 capacity mess hall, 1 large class room, 2 showers, and 6 buildings. C Company spent the night at XT278912.

(The Viet Cong used batteries to detonate mines see page 198)

USA-When the Battalion left base at 7:00am it was Thursday November 17 4:00pm in California. While the Battalion was still sleeping, I was on Highway 50 driving to beautiful Lake Tahoe in the High Sierra Mountains. We stopped at Echo Lake around 2:30pm. We arrived at Lake Tahoe around 6:00pm and had dinner and saw a show at Harvey's. Not surprisingly 40 years later, I do not remember what we saw. At about the same time, Company B was engaged with the Viet Cong many time zones away.

NAM-November 19, 1966 was a Saturday. Company B departed at 12:30pm and moved to objective Jack at XT270950. They found a Viet Cong base camp at 1:25pm. They found and destroyed 4 huts, 7 bunkers, 15 foxholes, some miscellaneous clothing, and 1 500-pound bomb. The company closed at the battalion base camp at 4:00pm.

(I must note that the true danger in the jungle existed when things became monotonous. You'd tend to relax and then pop! You'd fall into a trap of some kind!)

There were 7 bunkers like this around the Viet Cong base camp

USA –November 18, 1966 I was driving around beautiful Lake Tahoe. We drove through Tahoe City on the north side of the lake and made our way to the city of Truckee. We stopped in this small quaint mountain town for lunch. The battalion would have been getting up about now. From Truckee we took Highway 80 down the mountain through Sacramento and back to Napa. We arrived there about 6:00pm; it was a long day of travel, but a short day in Vietnam.

I hope you've gotten the idea of how normal the activities were here in the good old USA, compared to what we faced on a daily basis in the jungles of Vietnam. Even for me who had been in the states less than one week. I had immersed myself into my surroundings and removed myself from the daily unpleasantness in Vietnam. I felt a little ashamed of myself; I guess I am just human.

NAM-I want to share what Company B endured the end of Operation Attleboro. November 20, 1966 in South Vietnam there was no such thing as "Sunday Chicken Dinner". It was just another day. The Battalion Reconnaissance in Force continued at 7:45am on to

Fire Support Base #3 at XT336924. By 2:05pm, all elements had closed into the new base area without incident. Now they paid for getting into a new base camp by running three Ambushes and Listening Posts during the evening. B Company provided one Ambush, Company A provided the second and Company C provided the third that night. No contact with the Viet Cong was made and all Ambush details returned to camp at 6:00am.

NAM-November 21, 1966 a Monday Company B remained at Battalion base camp to secure a Landing Zone for the airlifting of an Artillery Battery into the base camp. Company A found a foot bridge and a docking site that would handle 10 sampans at a time. At XT329919 found a Viet Cong base camp and destroyed it. One Track was hit with an RPG2 Russian Rocket resulting in two Wounded-in-Action who were dusted off. C Company had found and destroyed a VC base with a bunker and tunnel complex accompanying 400 to 500 Viet Cong. The area included 500 lbs rice, 100 lbs peas, 100 lbs salt and documents. At 4:44pm they received small arms fire at XT348948. Fire returned produced negative results the company returned to base. An ambush at 9:40pm received three rounds small arms fire, a Weapons Platoon reciprocated with an 81mm mortar barrage producing a secondary explosion at the Viet Cong position.

NAM-November 22, 1966 a Tuesday B Company departed at 8:00am to conduct a local Patrol in Zone. A platoon located at XT346922 received small arms fire from the west at 8:55am. A check after return of fire showed no results. Three huts were destroyed at 9:20am at XT348925. They found a dock site with heavy Ox cart tracks, indicating loading and unloading activities. At 12:26pm the company found miscellaneous documents in a hut at T347918.

The company then returned to the Battalion Base.

NAM-November 23, 1966 a Wednesday, B Company departed at 8:25am, but due to mechanical break downs and problems encountered navigating the various crossing sites, B Company didn't arrive back at Battalion Base until 8:25pm that night.

I'll just bet rain had something to do with the long day.

NAM-November 24, 1966 a Thursday was the last Thursday of the month. Traditionally and through Presidential proclamation this was set aside as a day of Thanksgiving. Throughout the day Company's A and B remained in base and out-posted the area. Company C departed at 7:00am to establish a Fire Support base at XT185765. At 8:12am one track hit an anti-tank mine at XT188768 with minor damage. At 8:22am hit a mine at 308855 with heavy damage and five Bobcats were Wounded-in-Action & dusted off. Company C secured & closed a base at 9:25am.

Thankfully it was a quiet day for all but C Company.

As the evening came, you could smell food being prepared. The Battalion was going to have a hot meal prepared by the cooks. They were to feast on roasted turkey, mashed potatoes, yams, and cranberry sauce, all the traditional trimmings. Before supper-time came, it was raining a little, and before it was time to eat it was raining elephants and hippopotamuses. The boys went down the chow line getting their plates filled with food and water at the same time. By the time they got their food, the mashed potatoes were floating in a sea of rainwater.

Those types of experiences at holiday time were devastating to some GI's and just a disappointment to others. While the United States Army did its best to help them celebrate the holiday the one factor they couldn't control was the weather. It was a good idea for the soldiers have a great sense of humor and take some things in their stride!

## Happy Thanksgiving?

Yesterday was Thanksgiving. At least it stopped raining.

NAM-November 25, 1966 a Friday the Battalion conducted a Reconnaissance in Force to XT147685, the new base camp. (See Map B # 5 Page 315.) B Company departed at 7:55am as lead element of the Battalion and at 9:52am, One Armored Personnel Carrier hit an anti-track mine at OT234771. Extensive damage was done to the vehicle and three were Wounded-in-Action and evacuated. B Company returned to base minus three Armored Personnel Carriers that were mired in mud just outside the perimeter. Operation Attleboro had ended.

USA-Back in the United States it was Thursday November 24, 1966 and I was at my brother's house in sunny Napa. It was 4:55pm and we were sitting down for Thanksgiving dinner. We were inside and the only water was in the glasses on the table along with all the traditional goodies that go along with the holiday. Everyone was thankful, especially me for being alive! The importance of food in our daily living cannot be denied; it seems like just about everything revolves around food.

NAM-November 26, 1966 thru November 30, 1966 the Battalion as usual was not allowed to leave the field for Cu Chi base camp. It was being trained in Extraction Techniques by performing exercises in an area east of Trai Bi. At that time the battalion had been out in the field 35 days straight without rest. B Company recovered an Armored Personnel Carriers that had been stuck in the mud the day before. Then the whole company headed for the Trai Bi area to begin the extraction training.

USA-It was Friday November 25$^{th}$ on the West Coast and I was enjoying my leave. There wasn't anything-special going on, unless you count being safe and alive in the USA!

NAM-November 27, 1966 a Sunday the Battalion was having training in extraction.

(That wasn't learning to pull teeth. It was techniques in rescue.)

USA-In California it was the Saturday the 26$^{th}$ of November and I spent the morning going to church with my brother and his family. We had a great dinner after church.

NAM-November 28, 1966, a Monday, the Battalion conducted Extraction Techniques.

(I am not sure exactly what they were learning.)

USA-At the same time it was Sunday the 27$^{th}$ in California, and I was getting ready to fly to Chicago for the second part of my family -get-together. I hated to leave California because it was nice and sunny and comfortable, but the rest of my family was patiently waiting for my return. I boarded a plane for Chicago. The flight cost me $55.00 one-way! The weather in Chicago was getting cold, windy and ready to snow, but my two sisters, two brothers, grandmother, aunts and uncle were now expecting me. I really wanted to see them and my friends. When I arrived at O'Hare Airport it was evening and it was cold and windy. The weather didn't discourage me from having a great time visiting them!

## November 1966

NAM-November 29, 1966 a Monday the training continued.

I hope all that effort was worth the boys not having a break from the field. I didn't know what was going on in Nam when I was back in "The World". I just found out this year from the After-Action-Reports and thought it would be an interesting comparison of the two life styles.

USA-Chicago, Monday November 28, 1966 I was visiting my family and having a great time, but feeling a bit guilty and thought and prayed a lot about the guys in my unit. There is nothing more precious than family and it's just too bad that it takes us too long in life to realize it, until something shows you the value! The support from my family with letters and care packages was an expression of a deep and rich love for me. I would like to take this opportunity to thank my family for all their love and support in my life, during those especially difficult years.

NAM-November 30, 1966 a Wednesday and the Battalion was wrapping up the extraction training and preparing not to go home to Cu Chi, but preparing for another operation. The unit was to remain out in the field to begin another operation without a break.

USA-The winter of November 29, a Tuesday in Chicago, was a cold day, but I was warm inside with my family. The days can be dreary and it doesn't matter if you're safe and secure, which was never the case when I was in Vietnam.

NAM-the troops in Vietnam were already into December 1, 1966.

USA-The month ended on Wednesday the 30th in Chicago, but in Vietnam a new month had begun and I was nearing the last days of my respite. Each day was a gift that nothing could destroy, not even death, in the near future. I judge myself fortunate to have had them. I hoped that the days were going well for the guys in my unit and the Viet Cong were hibernating or shooting off the mark!

\* \* \* \* \*

The number of Wounded-in-Action this month was sixty-nine men with only twenty-nine returning back to action.

The field operations for November claimed five Bobcat lives. They were:

    Riccardo B Dickerson    Milburn H. Starnes

    Dock J. Pinion    Terry Lee Walls

    Fernando Luis Torres

Hopefully their sacrifices will be recognized by the nation that sent them in the cause of Freedom.

# December 1966

December 1, 1966 the 2nd Brigade began an operation in the Hau Nghia province to interdict the Viet Cong harvest, movement, and storage of rice near the Ho Bo and Boi Loi area complex.

Rice Paddies

This mission was to locate and destroy Viet Cong forces, base camps and supplies. The Viet Cong like to eat just like GI's, so they weren't going to give in to our wishes without a hell of a fight.
I have found no further information other than this operation continued through to the end of the 6th of December 1966.

Remember that Vietnam is one day ahead of the United States. My activities while on leave are designated as USA.

USA-From December 1st-6<sup>th</sup> most of my time in Chicago since the end of November 1966 is a mystery. The cold weather was of no consequence compared with the joy I felt being with my family. I hated to leave because I knew what awaited me in Vietnam. I didn't dare tell them what things I had seen, felt and experienced, or else they would have probably locked me in the basement! The things I did escape my memory and remain a cloud in my memory, which is a pain to someone who has remembered so many specific incidents. I visited with my friends from the neighborhood where I grew up before moving to Elk Grove Village, Illinois.

I do remember a young lady that I had met, but I don't remember her name or how we met. She did live across from Amundsen High School on Foster and Damen Avenues in Chicago. I really appreciated her writing me, and if I had the letters she wrote then I would mention her name.

```
NAM-December 7, 1966 the Battalion moved from the
location in Hau Nghia to various locations in the
Ho Bo the Mech executed a ground link up with the
2/27th Infantry at the Forward base north of Trang
Bang XT48427, Recon Platoon had two Armored
Personnel Carriers hit anti track mines XT509240
four Bobcats being wounded.

NAM-December 8, 1966 the Battalion was conducting
a Reconnaissance-in-Force. B Company, 1st Platoon
was deployed to assist the 2/27th Wolfhounds who
had engaged the enemy and had three Killed-in-
Action. B Company sustained two Wounded-in-Action.
```

The squad came to an island of dense foliage. Butch then moved by a huge tree and told Roy Love to deploy his fire team to the right of the track. They moved into position then the enemy fired at them. Tim Fyle, new in the field, and on his right Sullivan also new was hit with two rounds in the neck. Butch and Roy charged into the island laying in a burst of fire, Roy killed two Viet Cong and

Butch killed one. They dragged the bodies out. Butch looked down at Thomas Sullivan and saw that he had two large holes you could see through, and he was losing a lot of blood. Doc Ochoa was working on him. That was the last time they saw him, he was dusted off with the wounded Wolfhounds.

Thomas Michael Sullivan WIA 12/8/1966 Died 03/31/1967

NAM-December 9, 1966 units from 1/5th Mech conducted a Reconnaissance in Force from XT601307 toXT53014, and secured a Landing Zone for the 1/27th Infantry. A firefight took place XT526314 and shortly after an Armored Personnel Carrier from Company A detonated a mine resulting in one Bobcat being killed and three more wounded.

NAM-December 10, 1966 Company A secured a Landing Zone for the 1/27th Infantry and then joined the rest of the Battalion in conducting Search and

Destroy operations. During the day three Armored Personnel Carriers detonated mines resulting in seven Wounded-in-Action.

NAM-December 11, 1966 Company A located 3 underground fortifications containing numerous electrical items and medicines.

(I guess Charlie's going to have to live with that Asthma after all.)

USA-I left Chicago on December 10th 1966, because I had no viable reason to avoid a trip back to the land of enchantment, "Vietnam". So off I went for Oakland, California at around 4:00pm. The flight was about 5 hours, so I landed around 7:00pm. My poor brother had to pick me up, and by the time I got my luggage and we drove to Napa it was about 9:00pm. We got to bed late. I was going to spend as much time as possible the next day with my brother up to the moment I had to report to the Army in Oakland.

NAM-December 12, 1966 all three companies conducted Search and Destroy operations and Recon Platoon secured a river crossing at XT525345. This day there was no enemy contact.

USA-It was December 11, 1966 and I was going to spend my last day in the USA with my brother Guy. The day was very precious to me because it might be the last time any of my family would see me. They weren't too happy, but I had to leave. I wasn't exactly scared. I was more dreading the idea of it. We departed Napa for Oakland Army Terminal. When I arrived there it was early afternoon. When I got there they wanted to put me on Kitchen Police and wash dishes. I told the sergeant that when all these combat virgins had done Kitchen Police I would do it, but not until then! Wow, that was a big step for me, but I didn't care. He decided to pick on some other poor slob. I had to stay there until the next day's flight, so I took a rest.

NAM-December 13, 1966 Company A located 7 underground fortifications containing supplies and ammo. A Bobcat from Company B died from wounds he had received earlier when the Armored Personnel Carrier he was driving hit a mine.

The Bobcat that died was Specialist 4 Melvin L. Sherrell. He was from Portsmouth, Virginia, and he was a member of the 1st Platoon, 3rd Squad, "The Pretty Boy Squad" B Company. Earlier in the day the Armored Personnel Carrier, that he was driving hit an anti-tank mine. His legs were mangled and they weren't going to stay on because they were all torn up. The guys that got him out were the ones who carried him to the dust-off location. They said he was complaining that he couldn't feel his legs. When they lifted him up onto the chopper he looked down at his legs then passed on. He wanted and deserved to go back home to his family, but for some reason it was his time to depart. He had a choice. He could have run away to Canada, but he chose to serve his country. The hero is someone who pays a price for our Liberty.

Melvin Sherrell seen running the hole. Killed-in-Action 12/13/1966

USA-It was December 12, 1966. We left Oakland Army Terminal

at about 10:30am for Travis Air force Base. The ride on the bus took about 80 minutes, but it felt like forever. I felt even more like cattle going to the slaughter than I did in October on my first trip there. When we arrived at Travis there wasn't a brass band to send us off. We were processed and then waited to board the plane.

Walking up the stairs to the plane was like walking up the 13 stairs to the gallows! They used to say "Thirteen steps to a broken neck" when they were going to hang you. The number of steps to the gallows.

This flight was much better than the first time because it was a real jet airplane, not like the slow propjet in October. I don't remember the trip except that it took about 32 hours and I was really tired after the trip.

NAM-I arrived at around noon the 14$^{th}$ of December 1966 in Vietnam, when the plane finally landed on the runway: nobody cheered Hurrah!

I don't remember the details of getting back to Cu Chi, except that they dropped me off on the road east of B Company, right where the Shit House stood. I hoped it wasn't a bad omen! The first person I saw who happened to be back in base camp yelled to me something about missing some action the day before.

This day, 1/5$^{th}$ Mechanized Infantry had been conducting Search and Destroy operations in the Boi Loi Woods along the Saigon River in the day. No enemy contact reported.

NAM-December 15, 1966 the Battalion was conducting Search and Destroy operations in the Boi Loi Woods and no enemy contact was reported.

I was "Back Home in Cu Chi" and this day was sort of a free day. The Battalion was coming back soon, so they kept me in Cu Chi. Early that morning when the Post Exchange was open I went there to get some personal items. I ended up buying an oil paint artist's set and some canvases. I also remember the Post Exchange had snacks, so I know that I bought some junk food. I remember being hungry for peanut butter and jelly sandwiches. I couldn't find bread so I bought a can of corn tortillas. I returned to the company area and tried one of my PB and J tortillas. I liked it enough, but it was not the same as with real bread. I did start a drawing for a painting that day.

The "Goodie Store"

You are probably curious about how we paid for things at the Post Exchange, Barber Shop, Laundry or the most important place for Beer and Snacks, the Enlisted Men's Club.

We weren't slaves, although we felt like slaves at times, we did actually get paid. After all, this wasn't the US Continental Army under George Washington. Those boys had to fight harder to get paid than they had to fight the British Dragoons!

We didn't use US Dollars because of currency problems in a foreign country. We actually got paid with what was called an MPC, or Military Payment Certificate, once a month. The military didn't do anything fancy like automatic deposits into our checking accounts. Remember this was 1966 and 1967, you know the olden days. There are some examples of what the certificates looked like on the next page. My friend Keith Arnold, a US Marine Sergeant who served in Iraq, told me that when they got paid the money was transferred into their checking account and they used ATM

Visa cards to pay for things. I thought that was interesting. Tim Fyle e-mailed the copies of two MPC's to me, and they were in such great shape I wondered if he was thinking they might go back in style and he could use them at his current Post Exchange. I had kept a 50-cent certificate for almost 35 years!

Thanks, Tim, for those copies.

Military Payment Certificate, one dime

I don't remember getting paid but once or twice, but I doubted they paid us out in the jungle. I still wonder what I did with all that money I was paid.

Actually, all soldiers in Nam got combat pay, but those REMF's (Rear Echelon Mother Fuckers) usually worked one shift, whereas the real Combat Veterans worked two and three shifts every day in the jungle! I think we should bill the United States Government as a group for those two extra shifts. At 10% compound interest, that would amount to a tidy sum! What do you think?

> That reminds me. What happened to my pay while I was on bereavement leave for the month of November 1966? Where's my MONEY? How much was it anyway? This might sound funny to you but I do wonder....

*December 1966*

December 16, 1966 the Battalion conducted Search and Destroy operations in the Boi Lo Woods with no enemy contact.

I was in the base camp and had done a painting that afternoon. There were 2 or 3 others back at base camp, and I ran into my worst nightmare, the 1st Sergeant then... The reference to the "Bad Omen" leads us to my next story.

Shit Burner's Detail
I received the bad news from the first Sergeant that he needed me to perform an important mission. I never really got along with him, so I was suspicious. That bastard put me on shit-burner's detail with the help of two other grunts. This was an education in Hazardous Waste Material handling methods, U.S. Army style.

There are two subjects that one should not discuss in polite company, "bull", and (this story is full of it) "Shit" to be precise. This is not something that most people have a conversation about! Now let's be honest: aren't you curious about what the Army does with shit? Haven't you wondered what they do with all that waste? No, not government spending, but human waste products! What the Hell do they do with it, since we were not located anywhere that could accommodate the massive amounts of human waste collected.

You might think that I am crazy, and maybe I am, <u>butt</u> you are going to learn how it is handled; and then you can say, "I know SHIT"!

July 2006, while attending a Vietnam Veterans reunion of the 1st Battalion 5th Mechanized Infantry Survivors of the Battle for Cu Chi I was the honored recipient of the coveted "Annual Shit Burner's Award"! It gives me reason, if not the credentials, to talk on this subject un-professionally speaking!

Sometimes even after years of attendance at Army reunions, relatives sit in quiet contemplation wondering,

"Just what the Hell are they talking about?" I feel it is my duty to enlighten an ignorant world about this subject.

I WOULD LIKE EVERYONE TO KNOW THAT ONCE, ONLY ONCE, DID I PERFORM THE DUTIES OF SHIT BURNER FIRST CLASS!

In our country we are spoiled because we use facilities that are inside and sanitary. We've all seen old movies displaying the use of the old traditional method; polite people didn't talk about it then either! A little house out back of the main house hence, "Out House" The general dimensions could be about 6 feet wide by 4 feet deep and around 6 1/2 feet tall. Inside there is a platform (wooden top board with a round hole cut out of the top where you sit) about 3 feet high, at the back of the edifice, and about 2 feet deep-front to back.

The business end, so to speak! Oh yes, it has a front door usually with a crescent moon cut out of it somewhere near the top. This edifice sits atop a deep hole in the ground for the remains. When the hole gets full the house is moved to a new location. The old hole is covered up.

Does any of this ring a bell?

On that particular day, I was just in the wrong place at the wrong time. This was my day to learn about Burning Shit. If it sounds crude, you're right. TRY DOING IT!

And here's the rub, what do you do in an area that can be saturated with rain water that comes down in bucketsful at the drop of a hat and allows all that toxic waste ("Buried Treasure") to float to the surface and pollute the entire area? Not a sanitary proposition to say the least.

Well the U.S. Army Fecal Engineers (did they actually have such a unit?) arrived at a solution. Design a building with enough room for 5-Butt units on the top of the inside platform, and put a door on each side to enter. Also, design a collection receptacle by taking an empty 55 Gallon drum used for diesel fuel. Cut it 2 1/2 feet from the bottom and weld two u-shaped bar handles near the top for handling.

The outhouse needs to have a series of doors at the back near the bottom for loading and unloading the collection receptacles. Provide 5 of these receptacles per out house and there you have it! That solves the collection process. Now what? Since diesel fuel doesn't explode as gasoline, it's the perfect disposal tool.

The BM 5 Multifunctional Waste Collection and Disposal System was now ready for use!

For proper management, open the bottom back retention doors and insert the A-1 Collection Receptacle Unit, be very careful that the handle is exactly at the back for safer handling.

BM 5 Multifunctional Waste Collections and Disposal System

The company had been in the field for over a month and a half. So I couldn't understand why the latrines would need servicing. I am not sure if the drums were full or if the First Sergeant checked them, but I was in the wrong place at the wrong time, so I was it.

Ah, shit! Luckily I wasn't going to be alone. There would be two other unsuspecting slobs just as unlucky as me. No words can describe how base and degrading this job was; it was more made-to-order for GI's who had a knack for screwing up! Shit burning compared to what?

We had gone over the basic design of the BM 5, so disposal techniques were an important part of our education. We've already discussed the first stage in this process, loading the unit with 5 A-1 Collection Receptacle Units:

- \* Open the back bottom door
- \* Insert the A-1 Unit's handle facing outward
- \* Close the door and latch it
- \* Repeat process 4 more times

We were in the shit collection business!

The next area of concern was monitoring the collection process to make sure there was no overflow (extremely important). Who-the-Hell's job was it to monitor this function? I honestly don't know.

In most organizations shit runs downhill from the top. For us, the First Sergeant was at the top. After all he handled all the shit jobs from up above! (Just kidding, all you top sergeants get a sense of humor, please!)

Time for the disposal technicalities; when the A-1 Collection Receptacles were full, some poor unsuspecting slob, either through screwing up or being unlucky, was chosen. He then became "Fecal Orderly". The U.S. Army never assigned an MOS (Military Occupational Specialty) to shit- burning. If they assigned an MOS, then how would the Officers and the Top Non-Commissioned Officers go about meting out punishment?

The disposal process instructions were as follows:

- \* Drag water hose 15 feet from the BM 5
- \* Find a clothespin for your nose
- \* Open the back bottom door
- \* Grab the handle at the top of the A-1

* Carefully pull it out and drag it 15 feet away from the BM 5
* Repeat the process for the next 4 locations at the BM 5
* Space the individual A-1's apart for easy access
* Pour diesel fuel into the 5 A-1 Units, fill close to top
* Light a match, quickly drop into each A-1, turn body away, and don't look down
* Double-check that each one is burning. Be ready to hose down the BM 5
* Remember to stay up wind of the A-1 Units. Watch for wind shifts

You're a shit burner!

Aaaah, it is Shit-burning time in Cu Chi

Unfortunately our job was not quite done. Next we had to stand guard over the A-1 Units and the BM 5 until the burning stopped. By now huge volumes of black, billowing, acrid smoke were rising into the hot thick air sending out the signal. Aaaah, its shit burning time in Cu Chi!

Once you had been anywhere near where shit burning was taking place you never forgot the smell. Just imagine you are at a dairy farm at milking time, and a diesel truck is running as you breathe in a good whiff: you, too, can enjoy the experience! I wondered what it would be like if every company in the entire 25$^{th}$ Infantry division lit up all their A-1 Collection Receptacle Unit at the same time. It would be like the eruption of Mt. Saint Helens, only far more lethal! We should have spent the time and effort to learn how to capture that thick, black, smelly, billowing acrid smoke into a large holding tank. Then drive it to the large tunnel complexes, and with a giant powerful pump, secretly pump it into the tunnels. We could have taken the Viet Cong out for good!!!

Field Fecal Facts
Field techniques were quite different and much cruder. First, men have a much handier system for liquid waste elimination. Just unzip or un-button the storage unit, remove the tool, aim and shoot. A cardinal rule is not to aim or shoot near the sleeping quarters on the ground or you may get shot.

We made enough noise with the Armored Personnel Carriers, so we didn't worry about Charlie sniffing out where we stayed! There was also no concern for sanitary conditions. After all, sanitary conditions in the jungle didn't exist.

The second field technique was handled in its simplest and basic form. The most important factor was timing, because the whole company was not going to stop and wait for you. And if you messed up and fill your pants, the other guys would throw you out of the track! More simply put, we went when we had a chance.

The best times were in the morning before you left the base camp, when you stopped to eat, or at night when in the base perimeter. We could never wait until we were on an Ambush or Listening Post. But then again, we were probably scared shitless. It would be like a flashing light in a dark night! Whew!

The primary "Squat and Leave It" technique was as follows:

* Dig a small hole:
* Drop your pants
* Squat over the hole
* Take care of business as quick as possible
* Wipe

* Pull up your pants
* Throw dirt over the pile
* And leave it

There were some things to consider before you began the process in order to have a good experience. While squatting, it was very important to make sure that the liquid waste elimination tool was aimed in the proper direction, as a malfunction of it would cause your pants to get soaked. Your experience until it dried would be both embarrassing and uncomfortable!

Another good point is if you screwed up a lot and got punished with Shit-Burners Detail. Your first impulse would be to burn the shit. This was a negative. Burning would be bad from three standpoints. 1) It would use up fuel. 2) It would be cruel to the animals. 3) It would be a signal for the Viet Cong if they didn't already know where you were!

You needed to dig the hole a little deep and cover it over. You wouldn't want to step in someone else's pile, would you? This was especially important when staying at a base camp for more than one day.

There you have it. Now if most people were honest, they would admit to wondering about how this function was handled. We got enough of it during our tour of duty.

An interesting point about this subject is that current military methods of handling waste materials have changed. Recently I was talking to a young US Marine Sergeant, Keith Arnold, at my office. I was telling him about our crude methods. He was appalled. He said that they had porta-potties in Iraq! My, can you see how things have changed in war?

December 17, 1966 the Battalion was still conducting Search and Destroy missions in the Boi Loi Woods. Miscellaneous enemy supplies and other equipment were located in enemy fortifications and tunnels The items were destroyed or removed as appropriate.

It was probably B Company, because the words without the unit named usually indicated B Company. The battalion had completed its mission in the woods and would be back at Cu Chi the following morning. I had completed another one of my mystery paintings.

December 18, 1966 the 1/5$^{th}$ Mech conducted a convoy moving to Cu Chi base camp closing at 9:00am.

December 19$^{th}$ Company B provided security for villages north of Bao Trai in the area of XT560069 northwest of Cu Chi. This in response to recent threats made to the villagers.

This was my first day with B Company in the field since I returned from bereavement leave in November.

December 20, 1966 Company A established a company base at XT629198 near Bao Trai northwest of Cu Chi base camp. (The 5th Mech was the Division Reaction Force and was providing a presence around the base camp due to the Christmas show being given by Bob Hope.) B Company secured Battery A of the 1/8$^{th}$ Artillery at Duc Hanh and Company C prepared for Night Ambushes.

December 21, 1966 the 1/5$^{th}$ Mechanized conducted Company-sized Ambushes and Patrols. At 11:20am Company A received mortar and RPG2 Russian Rocket fire, resulting in ten Bobcats being wounded.
The artillery unit returned the fire with unknown results.

December 22, 1966 Company A conducted a Search and Destroy operation XT600197 to southeast toward Cu Chi. Company B established a company base north-of west Cu Chi at XT631206. Company C continued to provide security Northeast of Bao Trai at Duc Hanh at XT570070.

## December 1966

December 23, 1966 Company B conducted Search and Destroy operations around their forward base camp. Company C continued to provide security for the 1/8th Artillery unit.

December 24, 1966 Christmas Eve Company A and the Recon Platoon prepared for future operations sitting on their Butts at Cu Chi, waiting for the Bob Hope Christmas Show and Companies B and C were stuck doing Search and Destroy Operations!

December 25th 1966 Christmas day B and C Companies had finished breakfast, but were still out in the bush until a little later when we returned to Cu Chi around 10:00am in the morning.

We were looking forward to lunch. The reason will be explained a little later. This was Christmas and as luck would have it, actually it was by design of the Colonel of our Battalion; the 1st of the 5th Mech was responsible for the 25th Division's security. I don't know how it was determined who would go to the show or who would be on duty patrolling outside the base camp area. I was able to go, and I can't remember why.

I know for a fact that Butch Petit was one of the guys that went out that day so others could go to the show. That's leadership!

I had just returned to Vietnam about 10 days earlier from the "bosom of my family", a one month leave due to the passing of my father. It was Christmas, but peace on earth and goodwill were distant memories.

This country owes a huge debt of gratitude to the USO (United Service Organization), and especially to Bob Hope for the many, many years of service and joy he brought to all the GI's of many wars and during peace in foreign lands. Many times he was risking his own life, let alone the fact that he was not usually with his family for the holidays. It must be difficult to always be on your best behavior and still remain human, I am sure he must have slipped a time or two. I guess he was human after all.

There was excitement about lunch (okay, maybe not excitement) at B Company 1st, BN, 5th Mech Infantry, for we were to have a special guest that day. No, it was not Ann Margaret (drat!), but Phyllis Diller, Bob's partner in crime. She was to visit our mess hall today. What had she done wrong? Anyway, it must have been scary for her, but she lived up to her reputation, she was one crazy woman! Thanks, Phyllis, for the memories.

That afternoon on Christmas day was exciting for the GI's of the 25th Infantry Division. After all the years growing up watching Bob's holiday visits to all kinds of foreign lands visiting our troops, here I was experiencing it in person. It was a big deal after watching all those shows from years past for the benefit of troops. It was a thrill to be there. I only remember walking into the area where the show was to be held. Thousands of GI's were already there. I guess we were late. Then I heard the beeping of a jeep horn behind me. When I turned around to look, there was "Good Ole Bob Hope" in the front passenger seat not more than 5 feet away. Of course everyone was yelling "Hi Bob!" including me. I was close enough to catch his attention and to exchange greetings.

Phyllis Diller and Bob Hope
Picture taken at Cu Chi during the show

Out of all the shows and all the GI's that had attended, I wonder how many of them got to speak personally to Bob Hope, and I was one of them!!!!

## December 1966

The show pretty well followed its usual format with various entertainers. Bob's wife Delores accompanied him on the tour. That nutty and sometimes strange comedian Jonathan Winters, the lovely Ann Margaret, Miss America Anita Bryant, beautiful Joey Heatherton and last but not least, without her husband Fang, the incomparable Phyllis Diller! Somehow, when you see a show live it always comes across as something more special. I believe that Les Brown and His Band of Renown were there. There were also lots of music, comedy, singing, and dancing girls. Yes I know, the girls were especially well received by the audience. What can I say? Boys will be boys, especially under these circumstances! Christmas takes on a whole different meaning when you are far away from home and in harm's way. Home became a distant memory and very unreal.

Christmas that December 1966 was a brief memory and then it was back to business in Vietnam for the men in the field.

Oh, by the way, I'd like to tell you about my special all night date with Ann Margaret, but... (You will read about it in May 1967)

After the show it was mayhem getting out of the Lightening Bowl, now the Cu Chi Christmas Show is a memory. Un-believable another traffic jam in Vietnam.

While we were enjoying the show our buddies were on the outside of the base camp keeping the Viet Cong away from our guests. I can't switch with them now, but I wish they could have enjoyed the show.

```
December 26, 1966 the Battalion was right back out
in the thick of things. Companies A & C conducted
Search and Destroy operations northwest of Cu Chi
base camp near XT6319, while B Company and Recon
Platoon set up blocking positions near XT6220.
There was no enemy contact this day but extensive
enemy supplies and materials were destroyed.

December 27, 1966 the Battalion conducted Search
and Destroy operations in the same general areas
of the previous day.
```

December 28, 1966 the Battalion conducted search and destroy operations in the same area at 7:40am. A number of Viet Cong were engaged at XT627183. One Bobcat from Company A was Killed-in-Action and one was wounded-in-Action. A Bobcat from Company B died at the hospital from previous days wound.

December 29, 1966 the battalion conducted search and destroy operations. Company A established a forward base at XT630174 and all elements closed at Cu Chi base camp at 4:40pm.

After Midnight Mission
On December 29, 1966 we had spent the day getting ready for a future operation, we didn't know where, but we knew it would be soon. Since I got back from bereavement leave we'd been in and out of the field like Yo-Yo's! If it weren't for us being out in the field so much of the time, I would have been developing into a first class alcoholic. This night we were going to "party", come hell or high water! We had ample time to clean up and have a hot dinner.

We were not allowed to bring alcoholic beverages out in the field, but back at base camp it was a different matter. The Enlisted Men's Club sold ice-cold beer, just about as much as we could drink.

I usually had about 20 beers a night, and this night was no exception. It was as hot as hell and we had big thirsts, so we drank and we pee'd and we pee'd and we drank all night long until the club closed. The club had a juke box and played songs like "The Green Grass of Home", "California Dream 'in", and "Unchained Melody" to name a few. I don't know if the songs helped or made our circumstances seem more hopeless: anyway, the jukebox was always playing. Besides beer, hard liquor was available, not at the Enlisted Men's Club but in someone's hooch.

One of my favorite drinks was Rum and Coke. We had found a very interesting use for the U.S. Army canteen cup! It was a simple concoction of ½ Rum in the cup followed by ½ Coke, stirred not shaken, and gulp. The idea was drink, get drunk and pass out.

That way, you'd be able to sleep in spite of the heat and the dive-bombing mosquitoes!

There was mosquito netting, but they were quite adept at breaching those defenses, by slipping through the opening in the netting when you were just getting in and then lying low until you started to sleep. Then they would continually assault you! Critters always made our co-existence interesting, and there were all kinds of unknown and exotic insects to contend with in Vietnam.

B Company Mess Hall

Now, to continue to the story of our Midnight Mission!

The first day I arrived in Vietnam I thought that the U.S. Army was trying to starve me to death for about the first 15 hours. Like I said before, the army calls meals "mess", which means take first class ingredients, give them to the cooks and they make a mess out of it! Just kidding, I don't want to be looking over my shoulder the rest of my life for some half crazed cook trying to frag me!

I wouldn't want to be a cook in the Army for anything in this world; actually, I respect them. It took a lot of nerve for them to do what they did. Just imagine, trying to cook meals just like Mom for a hundred guys, the real "Mission Impossible"! Well, food was always an issue, right GUYS?

This one night, one of the few in base camp, we were HUNGRY, as usual, and unsatisfied. The all-night diner wasn't open. Come to think about it, I don't think there were any in Nam except maybe in the rear echelons or for officers. So after our usually voracious thirsts and constant imbibing alcohol, we were as HUNGRY as Bears! I can't or won't say or don't remember, yes, that's it, I don't remember, but weed (Mary Jane) could have been an additional catalyst for Giant HUNGER Pangs! I was just damn HUNGRY!

It was late (about 2:00am un-military time), and dinner had been almost 8 hours ago. Where, oh where, to get some FOOD?? The Post Exchange is it open? No, it's closed now. We were getting more desperate by the minute. WE NEED SOME FOOD, NOW!

Ah, the mess hall. Maybe, just maybe, they have some food. But this late? No way, no siree! We would have been happy to pay for the food, but at 2:00am, that was impossible. Pangs won over reason! We decided to go on a Search and Forage for Food Mission, as un-authorized and completely against military regulations as you can get.

Brave soldiers never shrink from any mission, so we employed all our energy and all our expertise into it all the same. I am the kind of person who, if ever I was to attempt something wrong and risky, I would get caught; end of story! This time I had expert and talented leadership in covert operations, so I thought. No, I didn't think, I just followed.

We assembled ourselves, all three of us, laid out our plan, synchronized our watches. We did have watches, didn't we?
We gathered our equipment, flashlights, one screwdriver, a pair of pliers and set out on our "Search and Forage for Food Mission".

We went out the back door of the hooch. That was the side that when you look out there, staring you in the face in the distance was Nui Ba Den the Black Virgin Mountain. We turned to the left and went beyond the B Company hooches, turned left and went until we were as far as the back side of the mess hall that faced A Company. We turned left again until we came to the back door of the mess hall.

## December 1966

We made a quick check for other personnel in the area and then entered the mess hall. High-level professional tactics were employed. We got in the mess hall undetected. It was my duty to be the lookout for officers. Ha! Ha! Ha! At that hour? Or Non-Commissioned Officers, which was a greater possibility, or anyone for that matter.

We were stealthy, or so we thought throughout the mission by not making a racket! The mess hall wasn't a solid building, so we had to be very careful and quiet. We were kind of laughing under our breath. We were being bad boys and we knew it, but it still was very exciting.

I had to keep them from making too much noise, as is the case a lot of times when someone is drunk or high from other stimuli. They don't have full control over their volume, or haven't you ever noticed? I was nervous as I had never gone to the edge of doing something really wrong (legally speaking). My experience of being in trouble was extremely limited. I had always been kind of a shady "Goodie Two Shoes" (I don't understand the full meaning of this term, but it fits).

My compadres had been working for about 10 to15 minutes on a refrigerator door lock but it seemed like 2 hours! I thought I had heard a noise, so I had to get them to stop and lay low until I could make sure. I didn't see anyone, but I wasn't taking any chances. It didn't seem that anyone was around, so they went back to work on the door, trying to open the lock to get at the food. We rationalized that it was food that was meant for us ultimately, so in that sense it belonged to us. We were just appropriating it early! Mind you, we were still drunk and could screw up this mission very easily except for our vast stealth, expertise, and self-preservation. Finally they hit pay dirt and the lock was sprung. It's a miracle that we didn't wake up the whole 25$^{th}$ Infantry Division. I can't remember what food we managed to get a hold of. I think it was cheese, lunch-meat, possibly bread, but a big score for hungry GI's! Who remembers what it was after forty years.

We weren't stupid enough to eat our ill-gotten gains in the mess hall, so we decided to leave the same way we got in. We went out the back door, turned right, went to the end of the mess hall, turned right and continued to the back of B Company's Hooches, turned right walked until we came to our home & entered through the back door. All this was done quickly, and quietly, in the most stealth manner. We were guilty of a crime, so we kept a low profile of activity.

The spoils were divided among the "Three Banditos", and we began to devour our ill-gotten food. We didn't care about anything at this point. We had FOOD! Needless to say there wasn't one crumb of evidence on the floor, just in our bellies. I don't remember if anyone else was awake in our hooch at this point. We were, and that's all that mattered. To be sure, we needed to wash down the food, and what a better way than with the alcohol drinks of our choice. Bellies full of food, more booze and Morpheus beckoning us, we gradually one by one drifted off to sleep....Happy Dreams.

On the morning of December 30, 1966 we were still sleeping off the evening's mission. When we finally got to bed we were still under the impression that we would have the next day off too, and they'd let us sleep in. We were back home in Cu Chi, so we thought that the "Brass" would take a little pity on us (and I mean a little). However, they got us up just after the roosters!

I was sawing wood like a lumberjack with a buzz saw when we were rudely interrupted. Someone yelled formation and we stirred and some got up, but not me. I just rolled over and dozed off again. I didn't care! Then the First Sergeant yelled loudly "Antinnti, get your lazy ass out of bed!"

Then the realization hit me. Oh shit! I'm late for formation! I jumped out of bed, winced and held my head. It felt the size of a beach ball. I stumbled around and found some clothes and fumbled with my shirt and tried to get presentable. I ran like someone was burning my butt with a torch running behind me! I must have looked like hell, because the First Sergeant ripped me a new asshole and he didn't like my shave. What shave? I hadn't gotten that far.

Was it worth it all? Yes, it kind of made up for my first day when the US Army tried to starve me all day. The events in the wee hours of the morning were not necessarily justifiable, they were retribution! Really, to be honest, it was an unforgivable action

*December 1966*

brought on by Maddening Hunger Pangs and Alcoholic Stupidity. I claim temporary insanity.

In any case, we were in formation, and then the First Sergeant announced that a person or persons unknown had broken into the mess hall and had stolen some food. Gasp! They wanted any information as to who might be the perpetrators and were looking to prosecute! Everyone kind of looked around at each other like "Can you believe that, who would do such a dastardly act?" We did a great job of acting, as no one suspected us, I think.

They did some hard looking at everyone trying to figure out if any of us angels could have done that dastardly deed. They probably had an idea, but no proof, so the issue gradually faded away. I bet it pissed them off, though. I just bet there's some squirrelly little bean counter that's hot on the trail after forty years and closing in on his guilty prey, as you read this. To my accomplices, I'll never divulge who you were, even under torture!

Besides, I think the statute of limitations applies, but I'll check with my attorney before this goes into print. Right, Butch?

Today this is a funny, but sad story, because we would normally never consider such actions had we not been where we were and when. Jail compared to what? We were expendable and we knew it, so what the hell! I would regret this incident, but in the Grand Scheme of Life it wasn't as big a deal as it seemed. When you consider how we were treated in our daily grind in the field. It all evens out in our rationalization. When we went on those long operations they ran us ragged to hell and back!

Not long after our midnight mission, the U.S. Army got smart and placed a guard on duty at our battalion mess halls.

```
December 30, 1966 Company B established a Forward
Base  Camp  at  XT630163.The  remainder  of  the
Battalion conducted maintenance at Cu Chi.
```

(I can't help wondering if the midnight raid had something to do with B Company going out a day early.)

December 31, 1966 New Years Eve, Company B was still out in the field and conducted daylight Ambush Patrols. Three Viet Cong fired on a Company C patrol at 4:00pm. There were no casualties.

Isn't this a great way to spend New Year's Eve? No girls and no booze, just the Viet Cong.

Boy, this army stuff sucks!

*   *   *   *   *

There were twenty-nine men Wounded-in-Action this month.

During the month of December 1966, eight good men from the 1st Battalion 5th Mechanized Infantry 2nd Brigade gave their all so we might live secure and plentiful lives in the United States of America and they are:

| | |
|---|---|
| Melvin L. Sherrell | Dennis F. Delasandro |
| William L. Mc Laughlin | Joe Munoz |
| John William Earnesty | Larry Moss |
| Luis Alvarez-Delgado. | John Curtis Williams |

# January 1967

January 1967 started out like any New Year. No wait, we were in Nam. Happy New Year! What's so happy about it?

The 1$^{st}$ of the 5$^{th}$ (Mech) Infantry spent New Year's Day not in front of the TV watching college football bowl games, but out in the Fil Hol and Ho Bo Woods. We had no contact with "Charlie" which made it a great day! We discovered some of Charlie's digs, supplies, and tunnels. You know the normal things everyone does for a gala holiday.

January 2, 1967 I celebrated my 20$^{th}$ birthday by going on a Search and Destroy operation starting at 6:00am. Happy Birthday to me! My birthday present was no enemy contact, no Ambush, and no Listening Post.

January 3, 1967 we spent the day on Search and Destroy patrols again in the area between the Fil Hol and Ho Bo Woods, without enemy contact.

January 4, 1967 the Battalion conducted Search and Destroy in the morning, then moved out for Cu Chi base camp and arrived around 3:00pm.

B12 in the Fil Hol

January 5, 1967 the Battalion was conducting maintenance and prepared for future operations. The track drivers and mechanics performed repairs & maintenance on the Armored Personnel Carriers.

All other personnel cleaned their weapons and prepared equipment and then almost were able to catch up on some much needed sleep.

January 6, 1967 the 1st Battalion Mechanized 5th Infantry became attached to the 196th Light Infantry Brigade. Troop B of the ¾ Cavalry became OPCON to the 1/5th (M). The Battalion moved to the area north of Trung Lap in preparation for Operation Cedar Falls.

So much for that "catching up" on sleep in one day!

January 7, 1967 Operation Cedar Falls officially began. We were up by the Saigon River and our home away from home, the Ho Bo Woods. The 1st Infantry

Division, 173rd Airborne, 11th Armored Cavalry and several ARVN soldiers from the Army of the Republic of Vietnam units started an operation searching the Ben Suc, Thanh-dien Forestry Preserve and the Iron Triangle. All were Viet Cong strongholds. At 10:05am Company A at XT640284 sustained three Bobcats Killed-in-Action and twelve Wounded-in-Action from 2 explosions. One was an 8" or 155mm ordinance and the other was a Viet Cong Claymore mine both command detonated.

January 8, 1967 the 1st of the 5th Mechanized Infantry was on the eastern flank side of the Saigon River north of Rach Son Creek in the Ho Bo woods. That evening on an Ambush Patrol Company B 1st Platoon Third Squad had three men Killed-in-Action when something went awry, a fourth man from C Company also died.

Arnez Franklin Miller Killed-in-Action
01/08/1967 (sitting under the Flag)

I don't remember this incident because I wasn't on the Ambush. Most of those guys were "greenies" not really experienced. I was on perimeter duty at the foxhole between two Armored Personnel Carriers. I vaguely remember hearing of it. During this part of Operation Cedar Falls we didn't get to rest or stop.

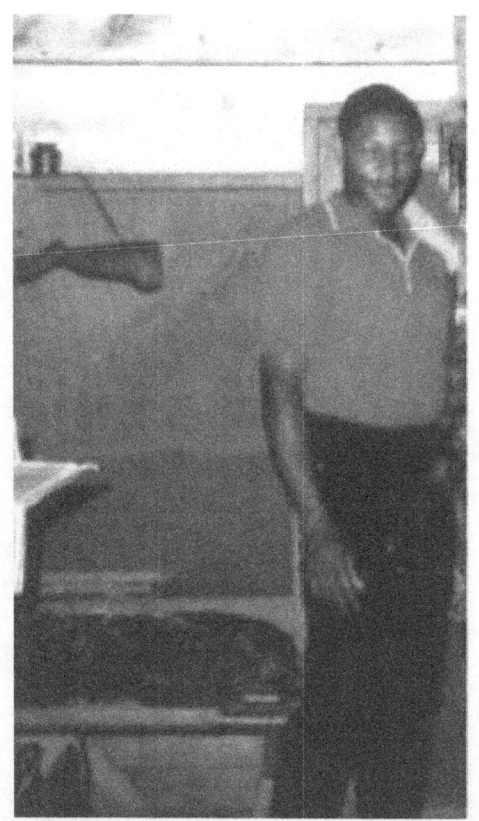

Lynn Arden Harris Killed-in-Action 01/08/1967

January 9, 1967 the Battalion conducted Search and Destroy operations in Zone and maintained Blocking Positions along the Saigon River. The Battalion had two Armored Personnel Carriers hit mines during the day resulting in six US Wounded-in-Action.

The following recounts what I experienced on this day. It was another lovely day in South Vietnam. We were in our favorite home away from home, the Ho Bo Woods. The Saigon River was about 10 meters away. The river looked peaceful enough and calm, but under the surface it was moving along at a good clip. Our "resort area" had the usual accoutrements associated with a first class military resort, dead bodies resting in lipid pools surrounded by lush vegetation along the river. Snakes of all kinds were present including the GI's "friend" the Iridescent Green Bamboo Viper. Every type of nasty insect biting you and don't forget the ever present leaches! Dried up rice paddies lined the area next to the river, it was quite pastoral.

The third squad was going to patrol up the river a ways to secure the area. This usually meant that you were going to see if you got shot at! We walked for a while enjoying the scenery, but ever diligent and watchful for any sign of "Charlie" and, mindful of the terrain for booby traps and Viet Cong hideouts. When on this type of terrain you learned how to look where you step, and to step as lightly as possible. It was kind of like walking on eggshells. It was starting to get uncomfortably hotter (somewhere around 110 to 115 degrees) as the day went along. We came to an area that was more like a little lake, not too deep, and as our mission was to check out right along the river we went through the pond.

This is exactly how the "Lake" area looked along the river.

We gradually walked into that lake to about waist high or so. It was very refreshing and the water helped cool us off. We were grateful. But everything has its price, and once we got out of the water it was time for a body check. We were checking for leaches, Yuck!!

We took turns, some watching for danger, the others checking our bodies for hitchhikers. This procedure was done by pulling down our pants and checking for those little suckers. It was time for a smoke, no not a smoke break. I would light up a cigarette, draw in, exhale and then proceed to burn the leach off my flesh. Your buddy would take care of any critters on your back and then repeat the process with the next guy. Then we were able to continue on our mission.

As we continued up the river I took over as Point man. I had gotten a little bit ahead of the other guys, and came to a lean to. It looked a little suspicious, so I checked it out. It didn't appear to have anything like tunnels or booby traps or signs of life. As I was leaving I noticed a thin iridescent green ropelike critter slithering along the ground at the back of the lean-to I had just been in! It looked harmless enough, but it was a Bamboo Viper. A bite from its fangs was fatal. That was another time to praise God f or my deliverance. Somehow I was spared again. That was too close for comfort. I warned the others and waved good-bye to my little deadly friend.

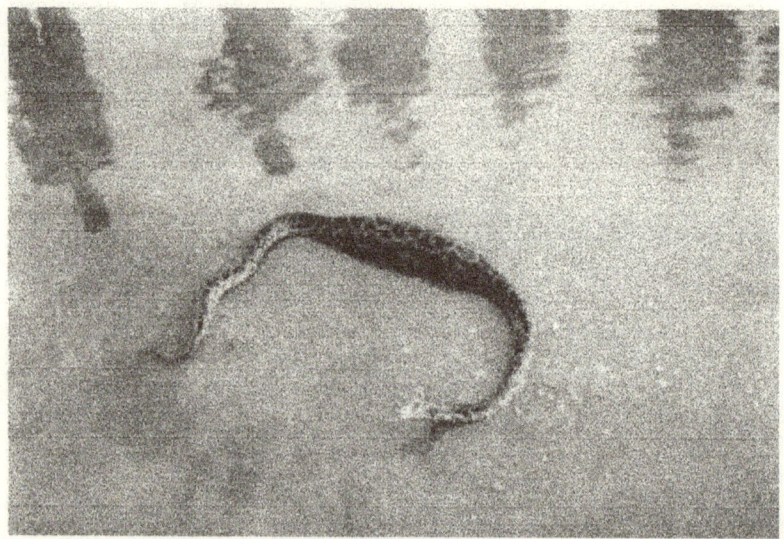

There are over 100 varieties of Snakes in Vietnam and of those only Three are non-fatal!
Had we known this fact we would have been more nervous about the water

We continued without further incident. Sometime around high noon we were beckoned to come back, so we turned around and headed back from where we came. This time when we came to the pond we went the long way to avoid our little water friends. We got back on the Armored Personnel Carriers to conduct a search and destroy mission farther up the river without incident.

January 10, 1967 the Battalion continued its mission of Search and Destroy and Blocking-in-Zone. 11:55pm Company A engaged two VC in a sampan resulting in two Viet Cong Killed-in-Action.

Do you know what that really means? Ride and/ or walk around an area, watching for mines and booby traps and Punji Pits, or finding "Charlie's" home and supplies and ammo, or "Charlie" takes a shot at someone, hopefully not you.

Another type of Punji trap

During the day the Battalion found and destroyed numerous bunkers and evacuated captured documents.

January 11, 1967 the Battalion continued its mission of Search and Destroy and Blocking-in-Zone, VIC Object Alpha. Contact during the period resulted in eleven Viet Cong Killed-In-Action, confirmed by body count.

January 12, 1967 the Battalion continued its mission of blocking and Search and Destroy. Company B acted on information from a Chieu Hoi (captured Viet Cong) and conducted search and destroy operation at XT613266 and XT625235.

January 13, 1967 the Battalion continued Blocking-in-Zone and Search and Destroy. At 1:35pm one Armored Personnel Carrier hit an anti-tank mine.

So we started the day at 7:00am. Once again we spent the whole day in the heat and the things the enemy could think up to make our lives miserable. Well, we found 9 Viet Cong bodies. We finally stopped around 7:00pm and set up our night's base camp. We had chow and then waited for what the officers could come up with to extend our day. Someone had to go on Listening Post or Ambush. Since we were always short of men, you could be chosen at any time. This was my lucky night to pull Listening Post duty and be the evening "Bait". (The Listening Post is an early warning device in case of an enemy attack!) This was about 80 meters away from the base camp perimeter, manned by me and two other pieces of cheese in a trap!

We set up as best we could as it was dark, but we were ready in case the enemy attacked. Should the Viet Cong attack we hoped to surprise them and not the other way around. It was our job to stay alert so they wouldn't cut our throats and continue to the perimeter. This still wasn't a very comforting thought for the three pieces of cheese in the trap.

We settled down for a short, peaceful, calm evening. I think not! We would start the evening of non-sleep at 10:00pm. We didn't get to sleep on Listening Post which made it difficult after a long day in the hot jungle until 5:30am and then not to sleep until this next night. Maybe a half hour nap before the Ambush came back. Then we were ready to begin another lovely day on vacation in our paradise, the Ho Bo Woods, yeah right!

## *January 1967*

The 13th was a Friday in Vietnam in 1967, and for some people they'd be scared to death. All in all, it wasn't a bad day especially since none of our boys got killed. Just being in Vietnam could make it an unlucky day. We couldn't worry about such things because it wouldn't have made any difference.

January 14, 1967 the Battalion conducted Search and Destroy operations in Zone, VIC objective Alpha and established a Blocking Position. At 9:30am a Chieu Hoi indicated a Viet Cong hospital located at XT639305. The area was searched with negative results.

January 15, 1967 the Battalion continued its mission in zone. During the day three tracks detonated mines at XT637241, XT661242 and XT622229. Company C engaged two Viet Cong, resulting in two Wounded-in-Action. At 4:55pm A Company uncovered 4 fresh graves, resulting in four Viet Cong Killed-in-Action by body count.

January 16, 1967 the Battalion moved to the zone previously occupied by the 2/1st Infantry and continued Blocking and Search and Destroy in Zone. B Company had no contact with the enemy. Company A had two Viet Cong Killed-in-Action by body count. C Company had eight Viet Cong Killed-in-Action by body count at XT653267.

B Company had moved into a zone previously occupied by the 2/15th Infantry. We were conducting Search and Destroy missions. We had stopped for a while and were told to get out of the Armored Personnel Carriers and move out on foot about 35 meters and scout the area.

This area had some trees but mostly large bushes in clumps with some open spaces interspersed. I had cautiously moved about 25 meters to the East, others were moving in the same direction but I was a considerable distance ahead. I came to a trail that ran to my right and my left. It was mid afternoon, and I was facing south because the sun was to my right. I walked a little farther and I came to a vast open area in front of me. I immediately got down so I wasn't a big target and looked the place over before continuing. To my right front was a small bunker with two entrances. I looked down that trail both ways before crossing to the bunker.

I slowly moved around to the right. I looked all around that entrance for booby traps and at the ground. The dirt was hard. While inside I looked for trap doors, tunnel holes and trenches. I found none. The front of the bunker was caved in. It made it so you couldn't look out on the sloping open valley that was about 10 to 20 meters lower in elevation. There were no booby traps on the inside roof, or the left side entrance.

After finding nothing, I decided to get the hell out of there. I crossed the trail and moved about eight feet by some bushes. I checked it out for surprises and then proceeded to sit down wait and watch.

I kind of blended into the landscape and still had a good distance view down the trail, both right and left. I rested there for about two minutes and soon a couple of the guys arrived on the scene. One of the guys was named Don, but I don't remember the other one. Don was standing on the trail looking down to the East. He was a short and thin with dark hair and dark skin.

I looked to the left and then I saw a person about 200 to 250 meters down that trail stop. He was dressed in black clothes that caught the afternoon sun and the sun's reflection made him stand out! He was small, and he was a Viet Cong! He looked at Don, and raised his arms straight from his sides and crossed them up and down twice. He was giving his comrade Don an Italian the all clear sign! Then he scampered across the trail, heading south into the thicket.

I fought it, but I couldn't hold it. I busted-a-gut laughing!! I was trying to say, while laughing, that they…they… thought…thought… you were one of them; they thought you were a goo, goo… gook… gook… too! Ha! Ha! Ha! Eventually, I calmed down from laughing, but I couldn't help chuckling under my breath about it. The whole

## *January 1967*

thing was very funny and ironic. It's a good thing that gook didn't know who it was or else Don could have been shot.

We got the call to go back to the Armored Personnel Carriers just after that incident. We further viewed the area to the left, front, and right for any signs of the Viet Cong, and then headed back.

It wasn't fair of me, but I couldn't help myself; I teased him about being a gook until it became evident that he was ignoring me, and no longer thought it was amusing.

I haven't seen him at a reunion yet, so I hope he has forgotten, but then if he reads this, I don't want to get fragged. Hopefully he won't get pissed when he reads this part.

These occasional episodes of humor helped us to get through a very tough part of our lives.

```
January 17, 1967 the Battalion conducted Search
and Destroy operation in Zones XT640280 XT633313.
We were still on Operation Cedar Falls, and our
activities were the usual. We were still a part of
a blocking force. Four Bobcats and a Helicopter
crew were killed as a result of a crash.
```

(Day 1) I was one of the lucky ones chosen for the evening's Ambush. It was somewhere around 8:00pm when we got the word. Well, there goes little chance for sleep. What's new?

We left through the perimeter toward the west; it was about 10:00pm, and dark as the ace of spades (to our advantage and "Charlie's"). We walked for a while through some thickets, then a field with short grass, when we came to a very thick grassy area. I don't remember who the Point man was, but it wasn't an easy job to navigate through. Remember, it was nighttime, but it was still hot compared to what we were used to at home. We were also sweating as much from nerves. This wasn't an evening stroll, it was a killing mission.

Finally, after about 3 hours of slowly and carefully trekking through jungle and fields, we arrived at our destination. I didn't know where we were, because I never saw the map the leader of the ambush was using. However, by now we had developed a second sense about how to get back to the Field Base Camp. We were on somewhat higher ground than the trail that ran through the area. We set up some Claymore Mines. It was then our job to remain alert and awake. By the time we set up the Ambush, it was around 1:00am. (Now remember: 5:00am to midnight is 18½ hrs, and I had the rest of the night before I might take a short nap on the track. Tired yet?) By about 3:00am sleep was tempting. Staying awake was a struggle. In case you didn't notice an Ambush meant NO sleep. At 5:30am we got the call to go back to the perimeter everyone got the Ambush site picked up and very carefully made our way back to the field base camp. (See Map A # 3 Page 314)

```
January 18, 1967 The Battalion conducted Search
and Destroy operations in Zone XT640280. At
7:00am, B Company XT671271 engaged one Viet Cong
swimming in the river, resulting in one Viet Cong
Killed-in-Action by body count. Company C at
8:00am continued a sweep along the northwest side
of Rack Son creek. Company A at 5:30pm discovered
an extensive tunnel complex at XT650235.
(See Map A #4 Page 314)
```

(Day 2) At 5:30am we had begun a new day after our "sleep over" in the jungle. By the time we returned there was little time to eat what was left of breakfast. We endured another full day in the muggy heat of Southeast Asia. Luckily for B Company nothing more unpleasant happened. We arrived somewhere around 8:00pm to set up for our night of perimeter watch duty. This night we did three 2 hours on and 2 hours off and had six hours sleep. (Note these were interrupted sleep hours not six hours of sleep straight through.)

(Day 3) After January 19th daily activities that night I was on Listening Post. We set up as it was getting dark and then began our watch. The next two hours were ok. It was about 1:00am and staying awake was becoming a challenge! Remember we hadn't had much sleep for many days. The next hour on watch passed without incident, other than critters that always managed to scare the shit out of you at least once a night. Then at 6:00am, we got the call to pack up and come back in. That night in the jungle we had zero hours of sleep. Any sleep was a luxury for the 1st of the 5th (Mech). We seldom got a short nap even for a half hour before we started on daily operations. I don't know what all the hurry was about we weren't going anywhere in particular. Many times a half hour nap would have made a big difference for us grunts.

Following is a brief recounting of our sleep habits:

| Day 1 | 24 Hours | 0 Hours Sleep | 24 Hours Duty |
| Day 2 | 24 Hours | 6 Hours Sleep | 18 Hours Duty |
| Day 3 | 24 Hours | 0 Hours Sleep | 24 Hours Duty |
| Total | 72 Hours | 6 Hours Sleep | 66 Hours Duty |

The 66 duty hours awake above were on the go all the time. Our sleep hours were always interrupted. We rarely got to REM sleep! REM is the dream stage where you experience deep sleep. Our sleep pattern was 2 hours on-2 hours off, resulting in less than 2 sets an evening. REM WHEN?

Compare this to a normal 9-to-5 job and its 275% more work hours and it's accomplished on 33% less sleep (all this done under extreme pressure and weather conditions). As if this short example isn't bad enough, remember this same pattern continued for two to three months at a stretch. Consider the average person works 8 to 10 hours, and then goofs off or relaxes at home after work. We had no "after work hours"!

What does this do to the human mind under stress, and what are the long lasting effects and costs borne by those who lived under the Vietnam Combat Sky? Ask, "How long could I keep this up and what would it have cost me?"

**You were right, Tim Fyle, we were supermen!!!**

January 19, 1967 the Battalion conducted Search and Destroy operations and blocked in Zone XT660300 to XT612256. Company B utilized RAG Boats to search the bank of the Saigon River, commencing at 9:20am. During the movement along the river eight Viet Cong bodies were found. Company A continued a sweep along the right side of the Saigon River. The day began the same as the day before except we didn't know were going up the river.

Not to jail, but on another Search and Destroy operation. (See Map A #5 and #6 Page 314) The early morning wasn't a surprise, but 5:30am was too early for me. The company loaded up at about 6:15am and began the daily grind of Search and Destroy.

The area looked pretty much like the day before, rice paddies and riverfront vegetation. We had been doing this slow but deliberate trek along the river to a place where the river was wider and turned a little to the right. The vegetation was getting thicker, and as we came to the turn, floating in the river at the edge of bank was what looked like a body. Yep, it was a body alright; a dead body that looked like it had been in the river a while, as it was all bloated. We didn't stop to check it out because we didn't want to check a booby-trapped body, so we radioed back to the Armored Personnel Carrier. We continued up river awhile where the river straightened out. The time was about 11:00am when we ended our river patrol on foot.

The area was flatter than before and had less vegetation, perfect place to board boats. The Company's Armored Personnel Carriers moved up to our location and we waited. Every river front resort must have some accoutrements, like water excursions. We were informed that we were going yachting in the afternoon. We thought that they were kidding.

When the boats arrived, we knew that they spoke the truth!
The Riverboats manned by Vietnamese appeared next to the shore and soon we were embarking on those vessels, underway up river. I don't have the slightest idea how we got on those

damned things. This was a different kind of yacht with a 50-caliber machine gun mounted. We went up river for quite a trip. Things sure looked different from the middle of the river.

Dead Viet Cong

We came to another flat and less dense area on the other side of the river where we could disembark. We were to meet up with an Army of the Republic of Vietnam unit to be part of a blocking force.

A blocking force is kind of like this: some people line up by the edge of a thick bushy area and start walking and yelling and beating the bushes, and the wild animals (Viet Cong) run away, right into the blocking force and are killed. We were to be the trap for Viet Cong!

We went on foot about 200 meters farther up river where we met up with the Army of the Republic of Vietnam Unit. The area we were going into was thick undergrowth with a trail running through its bushes. As we were entering that area, we intermingled with

RAG Riverboat manned by Vietnamese

the ARVN Troops. I was using an M-79 Grenade Launcher (a weapon like a single barrel shotgun, only with a round that was 40 mm's, more like a mortar). There are two types of rounds that you can use. One is an explosive round like a grenade that blows up, and the other is a canister round more like a shotgun round with little pellets or BB's.

The main problem with an explosive round is it doesn't take much more than a very small thin twig to ignite its fury. It is dangerous to use an explosive round in thick underbrush. This will make more sense in a minute.

The area we were in was thick with plants growing every which way, and so thick in places that you had to move plants out of your way. I noticed that one of my counterparts in the Vietnam Unit was also carrying an M-79 Grenade Launcher. My weapon was loaded with a canister round, and I just wondered which type of round he had loaded. He wouldn't let me look in his weapon to see which

type he was carrying, so I tried to show him (since I didn't speak his language) the two different rounds.
First I took out my canister round and showed it to him nodding my head up and down indicating yes. Then I showed him the 40 mm explosive round and turning my head left and right indicating no. I even smiled when I nodded, yes and frowned when I turning my head left and right, no. I had no luck. I even took an explosive round in my two fingers and showed it to him, flying through the air, striking a tiny twig and exploding.

He just smiled and wouldn't take the rounds out to make the switch. I felt like ripping the M-79 out of his hands and opening the damn thing to see what he had loaded in his weapon. I was exasperated and gave up!

I told my guys to let him go up ahead a far distance away from us. I wanted them to know that he probably had an explosive round in his M-79 and could kill us all if he fired it near our position. Hell, I didn't want him to kill himself and his buddies!

You probably have heard of people being killed by "Friendly Fire" (that's where someone is killed by his own side). Well, I didn't want to be killed by "Stupid Fire"! Nothing happened, for which I was thankful, and we went our separate ways when the mission was over.

We came out of the dense thicket a bit farther up river, and waiting for us was our water taxi to take us back down river. I don't remember how, but we did get back on the boats and started downriver back to our Armored Personnel Carriers.

While we were cruising downriver the Vietnamese crew decided to make tea. High Tea? No, just regular tea. No crumpets! A spot of tea would be delightful, but when one of the crew tossed the teapot with a rope tied to it out of the boat and into the river to get water, I changed my mind. Just four hours ago didn't we find a putrefied body floating in that very same river? What other of his companions or animals was floating in that river in addition to the normal nasty things constantly decaying?

I am not much of a gambler, not that my life couldn't end that very

second, but why risk it? We respectfully declined the offer and continued on our river soirée to our destination. We had come to the end of this day's journey on the riverboat.
Yo, ho, ho and a bottle of…hey, where's my rum?

After the cruise, B Company went on a patrol along the river when we returned we found three Viet Cong Killed-in-Action. At 3:50pm B Company at XT671259 engaged seven to ten Viet Cong with unknown results. At 4:20pm, B Company captured three Viet Cong women and accounted for one Viet Cong Killed-in-Action by body count.

All in a day's work! What a job.

I now know why I didn't choose the Navy.

January 20, 1967 the Battalion continued Search and Destroy operations in Zone. C Company departed base at 8:00am to effect a link up with Company A. Company A continued to search the tunnel complex XT649234. At 8:55am sustained three Bobcats Wounded-in-Action from a booby trap at XT650235. At 2:00pm B Company had one of its Armored Personnel Carrier destroyed when it caught on fire from a flare at XT661281.

January 21, 1967 the Battalion conducted Search and Destroy operations in zone Vic XT640280. Company A continued exploring a tunnel complex at XT650235. The tunnel complex main tunnel was 600 meters long, and 10 branch tunnels. The complex was 1500 meters southwest from the Saigon River and just north of the Rach Son Creek. The search lasted 4 days with over 60 lbs. documents found. At 1:15pm Company C had sustained four Bobcats Wounded-in-Action from a booby trap at XT653238. At 6:10pm Company C had three Bobcats Wounded-in-Action from an anti-tank mine at XT659238.

```
January 22, 1967 B Company conducted Search and
Destroy operations with no enemy contact. The
Battalion located at XT653267.

January 23, 1967 B Company conducted Search and
Destroy operations with no enemy contact.
```

(The Viet Cong must have been scared of our reputation!) (See Map A #9 on Page 314)

That afternoon, around 1:30pm, we were supposed to have a special visit from General Westmoreland in the field. We had been responsible for securing the area because Generals don't usually visit with line units in combat areas. He must have been interested in the tunnel find earlier in the week. Actually, I never saw General Westmoreland, that day.

The other visitors in this next story were more impressive than the General. Generals rarely venture out into the bush unless it's for a very special purpose; I guess it would be a major feather in the cap of a Viet Cong to kill such a high ranking officer.

Donut Dollies
Here's the way it worked. War was in progress, there were not enough soldiers. There was a draft. You got your letter. You got into the service (unless you snuck away to Canada and then became President). You went to war and served, whether in combat or elsewhere. For those who joined, it was their choice.
There were people who volunteered for all kinds of service for a variety of reasons, and that's admirable.

Then there were the "non-combatants" who volunteered in combat areas and put themselves in Harm's Way. They were a special lot! They were called "Donut Dollies". They were young ladies from the American Red Cross who volunteered in the service for the benefit of their countries servicemen. I only saw them a couple of times. There are two girls in the accompanying picture. If you look on the shoulder patch you'll see that they worked specifically with the 25th Infantry. Before I met them, I had no idea that they existed in a Base Camp like Cu Chi, so close to heavy military combat activity.

Their job was to bring a little bit of Home to the boys in the services that were far away from home.

These girls were nice enough, not exactly raving beauties, but special enough for just being there. I am sure, given the vast number of men around, that some may have different stories to tell. Look what they risked by being there, with an enemy who could care less about the lives of those young ladies.

The two Donut Dollies in the picture were at our Motor Pool just after we came back from a mission. They are by that old jeep that I used to pick up parts for the Armored Personnel Carriers in camp. Actually, I had no driver's license in "the world", as I had never gotten around to learning how to drive. Well, that jeep was my teacher and I taught myself how to drive. It was stick shift no less. Try learning how to drive on dirt roads in the dry season where they spray diesel fuel on the roads to keep the dust down. Add a little water, and wee! (Back to the story, I took a little side trip down memory lane.)

About four or five of these girls were there. The girl in the picture with the pigtails kind of took a shine to me, or thought I needed special help. Anyway, she was a different kind of person which made me a little nervous. Her nickname was "Claymore".

Need I say anymore? I don't remember if I hid from "Claymore" or not. Looking back, it seems a bit odd that those girls would have been allowed to visit us in an area of such potential danger, but there they were! It was strange to see them walking across the field in their uniforms. I wonder if they had an idea of the danger that could be lurking in the jungle. Since we were on the Perimeter we didn't have them visit us that close to danger.

We the men of the 1$^{st}$ Battalion 5$^{th}$ Mechanized Infantry, 25$^{th}$ Infantry Division A, B, C and Headquarter Company, salute each and every one of you girls: The "Donut Dollies" of the American Red Cross, Cu Chi Vietnam.

There is a special section on our Web Site for entertainment, and the "Donut Dollies" are shown there as well. We could use more pictures and names to give them proper credit.

January 24, 1967 the Battalion continued to search a tunnel complex and defend in zone, utilizing Daylight Patrols and Night Ambushes. Company C engaged an unknown number of Viet Cong result one VC Killed-in-Action and 2 Chicom AK-47 rifles captured at XT642249. At 12:55pm, B Company at XT 658247 engaged two Viet Cong resulting in two Killed-in-Action, 1 US Wounded-in-Action and captured 1 M-14 Rifle and 1 Chicom Carbine.

Donut Dollies. "Claymore" on the left.

The documents taken from that complex proved to be valuable to further operations.

January 25, 1967 the Battalion was released from the 196$^{th}$ Light Infantry Brigade at 11:07 am and commenced an overland move to Cu Chi at 12:45pm.

January 26, 1967 Operation Cedar Falls in the Iron Triangle was terminated.

January 27, 1967 the Battalion conducted training at Cu Chi Base Camp.

January 28, 1967 the Battalion began preparation for future operations at the Base Camp.

We almost didn't know what to do. This was our second day in a row back at the base camp, which didn't happen too often during my stay in Vietnam. The First Sergeant didn't mess with us too much, which was somewhat of a miracle because he was a bit of a power freak. I didn't do too much of anything except write some letters. Then it occurred to me that being away from the company was the wiser action. Out of sight, out of mind.

I decided to go to the Post Exchange and do some shopping for some snacks and personal items, and then maybe to the front gate to help kill the time. I don't remember doing any paintings at that time, but it is a possibility.

We knew it was just a matter of time, and then we were going to the land of Cong, again. It was always important to make sure our weapons were in good working order and that we had some clean clothes for the next operation. Even though we were tired, from lack of sleep it was still difficult to go to sleep; it had become a bad habit! We decided that tonight would be a festive evening. There was a movie, which I cannot remember, but "The African Queen" with Humphrey and Kathryn Hepburn somehow rings a bell. We didn't really care. It was something to do and we needed some entertainment! Considering the number of straight combat days we spent in danger it was the least they could have done and we did appreciate those little things.

For those of you who care we did get three hot meals a day while back in Base Camp. Hey, out in the field we didn't, so I wonder if the Rear Echelon Mother Fuckers got paid the same as us. If so, we need to put in a claim with the Government for our dangerous occupation.

Once the movies were over, there was still plenty of evening left. We went to the Enlisted Men's Club. The rest of the evening we exercised our drinking arms, ate salty snacks and washed it all down with Ice Cold Beer. All this time the jukebox blared away our favorite tunes and some not so favorite, but none fought over it! We drank and pee'd and drank and pee'd the rest of the evening until the club closed. After they kicked us out of the club we returned to the Hooches and let's see what happens...

```
January 29, 1967 B Company continued a much-
deserved rest by conducting maintenance. The
company spent some time cleaning out the Armored
Personnel Carriers and doing training exercises.
```

(what training?) I only remember strengthening my drinking arm at the Club at night!

```
January 30, 1967 one of the men from B Company was
killed north of the Sui Ben Moung River.
```

Maybe that was near the perimeter bunker just after the base perimeter on the Northeast side of the base camp. We got word that we would be leaving on another operation early in the next morning.

Butch Petit
We were moving out that morning, Butch Petit wasn't going with us because he was a short-timer, as well as "vertically challenged". He was so short in time that you would have to lay on your belly just to look him in the eyes and talk to him! We didn't expect to see him again as he was ready to ship home soon. We decided to have a party (not that we needed to have an excuse). We did the usual drinking and listened to more "Do Wop Music". Even though we were going out the next day, we still were up pretty late. Butch had a Class of 1966 Yearbook and we all signed it. I signed it, "Rich Antti, the Artist", just like in high school or college. The only difference was, if you flunked out of this University, you didn't walk on the plane home, you were carried!

In July 2004 I met up with Butch and the boys at a Reunion in Ohio and he looked about the same, maybe a few pounds more, but he looked good because he was the leader of "The Pretty Boy Squad" (B Company, 1st Platoon, and 3rd Squad)!

Butch must have been born for combat because he had a natural sense of combat leadership and an awareness of his current surroundings. I'll tell you that military discipline has its merit, which didn't fit us, but I would go into battle with our guys anywhere and anytime, even today.

Did we drink a lot? Yes, when we had a chance. It wasn't often, but never out in the field. Were we wild? Yes, we were living under wild conditions. What did you expect? Did we kill any civilians? Never! Never! NEVER!!

Butch Petit is a man I know, respect, and love as a Brother for who he is and what he continues to do for us Survivors of the Class of 1966.

We left Vietnam at different times, and for forty years we went our separate ways. But it's amazing that once we all got together, it didn't take long for us to be a family as if we'd been together all this time, since 'Nam!

Butch Petit as a Person of Honor and Duty in combat:

Let his record do the talking.

Sergeant Norman "Butch" Petit
Squad Leader, Tunnel Rat, Point man
Recipient of:

    Combat Infantry Badge
    Soldiers Medal
    Silver Star
    Bronze Star for "Valor" with 3 Oak Leaf Clusters
    Purple Heart with 1 Oak Leaf Cluster
    Presidential Valorous Unit Citation

Was he a perfect soldier who drilled perfectly, perfect in his demeanor, neat and tidy? I don't know about all that stuff I call window dressing. Think about this, it doesn't mean a thing if you and your men are dead!

Sat Cong 31 (confirmed)

Butch Petit going in the hole one more time

He was a hard ass when it came to doing the things that help you to stay alive. I count part of my being alive today as a tribute to the really important military training he provided us.

\* \* \* \* \*

This month there were forty-one men wounded-in-action.

The month of January 1967 seventeen Bobcats died in the field. They were:

    Danny C. Barnes    Willy V. Quast

    David Young    Lynn Arden Harris

    Arnez F. Miller Jr.    Carlos M. Rodriguez

    David L. Sheey    Herbert H. Crowder

    Herschel L. Epps Jr.    Larry G. Gray

    Frank J. Krebs    Donald L. Helton

    Leo V. Wilbert    Morgan E. Savage

    James B. Simmons    John L. Wilhelm

    Richard L. Parham.

We honor their memory and celebrate their bravery. Rest easy, our Brothers-in-Arms, rest easy...

# February 1967

February 1, 1967 the Battalion was OPCON to the 196th Light Infantry Brigade. Then to go the next day northwest of Nui Ba Den "The Black Virgin Mountain" as we called her, the Buddhist Holy Mountain. The Battalion was to operate in the area up to the far north and west border with Cambodia. The area was known as a Viet Cong stronghold with dense forests and dense thicket, a real jungle area. During the day one Bobcat died from small arms fire. We were to visit (not as welcomed guests) places like Trai Bi, south of Dogs Head, the Tonle Roti River border between Vietnam and Cambodia, and Fire Support Base Delta, to name a few.

## Convoy
We started Operation Gadsden on February 1, 1967. The Battalion, with a supply convoy, left Cu Chi base camp in the morning onto Highway 1 north toward Tay Ninh. We were close to

the middle of the convoy, and by 10:30am we had come to Trang Bang. Our section of the convoy came to Go Dau Ha onto Highway 22, where we came to a halt.

Tracks on Highway 1 in convoy

We waited for about 15 minutes and ended up with a small gathering of civilians, from where, I couldn't say. First small children, who for some inborn reason were interested in military maneuvers, like children from the beginning of warfare. They were particularly enthralled with the Armored Personnel Carriers.

Soon, I think because they had an efficient communication system, Mama Sans and more children armed with food approached the Armored Personnel Carriers! They were selling BLT's. You know, "Boar, lettuce, and Tomato Sandwiches"! They also had sodas. Now how did they know we would like that specialty sandwich?

I must admit that I was leery of their sanitary procedures, but given the conditions we were subjected to in the bush without a real bath for months on end I guess we didn't really give a shit! Charlie or chow, I don't think it matters which way we went if it was our turn to go! Hunger won over reason, as it usually did concerning GI decisions.

So I actually bit the bullet or "BLT" as you might say, and had one! The bread of the BLT sandwich was made with rice flour, boar, lettuce and tomato, and it was pretty tasty. Well I didn't die from my culinary case study, because if I had you wouldn't be reading this book. I didn't even get indigestion, heartburn, or the dreaded dysentery.

The column was stopped for about 45 minutes. Imagine that, a traffic jam in South Vietnam, will wonders ever cease? I wonder if there were some big tie up with trucks and Ox carts, and was the late morning BLT's they offered for sale the cause or the effect?

Working to help support her family by feeding always-hungry GI's

The sights you see along the road in Vietnam are not the same as in our world. They have a transit system on the highways, like Greyhound buses, but more like what you might see in a movie about the 1920's in foreign lands. The buses could be considered a close second to Jed Clampet's truck with Granny sitting in a rocking chair on the top, only it's a bus! This bus is about 10 years newer than Jed's truck.

The buses looked pretty rickety and chock full of Mama Sans, Papa Sans, children and even livestock. When you consider the hot temperature, humidity, animals and hygiene I would rather walk thank you! They also had what I called the "Death Taxi", a small Moped that had a small wagon attached with a bed with bench seats on each side and a frame on the corners and a cloth cover on the top.

The Far Eastern Branch of…………….

Most of the drivers drove like the devil was chasing them and they didn't care who they ran into. The Viet Cong had a transportation system for cargo, it was an oxcart pulled by water buffalo. It was his Semi-truck and Trailer rig.

After the catered lunch, the supply convoy said goodbye to our culinary crew and moved on up the road. The convoy moved slowly, and not very far down the road it stopped again. There must have been some activity, a bad road or Viet Cong activity up ahead! The convoy stopped in a farming area. There were women working in the field close to the road. One woman was quite near my Armored Personnel Carrier. She stopped her work looked up and spit. The next sight I saw was very interesting.

Beetle Nut
There are things that you remember without knowing the how or why. When you go to a strange country it is not unusual to see something different. Those things you think are strange are considered "Normal" to their population. The definition of "Normal" according to Webster's Collegiate Dictionary is, "Conforming to a type, standard, or regular pattern."

What I had seen on this day stretched my ideas of normal.

*February 1967*

Before I share with you the details of the present subject, I will share the results. There are many of us who served in Vietnam who experienced what I am about to share. The first time I encountered one of those women with her big open mouth grin it was quite a shock. They would get a big kick out of doing it. Are you curious? When she smiled with her big open mouth grin with that loud cackling laugh, her mouth was an eerie blood red! I am convinced that she did that just for the effect. Most of the time when Beetle nut chewers smiled it seemed to be a rule that they had several missing or ground-down teeth. When I first saw this I shrank back a little in quiet horror. I took a second look and became amused at my reaction. It may seem silly that I would react that way. It probably was because I was embarrassed. What was more appalling was what their mouths looked like later.

Those who have seen the musical "South Pacific" may remember the United States Navy men singing, Bloody Mary is the girl I love and something about "chewing Beetle nut". Well the incident in the paragraph above and the lyric in "South Pacific" have a common thread. It was Beetle nut! I recently learned that Beetle nut is and was used in several countries in Asia and the South Pacific areas, and it was also used in the United States by Native American Indians.

Mainly older Vietnamese women used of the fruit and leaves of the Betel Palm tree commonly known as "Beetle nut". The Beetle nut (Trai Cao) and the dried Betel Palm leaves (La Trau) are both mild narcotics. My Vietnamese civilian technical advisors provided me with additional information. The users would make a white limestone paste, apply it to the dried palm leaves, place the Beetle nut on the leaf and roll it up. They would then put it in their mouth and begin chewing. The red liquid inside the Beetle nut is released making the users mouth a blood red. They continued chewing this concoction. When they would spit, it left a red splotch on the ground.

After they were done chewing their mouths and teeth were stained black. They supposedly used it because it eased the pain from a gum disease. I am not sure if the chewing of the Beetle nut, leaf and paste was the cure, the cause or both, and it doesn't really matter. Those of us who saw this were appalled by that habit. It was their business, but the visual effects were disgusting!

I learned that they didn't have toothpaste as we know it, but they did use sand to brush their teeth to try and lighten the stain.

That's what I call "True Grit"! Ouch...

Many times we had seen the Vietnamese people leave the side of the road. We'd watch them like hawks, they seemed suspicious. Well, they didn't pull off a surprise attack. It was another kind of attack. It was an attack of nature! When you gotta go, you gotta go! But does it have to be out in the open? Well, given a challenge to be rude and crude, GI's were not afraid to share their talents and rise to the occasion. It was one of those times to see just how primitive we could get, and primitive we got!

---

Compare my relationship to normal civilities of today; I would never contemplate doing what I did in Vietnam. I am a respectable person and would never think of doing what I did in this story.

The wartime mentality of "Who cares?" and "What does it matter?" existed strongly in Vietnam, and to this day still carries on. When you consider how hurt we were that the American people didn't support us, our attitudes today sometimes reflect that same theme. We can turn that on at the drop of a hat and off just as fast, so don't piss us off! You might be surprised that Mr. Mild can become Mr. Asshole! I make no apologies. Our government trained us!

---

This word picture I am about to explain would have probably made international news if CNN had been there! We had stopped again, and it had been an hour since we ate our BLT's and drank our sodas plus the water before and after. Nature wasn't calling, it was screaming, "Please release me, I have to Pee!"

We couldn't leave our posts could we?

Now imagine this. Me standing on the top of the Armored Personnel Carrier which is about 6 feet high, and I am 5 foot 8

*February 1967* 131

inches which makes my head almost 12 feet in the air! This is quite a target! But I had to answer nature's call. So there I was, peeing off the side of the Armored Personnel Carrier! Now I did this discretely without exposing myself. Here I was peeing onto the ground. Talk about being pissed off! How rude, how crude. Who cared? When you gotta go, you gotta go!

War does strange things to people. Sometimes it brings you down to the lowest levels of human existence, and then sometimes to the highest forms of human endeavor. Also, you will find that some things you think are important in life don't matter in the greater scheme. It's your orientation to them. You may be shocked about my behavior. Come to think of it, so am I! That's my orientation to it today.

The convoy got going again, and we finally reached Tay Ninh along with the supply convoy. We never did find out the reason why we stopped, or if it was a coincidence that we stopped just at the time when we were hungry and they had the food already prepared.

The Battalion parted from Tay Ninh and proceeded up Highway 22 north towards the Cambodian border.

February 2, 1967 at 6:32am the $1^{st}$ of the $5^{th}$ Mechanized Infantry left Tay Ninh and assaulted to position XT055684. Lead elements of the $1/5^{th}$ (M) linked up with Company A of the $4/31^{st}$ Infantry at 10:50am. A bridge was air lifted to the site and installed by the $175^{th}$ Engineer Company. The $1^{st}$ of the $5^{th}$ (Mech) crossed over the bridge and continued to XT034717. The Battalion secured a Landing Zone for the helilift of the 4/31st Infantry into the area at 4:40pm.

It is interesting that today it takes months to build an overpass on a freeway and it takes the Army Corp of Engineers can build a bridge in a couple of hours. I know it is different but the ones the army builds is for heavy equipment crossing an uneven surfaces and under varied weather conditions including combat.

Engineers building a bridge we were to cross

Remember the engineers spent some of their time in the same jungles we visited from time to time.

Crossing on the bridge in the Armored Personnel Carrier

February 3, 1967 the Battalion commenced attack at 8:18 am to the area of WT 9869, which was very near the Cambodian Border south of "Dogs Head". At 9:00am the Recon Platoon was dispatched to sweep the flank of the Battalion.

At 9:06am a Recon Platoon Armored Personnel Carrier detonated an anti-tank mine with negative casualties. At 10:40am Company A located a TA/312 telephone in the area of XT995699. At 1:30pm B Company received fire from a 57MM Recoilless Rifle while repairing a track that had broken down in the area of WT999699. Two bobcats were Wounded-in-Action. A Recoilless Rifle round hit the Armored Personnel Carrier of the A Company Executive Officer, killing him and two others on the Armored Personnel Carrier. The Viet Cong managed to overtake and occupy the track, firing its 50-caliber machine gun. A man from B Company was wounded while attempting to take the Armored Personnel Carrier under fire. That Bobcat soldier died shortly after being wounded.

The Recon Platoon was dispatched to assist the B Company elements and while en-route received two Recoilless-rifle rounds resulting in two Bobcats being Wounded-in-Action. Fire was returned and the Recon Platoon proceeded to link up with the elements of B Company.

At 2:59pm an Armored Personnel Carrier from C Company detonated an anti-Tank mine in the area of WT 999701, resulting in thirteen Bobcats being Wounded-in-Action. At 3:10pm the Recon Platoon, while still providing security for the B Company elements, started to receive heavy small arms fire from an estimated fifteen to twenty Viet Cong in the area of WT000697.

The Armored Personnel Carrier was recovered at 3:55pm after air and artillery fire was placed into the area, and the Viet Cong broke contact. During this day, five Bobcats were Killed-in-Action and twenty four were Wounded-in Action.

The Viet Cong wore a mixture of the Black Pajama Gang and camouflaged uniform-type clothing.

It was noted that they fought with considerable determination and showed good discipline and fire control. The battalion closed at 5:50pm at WT977698.

He still was a bastard in my book!

I recently had the opportunity to talk with Allen Biggs a mechanic who was there that day and he provided the following details:

"The B Company track had some sort of engine trouble and the driver had the engine cover up and was trying to find the trouble. Our mechanic's track had pulled to its right side about 4 feet shorter from the front. I was at the rear of the mechanics track and heard the explosion and I grabbed my M-16 rifle, ran to the right side of the track and proceeded to fire at the enemy. That piece of crap rifle jammed leaving me exposed to the enemy without a weapon."

"Luckily, Sergeant Billy Williams had gotten on the 50-caliber machine gun and began shooting at the enemy who were shooting at me. I made my way to the back while bullets were zinging all around me to the left back of the track, and I then noticed the hole where the fragments had made a circle around the hole created by a recoilless rifle round."

"There were two men, Fisher and another soldier, who had been hit. Fisher was thrashing around in the Armored Personnel Carrier, so we got to him and lowered him down and calmed as best as possible while trying to stop his bleeding head wound. The other soldier was just sitting inside and leaning against the wall holding his left side. Sergeant Williams had called for a Medivac, and while we waited Ron Priebe helped me with the two wounded. Meanwhile two soldiers were setting up an M-60 machine gun position at the left side of their track. Then two Viet Cong ran past them. It happened so fast they didn't get a shot at them. We knew they were trying to get around behind us."

"We got the word that Recon Platoon had some help that was nearing. When they arrived I recognized two of them, Sergeant Arnie Queener Aka Spotted Bear and Sp/4 Jerry Curry. The track was approaching from the right front of our position. They began to help secure our position. The helicopter arrived. Ron Priebe and I carried one of the wounded to the chopper and got him loaded, and then went back for the next man. The pilot asked about the two Viet Cong that were wounded by the Recon tracks when we returned with some wounded from Recon. We checked but they were already dead. The chopper pilot then revved up and got the hell out of there!"

The quick and brave action of Specialist Fourth Class Allen Biggs, without thought for his own safety and caring for his fellow soldiers are in the highest tradition of the United States Army. Mechanic Allen Biggs was awarded the Bronze Star Medal for Valor. Knowing men like this is one of the great honors of my life.

February 4, 1967 the Battalion conducted Search and Destroy operations in the area surrounding their night base. At 9:10am B Company discovered an unfinished enemy base camp at WT976706. At 3:20pm Company C engaged two Viet Cong at WT996693, killing both. Among the items found with the bodies were 7 rounds of 55 mm HEAT ammunition and a tripod.

February 5, 1967 the Battalion attacked from Objective 4 to Objective 5 (along axis PLUM) commencing at 10:25am. Company C attacked along axis GRAPE en-route to link up with the 4/31$^{st}$ Infantry. Company C later diverted from this mission when the Battalion made contact. At 8:12am Company A's Ambush received fire from across the river in Cambodia. The Ambush returned fire and the action resulted in fifteen Viet Cong Killed-in-Action by body count. One body fell into the river and the other was hanging in a tree. Neither body could be recovered. The Ambush continued receiving fire until they were retrieved by Company A. Company A departed the Battalion Command Perimeter at 10:05am behind B Company en-route to objective 6, 10:33pm at WT96980 the company received small arms fire from their left flank. The fire was then returned with negative results. At 12:44pm Company A assumed the lead from B Company at WT983666. Company A became involved in a firefight at 1:35pm with an unknown size Viet Cong force fired RPG2's, rifle grenades and small arms fire. RPG2 Russian Rockets hit two Armored Personnel Carriers, and one detonated a mine. There were two Bobcats killed and eighteen wounded in the firefight. Company A had another man killed from a sniper. Contact was broken at 5:35pm. All closed the Battalion Perimeter at 7:37pm.

**I was with B Company at the time that the switch in position had been made, and Company A was attacked. Had we not switched it would have been B Company tracks that were attacked with wounded and fatalities, maybe even me.**

February 6, 1967 the Battalion moved overland at 8:30am from Vic WT995664 and conducted Search and Destroy operations in the southern portion of AO VICTOR. Recon Platoon screened from the coordinating point to WT986557 and located a VC rest area. At 10:15am B Company discovered four Viet Cong bodies Killed-in-Action at XT981667 and captured equipment at XT986657 including 50 lbs of documents, 3 Chicom grenades, 1 PRC-25 radio, 1 PRC-6 radio, 1 carbine and 1 AK-47 rifle. At 3:00pm B Company found two dead Viet Cong who had been killed at WT983668. At 9:01pm the Battalion base received 2 incoming rounds from the Northeast. Fire was returned by mortar and artillery fire, with unknown results. Battalion closed at WT995665.

February 7, 1967 B Company departed base at 9:40am to explore a B-52 strike Vic WT995685. A Company located an underground VC (Viet Cong) Hospital

Complex. Documents found identified units of the Staff Directorate of COSVN. Several dead Viet Cong were located during the operation along with some radio equipment, weapons, and ammunitions. Company A and Company C received fire from an estimated Viet Cong Platoon resulting in one Bobcat being Wounded-in-Action. At 2:25pm Company A again made contact with the Viet Cong, who were wearing Khaki uniforms. At 2:25pm Company A again made contact with the enemy at 3:01pm in the area of WT964670. Air strikes were placed into the area where the Viet Cong were firing from. After the Air strikes, Company A moved into the area and discovered twenty Viet Cong bodies and a cache of 18 tons of rice. All elements closed the Battalion forward base at WT995664 7:06pm. (See Map B #6 on Page 315)

About 15 years ago, I was in the kitchen cooking breakfast at home. I was making my specialty omelets with fresh garlic cloves sliced and sautéed in butter. When the eggs were starting to cook I added the sautéed garlic and cheddar cheese. I had just finished one of my Omelet Masterpieces and had started a second one. I heard the television from the living room which was playing some Vietnam War movie (which I usually avoided like the "Black Plague"). Something piqued my interest. This part of the movie had an actor recounting their experience, and he was talking about experiencing a B-52 bombing strike near the Cambodian Border.

I immediately said "We were up by Cambodia in February 1967 and were about 2 city blocks away from that strike" I thought for a second and then said "Then we went on a Search and Destroy operation in that area and came to a tunnel system with an Aid Station". I almost fell on the floor when the next words I heard from the TV set were "then we arrived at an underground tunnel complex". That was the damned craziest thing I had ever heard! What a strange coincidence, or was it the same event? Writing this just sent shivers down my spine!

## My First Tunnel

It was morning around 9:30am. The tracks were set in the perimeter and B Company started to move out on a Search and Destroy operation. We had been all morning then well into the afternoon when we stopped and turned into a line facing north. Suddenly we could hear in the distance the faint roar of jet engines, then the sound became louder and louder.

Bombing Strike

On our right flank high in the sky we could see the Bombers starting to make a dive towards the front of our position. We watched the bombers come farther down and then release the bombs and begin their assent up into the sky. The 500 pound bombs were quickly nearing the earth and to the bosom of our enemy. I saw the bombs hit and then the loud boom!

Shortly, the earth began to shake violently and twist up and down and reeled left and right. This happened when each of the bombs made impact with the earth, again and again! (When you see a bombing raid in the movies and the camera shakes up and down and reels left and right, that's exactly what we saw and heard that day.)

Bombing with dirt shooting into the sky

As those bombs exploded the dirt was hurled high into the air. Then a rainstorm of dirt pelted the ground below. Wow what a sight to behold.

It seemed that the Wrath of God was unleashed upon those unsuspecting Viet Cong. I almost (I said almost!) felt sorry for them. I can't and don't want to imagine what it was like for them. I'm sure it was 30 minutes of Hell!

I hope you can understand and appreciate our experience and that of the Viet Cong, even though they were our enemy. The movies can't recapture and do justice to the profound and awesome terrors of wartime bombing. Each time a bomb hit was a revelation of its power of destruction.

It was terrifying and exciting at the same time.

We moved out after 3:30pm to our right flank towards the northeast to the bomb raid area. As we moved out the sky still had dirt particles in the air like reddish brown smoke glistening in the morning sun.

Bomb Crater

As we got closer we could see that the area of that bombing raid was all torn apart. Large craters about 6 feet deep were all around us. The dirt was reddish-brown and along one side of each crater was a pile of dirt. The once majestic trees were scattered in piles of mangled, twisted, and broken pieces of green and brown foliage. The mounds of dirt reminded me of the Sand Dunes on the other side of Lake Michigan, only it wasn't sand, it was the soil of the jungle in Vietnam. There was something sick and sinister about the torn up jungle that gave us a creepy feeling. I guess all that energy expended and the chemicals in the explosives made atmosphere in the area feel heavy.

The First Platoon came up one area of the tunnel complex found by A Company, and I had an "opportunity" to crawl a tunnel. I was gamer than I was discerning in my actions! I didn't want to leave Vietnam a Tunnel Virgin! I thought to myself, "Wow, I wonder if

Butch would be proud to know I had the guts to do this?" It really didn't matter. I wanted to do it anyway. There are things we do that we wonder about later on in life. Just to go down in a tunnel takes some guts. This first event is the pinnacle of the bravest and most stupid things I've ever done in my long and illustrious life!

Tunnel entrances, down you go?

First, it is hotter than hell and there's an air of death that would permeate your senses. One would think that inside the tunnel in the bowels of the earth it would be cooler. The earth cools slower than the air does. So during the hot seasons the heat keeps the ground hot longer. The constant decay in the area provides a constant smell of death.

Imagine, yourself, right now, looking down into that dark abyss of a hole in the ground, about a two-and-a-half-foot opening. Your next action is to lower yourself into that hole until you get to the bottom, (Are you starting to feel closed in?). It's dark, really dark, and the odor of decay intensifies. The tunnel stretches out in front of you, going down on a slight decline. You can't stand up, you are surrounded by dirt and have limited mobility. You must navigate the tunnel on your hands and knees like a half blind RAT. You crawl on like the smelly vermin you are following. The pungent odor is musty and dank. Decay is all around you. It smells like a dead animal. This is not an exploration, it's a killing mission.

I went probably 12 feet or more under the grass and when it occurred to me that there may be an Armored Personnel Carrier or a Tank roaming overhead. What if it caused a cave in? It was a little late to think about that, so onward I went, seemingly deeper into the earth. The most interesting part of all this was I didn't even worry about the hidden trap doors, alternate tunnels, and punji pits with bamboo stakes laden with human shit. And don't forget the Bamboo Viper with its deadly kiss of death. Most people would never entertain such an excursion into Mother Earth would they? So why am I down here?

I had crawled about fifty feet into the tunnel. I had come to a fork in the tunnel to the right. I started to follow it to the right, but stopped. I shined my flashlight; I could see that it abruptly ended. I checked it out for being a trap door, but it wasn't, and there were no booby traps. Maybe it was the start of Charlie's spring remodeling or expansion program. All I know is it didn't lead anywhere, so I backed out of there and went farther down the original tunnel to the left. I continued with my 45 in one hand for about 20 feet then I heard a noise behind me. A lump the size of a beach ball came into my throat! Then I saw a flicker of light. This was not the time to deliberate or I could be dead! I was supposed to be the last one down and no one else was to follow.

Typical tunnel complex near water

Whoever it was had a flashlight, so I quickly deduced that if Charlie were sneaking up on me, surely he wouldn't do it with a flashlight. At about the same time I was exercising my option by

## *February 1967*

cocking my 45 Cal Automatic Pistol ready to fire. So I yelled out "Who's there?" It's me! Lt. Saliman. I yelled back at him, "You stupid Son of a Bitch"! I almost shot your sorry ass, Sir! That got a laugh out of him, and the beach ball in my throat began to shrink. I took a deep breath and let it out! We began to crawl farther. We crawled about 20 feet and came to an opening to our left. It was a fairly large room that was being used as a surgery center. The room was about 8 feet by 12 feet and was 5-6 feet high. There were no bodies, but you could tell from some bloody bandages and blood soaked into the dirt floor, that some medical aid was performed here recently it was an aid station.

It's strange that my memory of this has remained about the same all these years. And yet, I don't even remember anything about how, when or where I climbed out of that hole. What I've described is all I remember.

Now, what Lt. Saliman did wasn't in good taste, but I can understand his desire not to leave Vietnam a Tunnel Virgin. Why did he have to wait so long and why when I was down in that damn tunnel? The real scary thing about this story is the fact that beside scaring me to death, Lt. Norman Saliman had just three days left in Vietnam. He shouldn't have even been out in the field at all that day. What a crazy GI!

Lt Norman Saliman B Company, Platoon
Leader Killed-in-Action 06/12/1969

This may sound stupid to most of you reading this. Who would be crazy enough to descend into the bowels of the earth on their belly in a small hole? Well, I guess me! I was young, and I thought I was tough and ready to try anything. Does any of this make any sense to you? If it does let me know what sense it makes, I'd like to know. Hey, this could become a habit!

February 8, 1967 the Battalion commenced operation at 9:10am. At 10:35am Company A at WT982666 found ten Viet Cong bodies, five killed by small arms fire, four found in a bomb crater and one in a covered bunker. At 12:00 noon Company A Vic WT982666 found four VC bodies killed by small arms fire. At 1:35pm B Company received 3 rounds of small arms fire at XT010668. Then at 3:40pm Company B received auto-matic weapons fire from an unknown number resulted in one Bobcat Killed-in-Action, fire was returned with small arms fire and M-79 fire, result one Viet Cong Killed-in-Action. The Viet Cong was wearing a blue and gray uniform at XT010688 were the 680th VC Training Regiment.

I wonder if that was my M-79 that got that Viet Cong.

February 9, 1967 the Battalion continued to observe the TET truce period.

February 10, 1967 the Battalion continued still to observe the TET truce period. At 2:07am one of the Listening Post received 1 (truce) hand grenade at WT989650. Fire was returned with 1 round 81 mm illumination and 9 rounds 81 mm High Explosives with unknown results. At 1:35pm Recon Platoon received 10 rifle grenades Vic WT989650. Fire was returned with small arms and machine gun fire with unknown results. Elements located a training area with 44 structures, fortifications, 2 class rooms, 2 mess halls, and a 75'x 30 meter rifle range with complete with silhouette targets.

## February 1967

Possibly the Viet Cong in the 2 incidents of enemy contact weren't Buddhists?

February 11, 1967 the Battalion continued to observe the TET truce. At 1:31pm the enemy fired one round of small arms fire on a CH-47 loading, at WT973793. Gun ships were alerted and fired into the area Vic WT967697 after they received heavy automatic weapon fire from that area.

February 12, 1967 in the morning, B Company and C Company departed the Battalion base at 7:30am to secure a Landing Zone at Forward Support Base Delta in the area of WT0364. Headquarters Company and Company A departed at 9:49am and closed Objective 7 at 3:47pm. At 11:40pm Companies B and C departed Delta and arrived at the new Battalion Forward Base at 4:20pm. At 11:00pm the Battalion received 1 rifle grenade Vic WT984616. At 11:15pm 6 more rifle grenades were received at the same location.

We had settled in for a quiet evening's rest without an Ambush or Listening Post (at least for me). The evening seemed peaceful enough. Except for perimeter duty, we looked forward to 4 to 5 hours of interrupted sleep. The enemy, not wanting us to get too much sleep, decided to harass us in one of their usual ways. During this evening, those Viet Cong bastards intermittingly fired 7 rifle grenades at the base camp to deprive us of needed sleep!

We who were asleep in the morning started to stir about 6:00am, and as usual we were hungry as bears after a long hibernation.
We got the call for 50% to chow, so we sent half of our hungry bears to squelch their hunger pangs at breakfast. We had been refreshed from the heat by the fog and the morning dew. Sometimes we'd pay dearly for that little refreshment because if it got hotter faster than the days before, it would be so much more humid, kind of like a sauna bath!

Just a short note about fog, it can be very scary for most people in

the dark of night, but can be nothing less than terrorizing to some people in a combat situation. You can't see what's out there until they're right on top of your position! When you've had as little rest as we experienced it doesn't take much to startle your reactions.
Once we'd eaten, we waited to see what the day had in store for us. By now you should be able to guess what we were going to do. You're right, of course, search and destroy! We packed up what little we had, stowed gear and mounted up about 8:00am, ready to go, and waited!

```
February 13, 1967 the Battalion commenced Search
and Destroy operations in Zone southwest of
Objective 7 Vic XT990620 at 8:15am. Battalion
elements continued to find and destroy Viet Cong
ordinance fabrication facility base camp and cache
sites in Zone. At 3:15pm Company B Vic XT995624
uncovered a Viet Cong base camp. At 8:15pm the
Battalion Perimeter received 5 rounds of 81 mm
mortar fire. (See Map B #7 on Page 315)
```

<u>River Ambush</u>
We heard that we were going very close to Cambodia. We had developed a mystique about Cambodia, so we always got excited and kind of worked up being near there.

The area we left had very thick trees and under-brush. As we traveled the area started to have more open spots than where we had just been. The vegetation seemed to more resemble what we thought the jungle was supposed to look like and not the dull drab death-like foliage we'd become used to.

We came to an area that was open, and as we looked forward the trees and under-brush were lush and life like. There had to be a creek or river on the other side of the wood line. We stopped and then circled our Armored Personnel Carriers like our earlier day pioneers used to do with wagons. We moved into our defensive position, lowered our back tailgate and disembarked. It was time to begin our foot patrol. Our location was close to XT966642, only more west and closer still to Cambodia.

We weren't going on a picnic, because we were going to bring a

## *February 1967* 147

little more gear with us in the form of one more can of M-60 machine gun ammo and four more bandoliers, two for me and two for Luis! You know, sometimes we do things without thinking because we don't want to think of the alternatives, and besides, we had orders.

My first day in combat on Operation Kailua was in the Ho Bo Woods. I saw what can happen when you carry ammo or other explosive devises on your person.

Thoughts of that Viet Cong bastard's body parts flying every which way into the air just flashed through my mind as I write this! I am glad that I didn't think about it that day, or I would have been more nervous. This time it was I in my Army's uniform and I was carrying ammo just like that Viet Cong. Hmm?

Luis Milan-Anavita was the M-60 gunner, and I was going to carry some ammo and assist him. He wasn't exactly the biggest soldier, and he was carrying the biggest weapon because he was tough. There must be an unwritten law that states, "The heaviest weapon must be carried by the smallest soldier"! It wasn't that heavy except when you carried it awhile, and we weren't going on a short stroll. After a very short 20 meters, we came to a river.

Before we crossed, something told me this wasn't just the average run of the mill search and destroy mission. It was more like going to an Ambush site. We surveyed the river. As we got closer we could see that it was about 12 feet wide, and on the surface it seemed to be peaceful and meandering. Up ahead, some of the bigger guys went through the river and got through without much difficulty. Then Luis got in and took about 5 steps. I was following behind him.

He had made it to the middle, and the water was mid-chest deep. He started to drift to one side downstream. I took 5 quick steps and stopped him, and he moved three more steps and got a little higher. Then I started to also drift down stream! He grabbed me and gave a yank on my arm, and I took a couple of steps. Together we pulled each other through and navigated the current to the other side. Finally we made it without losing any equipment or anyone. It was teamwork. Meandering river my Lilly White Ass! Once you got in it was moving along at a great clip, almost twenty-five miles per hour in the middle! Where were those "Big Lugs" when we little guys were trying to drown ourselves? After our ordeal of the "crossing" (kind of feels like George Washington's Delaware River crossing), we laughed our silly heads off and it was funnier than Hell! Humor in hell: how's that for a concept?

What would you do if you were just in water for about 5 to 8 minutes and leaches were swimming too? We decided that a quick check for leaches was in order, so we performed the leach check. I guess they didn't have time to latch onto us, because thankfully no leaches were found.

Before you start making fun of the smaller guys, remember who was carrying the M-60 machine gun, the two boxes of ammo and the four bandoliers. That's right, the smallest guys in the unit. The only plus in carrying the ammo was that you did not have to be point man. A point man leads the platoon to the desired location or designated site, which can be dangerous because you are the prime target after the platoon runs into a firefight, and you get cut off from the others.

We had a strange feeling that we weren't on the right soil, but of course we weren't in the big "C" were we? Nope! American GI's never went into Cambodia, did they? We walked on a trail along the tree and brush line for quite a while, and were very cautious about how we stepped.

We came to a spot along the trail that had some higher ground to the left, and moved in to check it out and make sure of our position, and then set up an Ambush with two Claymore mines, one up the trail and one down. We set up two more Claymores, covering our back in case of an attack from that direction. We had two directions to watch, one in front, and one in back. This spot was our home for several hours, and it was nerve racking just sitting there waiting for your prey to get caught in your trap.
The place felt eerie, like we weren't supposed to be there, bad electric vibes, maybe a bad karma or bad aura. These feelings were common to just about every site we visited.

We had been there for almost two more hours and didn't even get a nibble on our trap, and the longer we waited the more tense we became. The day proved to be a bust as far as killing Viet Cong,

## February 1967

but no one had gotten hurt so far. We got the call to return. We retrieved our Claymore mines and loaded on the bandoliers of ammo. I picked up the ammo cans and we moved on down the trail back to the river.

This was not the time to relax just because we were going back to the Armored Personnel Carriers. The guys had no desire to become trapped in an Ambush of the Viet Cong's design.

We took great pains to keep a distance between ourselves so we didn't get bunched up. The point man continually watched the direction we were going to make sure we weren't the victims of an Ambush by Victor Charlie. The rear man kept a vigil on where we had just been.

When we arrived back at our old nemesis, the river, I had no desire to do a repeat performance of our "Water Ballet" earlier in the day. This time we gave up some of our burden of ammo to those big lugs that deserted us on our first crossing. We made it through the river with the help of the other guys interspersed between the two shorter ones of the squad. This took a while, so we waited in the water. The crossing was actually refreshing, because it was in the afternoon and it was getting hot and sticky.

We made our way back to the defensive position of our Armored Personnel Carriers. Once across, we did another check for leaches, mainly for peace of mind. Good thing I checked, because there was one of those little blood-sucking vampires on my left side. So I lit up a Lucky Strike and burned him till he dropped to the ground. Another casualty of war!

Then we left to rendezvous with the rest of the battalion at the Battalion Forward Base camp. Later we found that others in our unit had discovered several Viet Cong base camps and an ordnance factory containing bombs, artillery rounds, hand grenades and tools.

The purpose of our little diversion during the day was to be ready to confront the Viet Cong in the area as they made a break for safety in Cambodia. Apparently, the Viet Cong decided to evacuate the area via a different route, so we didn't get to kill any of those bastards that day. Later that evening we really wanted to kill those Viet Cong bastards because they were again fucking with what little sleep we could get by firing 5 mortars into our base camp!

February 14, 1967 the Battalion continued Search and Destroy operations in the area of WT0256 and 0358 for the day. No enemy action occurred.

February 15, 1967 the Battalion stayed in the same area, and all seemed calm until we were under mortar attack. The Battalion received an attack of seventeen mortar rounds at the base camp! No one was wounded. (bad shooting Charlie!)

February 16, 1967 the Battalion broke camp at 7:30am and moved to the bridge site at XT0559. We crossed the bridge at 8:00am and moved southeast to Tay Ninh. We were on the outside of the base camp and finished our day at 1:32pm.

We were going to get a night off! (This was the first rest time we had since the first of February, and boy was it needed!) There was still Perimeter duty but Ambushes and Listening Post that night were suspended. We actually had some personal time and could shave and take a "spit" bath & some clean underwear. We were hoping for a beer or two, I don't think that happened.

February 17, 1967 through February 21, 1967 the 1$^{st}$ Battalion 5$^{th}$ Mechanized Infantry continued to keep a presence with Search and Destroy operations in the general area of X0358.

February 22, 1967 the Battalion moved from the area of Trai Bi XT1375 to secure Fire Support Base Pershing (named for General Black Jack Pershing of World War I and the Mexican-American War) 3000 meters southeast where Highway 22 & 247 intersect. (See Map B on Page 315) This day marked the beginning of the 1$^{st}$ of the 5$^{th}$ Mechanized Infantry in Operation Junction City Alternate.

The date I wrote this was August 20, 2007. As I wrote this I remembered having a conversation with Tim Fyle, who was another former "Pretty Boy Squad" member, about this incident. He recalled some press clippings from a local newspaper in his home area about this historic jump. They were up in his attic in a box containing a scrapbook. He did not remember the date, so he was going to look for the scrapbook with the article.

We all remember events, but dates were fairly elusive, probably because we didn't keep track of dates. We were too busy! Shortly after our conversation, Tim sent me via e-mail a copy of the newspaper article in the Asbury Park Press, Asbury New Jersey. It states that elements landed into a Hot Landing Zone and encountered sporadic small arms fire. This didn't happen at our position they must be talking about further north. We were at the southern position of the western blocking force on the map.

Go Jump!
We had gotten up early and secured an area near our position. The area was a quite large open space, considering we were in a highly wooded area. The time was somewhere around 8:30 or 9:00am, and we began to hear a dull roaring of engines from the southwest. We had no idea what to expect. The roaring became louder and louder, and we spotted 4 large transport airplanes come closer and closer. About the time they reached our position, they were a little in front of us.

Normally we don't see that many airplanes, if any, but 4 at the same time never happened. The planes were starting to pass by, suddenly a stream of things were coming out of the side doors, followed by the opening of parachutes. Well I'll be, it was paratroopers. That's right, paratroopers! We didn't see them land because we were too far away. The next several sets of trees between us hid the ground, that's how big the area was. The men would come out first, followed by the parachutes opening their big canopies, followed by a quick jerk as it stopped the paratrooper's descent. Then they floated down toward earth. After the planes passed, it looked like it was snowing. Why in the hell were they doing this? Regardless of the reason, it sure was an exciting time for us.

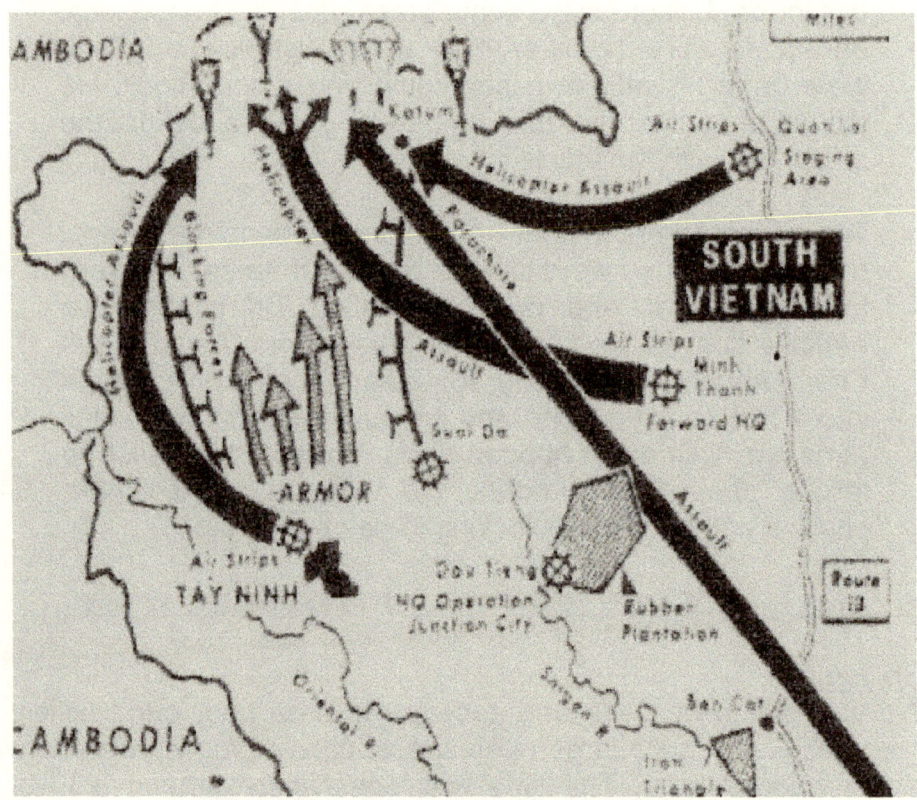

Map of Operation Junction City from Tim Fyle
We were located near bottom of left arrow

The 173rd Airborne Brigade, commanded by Brigadier General John R Deane Jr., accomplished this historic combat parachute assault mission with 3 Battalions and established blocking positions from Katum to the 1st Brigade area.

I had printed a report from February 1967 about Operation Junction City about two weeks earlier, but never read the report until recently. It has a title "D-Day, 22 February, 1967, Junction City", but it was just one operation after another for the 1st of the 5th Mechanized Infantry for over 3 weeks! We didn't know what the operation was called until later.

## February 1967

This jump was historic because it was the first U.S. Combat Parachute Assault since the Korean War (or should I say conflict? That's what the non-combatant pacifists want to call everything).

The morning of 22 February, 1967, 845 paratroopers boarded 16 C-130 transport planes at Bien Hoa and at 9:00am began the day's jump into 4 Landing Zones near the Cambodian border. There were only 11 minor injuries as a result of the jump and little enemy contact. They probably scared the hell out of the Viet Cong! Oh, by the way, General Deane was the first one to jump as the green light flashed, "go"!

The perimeter or blocking force area secured was quite large, containing our Brigade, units of the 196$^{th}$ Light Infantry, and the Big Red One Division. We remained at this perimeter position all day. Our battalion was to hold this position. A rumor circulated that an important visitor was arriving. You know the army never told us grunts shit about anything! The area had several large fields surrounded by tall trees and thick jungle growth.

About 11:00am I was 50 to 60 feet from the track at the perimeter. I had a blanket and was out there trying to get a suntan. We didn't usually had our fatigue jackets on. (Boy, someone really named that jacket right!) Here I was, as lazy as could be, when it occurred to me that I was bored. I decided I needed some exercise. My sport in high school was Gymnastics, so I figured why not. I started by taking off the jacket and then with single leg circles into splits, ouch (actually I can still do them today). Then a straight arm press to a handstand, and then some more complicated moves. It felt great and released my pent up energy. This does fit in with my brief military career. May 1966 I was the Fort Hood Parallel Bar, Floor Exercise and Pommel Horse Champion, so there!

I think Charlie left us alone because he was damn scared of some crazy GI doing crazy things. Especially things he'd never seen someone doing out in the jungle. At least that's my fantasy, so let me live with the delusion. I had finished my exercise then I was called back to the track. We were told that we were on alert and to keep a keen eye out for the Viet Cong.

We waited for almost 45 minutes and heard the roar of airplane engines coming closer. Soon it was upon our position, a huge C-

130 Transport Plane. What the Hell was it doing here? There was hardly enough room for it to land. Even worse was the thought of it flying out once it landed.

The plane made a big circle around the area waiting for clearance. I hope the people responsible for radar were monitoring enemy activity in the area. The C-130 finished circling in front of our position and to our left. We heard it coming. Remember, the trees were quite tall on the edges of the clearing. We saw that plane as it came over the trees and then drop almost straight down like a roller coaster. We turned our heads, gasped and looked just as it neared the ground to land. The plane then taxied through the field and into the next clearing. Then the pilot must have turned off the engine because we didn't hear it any more.

How the Hell is he going to get that huge plane out of here?

That plane was still there after awhile, so he must have waited to unload or was picking up someone or something. I really didn't care who or what it was, it was just another day in paradise and very quiet for us. We probably will never know the truth. We really didn't care because this day had been easy duty compared to Search and Destroy operations or Ambushes.

Eventually we heard the pilot fire up the engines in the distance; the engines roared as he revved them up. Then the plane sounded like it was idling. The plane was still in the other clearing but we could see it facing in our direction. We weren't as sure as the pilot that he could make it out. It was our duty to keep an eye out for the Viet Cong. We didn't want anything bad to happen so we did our duty to the letter.

Our attention was brought back to the plane as the engines revved up louder and louder. We glanced out towards the front for signs of the Viet Cong and then at the plane as it began picking up speed. The plane rolled fast and faster as it really picked up speed. We glanced out towards the jungle and then saw the plane nearing the end of the field, closer and closer and closer. We thought he's not going to make it! Tension was building to a fevered pitch as we looked at the plane again. The more we looked the more our bodies tensed up and our muscles were strained. It was as if we were sending our energy to help lift up that plane.

*February 1967*

It looked like the plane was going to crash into the trees, when... The pilot must have jerked up the yoke almost pulling it out of its mooring and that damned plane shot straight upward like a rocket and cleared those trees. Everyone cheered wildly! That was one hell of a pilot!!!

That was the most exciting thing that happened to us that day. It was more interesting and exciting than the Paratrooper Jump in the morning. I guess you could say we really were easily entertained.

It was usually difficult for our unit to tell when one operation ended and another started, because we were always left out in the field between operations. It was normal for the $1^{st}$ Battalion, $5^{th}$ Mechanized Infantry, $25^{th}$ Infantry Division to stay out in the bush without any rest until the next operation, while other units went back to the base camp to "Shit and Regroup", to use an old Army Euphemism.

Our unit holds records for the longest continuous field combat periods in Vietnam, a reputation we've all paid for dearly over the last 40 plus years. (See Map B # 8 on Page 315)

February 23, 1967 the B Company moved to 5000 meters east of Highway 22 where the Battalion established a forward base. Elements located 5 bunkers & 15 structures north of base. Two tracks hit anti-tank mines, five Bobcats wounded. Company A had one Bobcat die from his wounds. Found in the area was evidence of uniformed personnel as well as the 'Black Pajama Gang'!

February 24, 1967 elements of the Battalion located 2 base camps containing arms, ammunition and supplies. During the day, twelve Bobcats were wounded, and one Armored Personnel Carrier was damaged as a result of command detonated mines while engaging the Viet Cong at XT166804. Three were killed in the exchange and were identified as members of the $272^{nd}$ Viet Cong Regiment.

February 25, 1967 while searching a base camp from the day before located at XT154834, an unknown number of Viet Cong were engaged. The important items found after the firefight were 300 rounds 105mm Artillery ammunition, but no bodies.

February 26, 1967 shows no recorded activity day regarding the 1st of the 5th Mechanized infantry.

February 27, 1967 the Battalion secured Fire Support Base Foche for the 1/8th Artillery and the 2nd Brigade Command Post.

1/8 Artillery Fire Support Base Thanks Guys

We also found a place with water somewhere around that command post. The Battalion had been out in the field for a month. The typical day in our unit was to get up just after daybreak, eat and load up while waiting for Ambushes and Listening Posts.

The Battalion would be safe and sound in the bosom of the perimeter. Breakfast for those returning from Ambush or Listening Post was usually long after all the others had eaten. There usually wasn't enough food to feed a poor church mouse, and the cooks had finished their work. So if you were on one of those operations,

*February 1967*

you didn't eat much and the food was usually cold.

It's interesting that those on Ambushes and Listening Posts with no sleep couldn't get the two hours-on and two hours-off sleep that they did at the perimeter because they were the first elements that would make contact with the enemy. Perimeter watch was to be two hours on and two hours off, so from 11:00pm-4:00am=5 hours divided by 2 hours equals 2½ times at watch or only 4 hours sleep. Are you starting to get the picture? In short, we thought the U.S. Army was trying to kill us before the VC "Victor Charlie" could!

Once we were ready, it was Search and Destroy, trail blazing by knocking down the jungle with the Armored Personnel Carrier, and firefights, mortars, RPG2 from dawn to dusk. Once the brass decided where to feather our new nest it could be 8:00pm or 10:00pm. We were without doubt sleep-deprived!

How about doing a Listening Post duty one day, perimeter duty the following day, Ambush duty the next, and then repeat the cycle almost continuously. Bingo, this was what our life was like. Then you mix in the constant threat of death and red and black ants, all kinds of insects, and snakes. It's kind of useless to complain to a Combat Veteran with these experiences about, you being tired!

Bath
We were a hop, skip, and a jump away from the Cambodian Border, somewhere northwest of Tay Ninh. There was a big pond with reeds growing along the sides.

Bath time was very refreshing

We must have had another unit or two providing us with a more secure "safe" area! We weren't going anywhere for a while, and the pond water wasn't the cleanest, but it was wet and inviting! (See Map B #9 on Page 315)

The big brass must have taken pity on us or they couldn't stand the smell of us any longer, so we got what we wanted. Since we hadn't had a bath in quite a long time, we were ripe. So ripe we started to smell like the Viet Cong! We went for a swim armed with a bar of soap. I can still remember the eerie feeling. I walked into that pond with the mud oozing through my toes, wondering just what the bottom was composed of, or should I say decomposed of? Believe it or not it was refreshing. Ah, the luxuries of life. Draw me a bath, Reginald! We camped somewhere around that spot, that evening.

```
February 28, 1967 B Company conducted Search and
Destroy missions and Fire Support base security.
We came to an open field in front of us with the
Tole Roti River on our left about 250 meters. It
was the border between Cambodia and Vietnam. The
Viet Cong always moved with ease in and out of
Cambodia, but it was illegal for us to be there.
```

(Cambodia always seemed to be a mysterious and forbidding area. We had no idea why Cambodia was so mysterious, but it was and that's all that's important!) (See Map B #10 on Page 315)

### Water Buffalo
We looked out in front of us for about 350 meters and the field stretched out to our right for an even greater distance. We moved cautiously a little farther, checking it out for Viet Cong presence. There out in the field were about eleven water buffalo grazing in that peaceful field about 50 meters away from us. It was quite a pastoral view.

It's amazing. We stopped and dismounted our trusty steeds. Just kidding! We all started thinking how powerfully strong the water buffalo were, and we all came to the same conclusion. The Viet Cong used water buffalo to power the ox carts to haul supplies, ammo and weapons to their comrades farther inland. We were experiencing the Ho Chi Minh Trail syndrome, so we viewed those water buffalo as the enemy. We called in for orders concerning the water buffalo. We were not surprised when we heard the orders. We had orders to destroy the water buffalo, but we didn't necessarily like the idea.

The more we thought, the more we agreed that those critters needed to be destroyed. Maybe we could slow down the supplies, ammo, and weapons, and it seemed to be the logical course of action. I was of the same thinking, and besides, my M-79 Grenade launcher and I were itching for some more action. Well we counted to three and opened up on the poor critters. I aimed at one of the big ugly beasts, squeezed the trigger and let one go- "pop"! The 40 mm shell introduced itself to the head of the beast "tic", "boom!" and blew the top of its head clean off the body! When we were all done, so were the water buffalo.

Water Buffalo after the shooting with Bull in the foreground
Armored Personnel carriers moved up to secure area from the back of the picture from where we shot

According to Tim Fyle, when the shooting was done the water buffalo were laying in semi-circles with the bull buffalo in the back center. As the cows were dying they were looking at the bull. It appeared as if they were questioning him with--didn't we tell you not to help those Viet Cong?

There was another cow running away as fast as she could while herding a young calf to safety. Those water buffalo looked innocent enough, just like some of the people in the villages we'd passed out in their fields and rice paddies.

My buddy Tim Fyle

The friendly farmer smiling and waving his hand at you in the day time could very well be a Viet Cong at night with blood in his eyes and murder in his heart!

Today we have groups fighting for the rights of everything from Alligators to Zebras. I think that's ok, and if it is done right without someone else getting hurt, it's a service to all mankind and I applaud you.

***February 1967***

If you are one of those animal rights activists please don't think too badly of us. We were a product of our circumstances, environment and training. As I reflect, I would really regret the incident if it weren't for the fact that water buffalo were used to deliver supplies, ammo, and weapons to the enemy. Maybe we delayed supplies, ammo, and weapons, so possibly we saved lives. Maybe a relative of yours!

War is hell and if you weren't out there in the combat with us, try not to judge.

Thirty-nine years later I had the honor and privilege to attend a unit reunion of the Survivors for the Battle of Cu Chi 1$^{st}$ Battalion 5$^{th}$ Mechanized Infantry, 25$^{th}$ Infantry Division Class of 66 held July 2005 in Dayton Ohio. It was my first contact with most of them since Nam.

I was standing with Tim Fyle on my right side and we were talking to someone. Tim was talking, and said "The craziest thing I remember was we were up by Tay Ninh near Cambodia, and we decided to shoot some water buffalo, part of the Viet Cong supply line. Then someone on my left shot off an M-79 and blew the top of the head off of one of them"!

I piped up, "Fyle that was me"!

Well, him telling that story when I was standing on his left side again, just like in Vietnam 39 years ago, what a thrill! What a strange coincidence.

\* \* \* \* \*

There were seventy-seven men wounded-in-action this month.

February 1967 claimed the lives of nine of our Brothers-in-Arms:

    Jackson Thomas      Paul T. Short Jr.

    Marco J. Baruzzi      Raymond F. Demory

    James E. Bostock     Joseph M. Brady

    Henry R. Lopez       Jack M. Secrest Jr.

    Landon C. Ray

These men lived in danger almost every day in their tour of duty, and did what they had to without flinching. They never knew whether or not a new day would come. We who have served with them give them Honor and Respect.

# March 1967

March 1, 1967 the Battalion conducted Search and Destroy operations in an area 18 kilometers southwest of Katum. At 9:52am a track hit an anti-tank mine resulting in nine Bobcats Wounded-in-Action. C Company engaged the enemy, resulting in killing two and capturing one Viet Cong, with five Bobcats being Wounded-in-Action.

March 2, 1967 B and A Companies conducted Search and Destroy Operations to the northeast of FSB Foche. An enemy base camp was found and destroyed at XT165880. Company C provided security for the Fire Support Base.

March 3, 1967 Company A provided security for the base while Companies B and C conducted Search and Destroy operations in the area.

The Listening Post from Hell
We were up by the Katum area and the Battalion had no enemy contact. At 8:30pm I was selected to be on a Listening Post that

evening with two others. I had been on two prior Listening Posts with James Wisdom and James Flickenger. This one was the last one I would do with these guys. They were the real "Odd Couple". Wisdom was a scrawny, scrappy character with red hair. He had an attitude from the East St. Louis, Mo. slums. Flickenger was a 6'2" blond guy from Burbank, California, and maybe a little too cocky! Then there was me stuck right in the middle and wondering how I got there. We all got along though.

We were selected to be bait for a night because that's what a Listening Post really became. We got our stuff together and went about 80 meters out in front of the Perimeter and set up. The night was very dark. Because we were out in the jungle there was no incidental light from nearby villages. The deep dark sky was very striking, with the distant but brilliantly lit stars creating a great contrast.

Since the jungle was so dark we couldn't see a thing, but we could hear every little noise. Unfortunately, we could even hear the movement of large insects, not to mention snakes and small, medium and large four legged critters. Sounds like a wonderful evening, huh? For some reason, even though we were really tired, none of us could go to sleep. We had laid there for a while when I turned saw them with a blanket over their heads and they were lighting up cigarettes. A lit cigarette in the dark jungle is like firing up a searchlight! Guess who could see it?

I made them put out the "Fuck'n cigarettes", as the smell would also tell of our presence. They thought that I had gone soft, but really they had gone soft in the head.

When we settled we began to concentrate at watch. Flickenger was on the right side. I moved to the center of the position with Wisdom on the left. My Omega wristwatch my father gave me for High School graduation was the only one working, so we used it to keep track of time.

I sat up to get a good view, but keeping down so as to be a target. About an hour-and-a-half later I heard a muffled snap! Pop! I looked and then I heard another snap! Pop! That did it. I'll be damned. They had sodas out there on Listening Post!

Needless to say, I was pissed. I was with two crazy lunatics! I sort of wanted to live so I had to keep track of three potential enemies; Flickenger, Wisdom, and the Viet Cong. I don't know which one was the deadliest enemy.

The morning finally arrived and we got the call, so we packed up everything and then called in that we were returning so they would not shoot at us. We made it back to the Perimeter safely. This was the last time I ever went on a Listening Post or Ambush with either of them.

Somehow my Omega watch didn't make it back with us. We looked for it before we left but it wasn't found. It's probably still ticking away in the thick grass and driving the water buffalo crazy!

March 4, 1967 the Battalion provided security for the air extraction of the 2$^{nd}$ Brigade Headquarters' forward elements from the Fire Support Base. At 1:00pm the 1$^{st}$ Battalion 5$^{th}$ Mechanized Infantry was attached and OPCON to the 11$^{th}$ Armored Cavalry Regiment.

March 5, 1967 the Battalion Forward Base received a 120 round 60mm and 82mm mortar barrage. One Bobcat from B Company was Killed-in-Action in that attack.

I couldn't find reports for seven of the days from the 5th to the 12th we were attached to the 11$^{th}$ Armored Cavalry.

March 13, 1967 the Battalion conducted operations. C Company engaged the enemy result one Bobcat was Killed-in-Action by small arms fire.

March 14, 1967 we became OPCON to the 196$^{th}$ Light Infantry Brigade at the French Fort, located 7 km north of Nui Ba Den (The Black Virgin Mountain) at XT2868 at 6:30pm.

March 15, 1967 the Battalion was running convoys

near the French Fort; Recon Platoon was struck by an RPG-2 Russian rocket, two Bobcats Wounded-in-Action. At 4:40pm an Armored Personnel Carrier from B Company was hit by an RPG-2 at XT273722. Four were Wounded-in-Action and one died of his wounds later in the day. At 8:00pm the Ou Chi Base Camp received 50 rounds of 82mm mortar fire and 25 rounds of 75mm recoilless rifle fire.

March 16, 1967 between 1:35am and 2:00am, 150 rounds of 60mm, 82mm mortar and 75mm Recoilless Rifle rounds were received on the 196th Light Infantry Brigade command post at the French Fort. Four men were killed and 22 wounded including. The Battalion continued clearing the road with Convoy Escort from the junction of Highways 4 and 247 South to the French Fort.

March 17, 1967 we were OPCON to the 2/34th Armor Company C. 2/34th Armor became OPCON to the 1/5th (M) Infantry. Units conducted Search and Destroy.

March 18, 1967 B Company did Convoy Escort when a command-detonated mine was set off at XT193726. At 4:00pm the Recon Platoon was fired upon by a burst of Automatic Weapons fire on Highway 4 south of Prek Klok, with unknown results.

March 19, 1967 the attachments with the 2/34th armor were terminated at 1:00pm. One Bobcat from B Company was accidentally killed, cause unknown.

March 20, 1967 the Recon Platoon and Company C conducted convoy escort from Soui Da to Prek Klok after clearing and securing the highway. Companies A, B, and C conducted Search and Destroy operations in the area. Company A had one Armored Personnel Carrier hit a large mine at 10:45am at XT241805 between Soui Da and Prek Klok. Five

Bobcats were wounded and "dusted off" by Helicopter. All Battalion units closed the Battalion Base at 4:50pm.

March 21, 1967 the Battalion conducted Road Security and Search and Destroy operations in the area.

March 22, 1967 the Recon Platoon with personnel from the 196th Engineers cleared and secured the road from the French Fort to the Soui Da turnoff. Company B and C continued operations east of Highway 4. At 8:25am Company A hit an anti-tank mine resulting in 1 wounded. At 8:50am Company C had also hit and detonated a mine resulting in 8 Wounded-in-Action. An Armored Personnel Carrier at XT245815 from Company A hit a mine at 11:30am with 4 Wounded-in-Action and One Bobcat Killed-in-Action. All elements of the Battalion closed the forward base at 5:00pm.

March 23, 1967 Company A provided security for the Battalion forward base. B and C Companies ran Search and Destroy operations in the area. Recon Platoon and part of C Company conducted Road Security and Convoy Escort operations.

March 24, 1967 the Recon Platoon conducted Road Security and Convoy Escort on Highway 4 from the French Fort to the Soui Da turnoff. Company B remained at the Battalion base for security. C Company secured a Drop Zone for a re-supply airdrop. Company A Screened and Blocked from XT3074 to 3076.

March 25, 1967 Recon Platoon and one platoon from Company C cleared and secured the roadway and escorted convoys. At 1:05pm one platoon from C Company secured a Drop Zone at XT267786. The drop was 90% effective, 10% was damaged and recovered. One platoon from C Company secured a crossing site while the 175$^{th}$ Engineers installed an AVLB bridge. Companies A and B crossed the bridge and conducted Search and Destroy operations at XT3180 to 3178 with negative contact. Units closed the new Battalion Base at Prek Klok by 7:00pm.

March 26, 1967 the Battalion established Blocking Positions in coordination with sweeps by the 3$^{rd}$ brigade, 4$^{th}$ infantry division. At 11:20am an Armored Personnel Carrier from B Company struck a mine at XT295737, resulting in one Bobcat Wounded-in-Action. At 1:00pm one platoon from A company secured another drop for supply at XT269711.
(See Map B #11 on Page 315)

With all these supplies coming in, we knew we wouldn't be leaving soon. Around 2:30pm we were near a Landing Zone site about 800 meters from the base perimeter. We were at an open field that was about 200 meters by 300 meters. On one corner of the field was a big bomb crater about 4.5 meters across. When this crater was filled with water it looked crystal clear with the most vibrant blue tint from the reflection of the sky.

I was with 2 Spanish-speaking guys from Puerto Rico. One of them spotted a lone banana tree, or so I thought. Actually they were plantains, a member of the banana family. Who cared? It was food that was not from a can! They were green and I thought, "Darn we can't eat them, they aren't ripe." The other guy told me that was no problem because we were going to bake them. I thought that they were crazy! One of the guys told me that at home that's what they did with plantains when they were green.

Being an Eternal Pessimist, I told them that we had nothing to bake them in. I hate to tell you I was wrong, but I was. One of the guys came back with an old ammo can that was olive drab on the outside and a shiny brass color inside. He had found it in the back of the track. They rigged up a stove with a hole, some rocks on the sides, sticks, and a few small logs inside the hole. Then he added some C-4 (explosives), lit it and we had a fire. He added into the ammo tin the plantains.

Once the tin was on the fire he put the lid on top. We waited.

Bomb Crater filled with clear blue water

I had no idea when they would be done, but they had experience with this process. It took about 25 minutes before they determined they were sufficiently cooked.

Now I know you're just itching to know what they tasted like. They had the consistency and taste of baked potatoes. We had a feast!

I thought that this story would show first hand that we GI's could be resourceful if needed, and then someone might learn a little more about us. This was a different type of search and destroy (eat) mission! We were informed that we would remain there for the night, so we needed to set up an evening Base Camp Perimeter. The company was east of Highway 247 at XT295737 near the Black Virgin Mountain, which was also known as Nui Ba Den about 1700 meters away.

The Armored Personnel Carriers were arranged in the usual defensive formation. We were to set up an M-60 machine gun position between each track. We needed to dig a foxhole for cover.

We've all seen a construction site or a roadwork area with a Workman using a jackhammer that makes a lot of noise and vibrates a lot, shaking the hell out of the worker. It is used in many cases to

Nui Ba Den "The Black Virgin Mountain"

break up cement or pavement. This is very a very effective way to make a hole. Well, we didn't have one in the jungle.

What we did have was the good old GI entrenching tool. Using those shovels is like trying to demolish a three-story building with a small claw hammer. We had to use what we had, so I took out the shovel, opened it up as long as it could go, put my left foot on the left top ledge of the blade, and then attempted to use the right foot on the right ledge by jumping with my full weight to ram the blade into the earth. Clunk! Moved it over a little and tried it again. Clunk!

Some brilliant person remembered that somewhere there was a pickaxe. That was a great solution to our dilemma. I took that Pickaxe, swung it around then over, and with all the force I could muster, pulled it around, and down. Clunk! I moved it to a different spot, tried again. The point went down into the earth. Ah pay dirt!

What we had found was a big rock about 2.5 feet by 2 feet and 1 foot high, or so we thought. We pried it up and found that it was a bunch of smaller rocks or stones fused together. We weren't going to fight with any more "rocks" like we did with that one! We moved it to the front top of the foxhole. That gave us a hole to work with, except the area seemed to be made up of the same type of rocks. We weren't going to build a home there, so we scraped up as much loose surface dirt as we could to fill sand bags. We then set up the M-60 and placed the sandbags. With that done, we scraped out as much of the ground as we could from the bottom of our foxhole. When you take into consideration the heat and long days, we were drenched when we finally finished working. But there were no cold beers for refreshment.

I will never forget the ground around Nui Ba Den! See we had all kinds of enemies! We passed the evening without enemy contact.

March 27, 1967 Recon Platoon escorted the 3/13th artillery to Prek Klok. Companies A and C left the base at 7:30am. At 11:55pm an AVLB was placed across a stream at XT310804. Company B secured a drop zone for another two supply drops. One was at 12:30pm and another at 4:00pm.

It is amazing the strange sounds you hear out in the jungle. Many sound very similar to human sounds. While we were at the supply drop zones, I heard two more crazy sounds that I hadn't heard before. I don't know if it was a lizard, insect or bird, but this one sounded like "Piss...ahn...yaaa!" That's right, "Piss...ahn...yaaa!" I know you think I am full of crap, but that's what I heard! It was like a symphony of strange morning sounds with different critter accents. Another participant joined in the chorus and it sounded like "Fok u, Fok u! I don't need to say what we thought it sounded like, do I?

I suspect there is bound to be a television program about the strange creatures they've found in Vietnam. One day soon you'll be watching the Animal Planet or some such show about the jungles North of Nui Ba Den and you will find out I am telling the truth! These are some of the strange things that amused us while in very frightening circumstances. I call them Combat Comedy!

March 28, 1967 C and A Companies secured one Fire Support Base, then 4/31st Infantry relieved us at 11:15am. Company B and Recon Platoon secured a 2nd area at Katum, B Company had an Armored Personnel Carrier detonate a mine, causing extensive damage, with one Bobcat Wounded-in-Action. Battalion Command Post, Companies A, C and Recon crossed Fire Support Base at Katum. Company B secured another re-supply drop zone and stayed for the night. Recon secured an AVLB bridge at XT289865.

A typical supply drop, picture supplied by Arnie Spotted Bear Queener with Recon

We knew something was brewing.

March 29, 1967 the Battalion secured a landing zone for the airlift of the 2/1st Infantry Battalion from the French Fort. The 1/5th Mech conducted Search and Destroy operations and closed the new Battalion Base at XT276935 at 5000 meters, South of the Cambodian border and 6000 meters northwest of Katum.

## March 1967

I don't know about you, but I could feel the tension of all that activity, and I thought about all the additional Listening Posts and Ambushes. Things appeared to be building up to something big!

```
March 30, 1967 C and A Companies conducted Search
and Rescue operations in the area, and Recon
Platoon conducted a reconnaissance of the area.
Company C escorted a convoy from Prek Klok. At
11:34am one Armored Personnel Carrier from the
Recon Platoon detonated an anti-tank mine. Company
C engaged an unknown sized enemy force at 1:40pm,
57 mm, Recoilless Rifle rounds hit two Armored
Personnel Carriers. One Armored Personnel Carrier
was shot in the rear ramp with two rounds. Six
Bobcats were wounded. Gun Ships hovered and fired
giving cover and contact was broken. The Battalion
established a new base at XT281969, only 500
meters south of the Cambodian Border.

March 31, 1967 Companies A, B, and C conducted
Search and Destroy operations to the west of
Battalion base. The Recon Platoon remained in
reserve with the Battalion command group. Company
A made brief contact with the enemy at 8:30am,
exchanging small arm fire with negative results.
(See Map B #12 on Page 315)
```

Can you feel it? This was heavy shit, and it had been building for almost a month. The shit was about to hit the fan. We were in "Victor Charlie's" face, pushing him, and he was getting desperate. We were not too laid back either. Just reading this makes my blood run cold with the possibilities!

We were on Operation Junction City Alternate, somewhere around the French Fort area about 1500 meters from Cambodia, which is north of Nui Ba Den or the Black Virgin Mountain, as we knew her. The Battalion had been receiving a lot of action, mines and RPG2 fire. The previous day, Recoilless Rifle rounds hit 2 Armored Personnel Carriers from C Company. All in all, 6 Bobcats were wounded.

March 31, 1967 is a day I will never forget. It is burned into my memory. My day began early in the morning, which was true of every morning out in the field. I had my usual flirtation with Morpheus the Greek God of Dreams. After being out in the field for a long period of time with our grueling schedule and lack of sleep, we were all sleep-deprived! The morning began much the same as any day. My squad had not been on an Ambush, which meant we would be getting some breakfast this day.

Right about chow time I heard another of those crazy critters in the jungle. I don't know if it was a lizard, bird, or an insect, but it made the most darned noise. When we had a prepared breakfast we would be informed to send "50 percent to chow" so some could eat and those remaining could watch the Perimeter. Well, whatever creature it was, it mimicked the exact sound of "50 percent-to-chow" almost note-to-note in a little higher pitch!

The First Platoon B Company was to lead the company that day, and our Armored Personnel Carrier B13 was chosen to be the lead track. I was to be the Track Commander. Normally, the Squad Leader was the one who rode in the Track Commander's Hatch. Roy Love took over the squad when Butch Petit left for the "World" at the end of his tour of duty in Vietnam in February 1967. Roy later left the squad in the field around March 27, 1967 to prepare for his trip back to the "World". That left a temporary empty spot because a replacement hadn't been assigned. Someone was needed to be the Track Commander (just a term, not an NCO position).

I didn't know why, but there I was, bigger than life in the Track Commander's Hatch. What luck, in charge of the Armored Personnel Carrier and a chance to be the Leader, Wow!

We started out easy enough until we were told to turn left into the jungle, thick with trees and bushes. This was to be a horrendous 4 to 5 hours of knocking out a path through the jungle. Imagine it's hot and sticky, stifling thick air, and then add into the mix having to dodge falling branches and the ANTS! Ants were falling from those trees in bushels-full, lots and lots of angry ants fighting and biting for their lives!

If you've never had a sizeable clump of ants down your pants or in your shirt or on your head, I don't suggest you try to accomplish that experience. When this happens you just can't stand it anymore. You arm yourself with a can of insect repellant (usually DDT), and do what's known as the Ant Dance. While ripping your clothes off, you frantically spray yourself like mad while hopping around with all kinds of gyrations! Your goal is to kill lots of ants before they kill you. The ants were administering my Baptism of Leadership, or was I being punished?

I recall that miserable task of "Trail Blazing" and the pressure we felt. We started by knocking down trees and thick underbrush with someone, probably the Platoon Leader or Company Commanding Officer, yelling directions.

The jungle area north of Nui Ba Den was thick with trees and foliage. Try trail blazing through this area.

Occasionally we would run into a tree that was too big to knock down. We used the Armored Personnel Carrier as a ramming device, but if a tree was too big we had to temporarily change directions. I don't remember who the driver was. I think he was a tall and lanky guy, with almost bleach blond hair, and he had a slight overbite. The person I described is Clyde Simonson.

I had a map and a compass, but have you ever tried to read a map with branches and ants falling on your head, knocking you silly? To say the least, it wasn't the most pleasant task I've ever done. Have you ever had a map with coordinates, but no visible point of reference to tie with, at the same time being busy with all the other physical factors and that dammed engine noise? It was like being in a wind tunnel at hurricane speed carrying a big bag of feathers while reading a map twisting with the wind. We were so busy that the Viet Cong could have taken advantage of us quite easily, but luckily he wasn't that close to us at the time.

At about 9:30, after about 2 hours of experiencing the joys of trail blazing, we stumbled upon a small cleared area serving as a mini Base Camp, a safe haven for Charlie. It consisted of a couple of

Armored Personnel Carrier attacking the jungle
Trail Blazing

lean-to's, a cache of rice, a pig, but no weapons or ammo. Tim Fyle shot the pig and fixed it so they couldn't eat it. The rice was too much to just scatter so we took turns pissing on the rice until the rice pile was unfit to eat and then scattered the rice.

It's what's not for dinner "Charlie"! We then wanted to show "Charlie" that we had a burning desire to be friends, so we torched his little home in the woods. We mounted up and continued trail blazing.

The Third Squad continued on trail blazing, the Viet Cong were attacking (unknown at the time) B Company! At 10:34am, an RPG2 Russian Rocket struck one of B Companies Armored Personnel Carriers. The shot was fired from a trench line at XT229973; this location was 1000 meters from the Cambodian Border. At 10:52am another B Company Track was

This is what I call "Torch and Destroy"

fired at with an RPG2 Russian Rocket (bad shot) the Viet Cong had missed. The area then was taken under fire by 81 mm mortars and organic weapons fire. Then at 10:59am RPG2 Russian Rocket Rounds hit 2 of B Company's Armored Personnel Carriers. At 11:25am a RPG2 Russian Rockets fire hit another Armored Personnel Carrier. At 11:25am another Armored Personnel Carrier was hit by RPG2 Russian Rocket. Contact was broken at 11:40am.

We pushed our way onward for about another one and one-half hours until we came out of the jungle.

At about 1:10pm we crossed over Prek Klok Creek on an AVLB bridge. We proceeded a while along a road/trail until we came to an area that the US Calvary unit was in the process of setting up as a Field Base Camp. Then onward we went to a point near the end of that camp at about 1:40pm.

Bridge crossing Prek Klok Creek near Cambodia
Courtesy of Arnie Spotted Bear Queener

In the process of blazing that trail through the jungle with all the noise and activity, we had no idea what had been taking place behind us! It was quite a devastating morning as we found out later. The reason we didn't find any weapons or ammunitions at that base camp in the midst of the jungle was that the Viet Cong Sons-of-Bitches were busy using them on our boys!

## March 1967

I got a message to stay where we were, and the rest of the 1st Platoon passed around us, putting another Armored Personnel Carrier in the lead, and then they stopped in front of the column to await further orders. The coordinates near this place were XT229973 as shown in the After-Action-Reports.

It was time for me to give up my Commander's position in the hatch, so I changed positions with one of the guys in our track.

```
At 1:45pm Company B made contact in the same
general area. One Armored Personnel Carrier was
hit by RPG2 Russian Rocket Fire. Contact was
immediately broken.
```

The following information explains in detail the 1:45pm After - Action-Report:

I looked ahead at the rest of the platoon. On the right was a clearing between two wooded areas that was about 20 meters wide. The clearing consisted of short vegetation.

About **five** minutes after we switched the lead, I saw a Flash! Then heard a Boom!! Something hit the new lead track Commander's hatch from the right side (the position in front of the column where I had just been). From my position it looked like something lifted that Armored Personnel Carrier up on its right side about two feet.

The back ramp came down, and several men bailed out and wandered around in a daze. They were exposed to possible enemy fire, but made it all the way back almost to our Armored Personnel Carrier. I couldn't believe that everyone was just watching them, and no one was trying to move them to safety. I jumped off the track behind them. I helped them to get under cover and tried to quiet them down since they were easy targets for snipers. Two of those guys were from Puerto Rico, one guy from Chicago area. Another one, James Wisdom, was from St. Louis. James was holding his hands over his eye. He applied pressure on his eye socket with his hands as blood seeped through his fingers and ran down his face, onto his clothes and down on the ground. He was in too much pain to yell, so I yelled for a Medic and attempted to lead the others to a safe place.

Time cannot blank out my memory of those guys' faces. Their skin was either blackened from the explosion or maybe grease, or a combination of everything. They were in deep, deep shock and loudly half-mumbling and sobbing in repeated bewildered babblings! As they moved, they stumbled and fell, getting up and down again. It was a most depressing sight. They moved like zombies, and the look of shock mingled with the sheer terror filled their eyes!

I don't know why no one fired at that Viet Cong bastard.

The strange thing is that this event has accompanied me for the last forty years, popping up at various unexpected times, but never far from my conscious memory. I was talking with Tim Fyle about mid-May 2007 about this particular incident and he filled me in on some of the details that I didn't see from my vantage point.

While I was busy looking after the shock-stricken members of that unfortunate Armored Personnel Carrier who were wandering aimlessly back to my position, I was unaware of the details that were happening around that lead track. I don't know who the lead TC Track Commander was at the time we switched places.

---

Sometimes it is better not to know or remember the exact details, because most people don't want to hear what happened, although it's permanently recorded in our brain. To fulfill the purpose of these writings, you are reading of horrible indelicate things that must be told in order to fully understand and feel our experiences.

I found out later that day that an RPG2 Russian rocket had hit the Track Commander and he had been killed. That rocket hit that Track Commanders Hatch near the top and had separated his head from his body and sent it flying! He had just taken that position from <u>me</u> five minutes earlier. Wow!

The medics and others had the gruesome task of dealing with what remained of our soldiers. Just put yourself in the Medic's shoes or the other guys for a moment, who where frantically looking for the remains. Imagine trying to find the helmet and headset with the head inside! Oh how they must have felt at that moment, and the horrible memories. I don't believe they found his head.

Then imagine being responsible for removing the rest of his body from inside the Track Commander's Hatch, and preparing the body, for pickup by the helicopter. Could we have any idea of the pain they must have felt in carrying out the dictates of their duty? Not hardly.

My whole adult life has been haunted by the memory of this incident. People tell me to forget and let it go, but they never seem to understand or listen to me! Five minutes earlier, I was in the lead Armored Personnel Carrier as the TC Track Commander. Had we not switched; that would have been my death instead of the other guy's!

Five minutes more, just **five** minutes?

If I close my eyes, I can see that scene almost as vividly as the day it happened. Try living with that for forty years! Forget? Never!!!

This day Clay "Farmer" Messer and I both share a painful and horrendous experience:

"The morning of the 31$^{st}$ we were getting ready to start our mission when Lt. Dickey told me 'Farmer you're not going out today, you're too short. Schuler can drive today.' That day Lt. Dickey, Gary Schuler, Kenneth "Pappason" Breshears and another on my track B33 died."

"I am still alive today, thanks to the faithfulness of God and Lt. Dickey's kindness. I still can't get over it."

I am telling these stories so it can help others to express their true feelings, and hold nothing back. I will never forget these things, but writing this has helped to put this into a better personal perspective. I had blamed the unit that had secured that area for years, but have since put it aside. Charlie was a sneaky bastard, and very clever. So maybe it wasn't that Unit's fault after all.

I can't remember the names of the guys from Puerto Rico and have had no contact.

When I came home from Nam, and was in Chicago before I returned to duty at Fort Knox Kentucky, I got a call from the guy from Chicago. God, I can't remember his name (he is the man in the picture on page 219 after his hospital stay). He seemed a little strange when he talked, like he was a little off. He said he was going back and get those little gook bastards and kill them all, with kind of a sick, sadistic laugh! I can't say as I blamed him. Summer of 1969 I was a married man living in Napa, California. I had made contact with Jim Wisdom. Jim was a short, cocky, tough little character when I knew him in Vietnam. He had grown up in the slums of East St. Louis, Missouri, and with his tough attitude he was lucky not to have gotten killed long before Vietnam. Somehow we came up with the idea for him to visit us. I think it was because I thought I might be able to help him. He deserved to have a regular life and maybe a little happiness.

We invited him to stay, but he insisted on staying in one of the old hotels in downtown Napa, (kind of like the old flop houses you see in old movies about the Great Depression Era).

Jim was very bitter about life in general and specifically, about Vietnam. For him to make a good life probably was going to take a miracle. I visited him at his hotel, and it was like he was still in Nam. The room was a mess, and he was still eating tiny Vienna sausages out of a can. It almost broke my heart! The thing he got the most kick out of life was taking his glass eye out of its place and doing tricks and jokes with it. If anyone has seen a short character like this with red hair (if he hasn't lost it all, or it has turned gray), please contact me. I don't remember how we lost contact. He just drifted into anonymity. How sad!

The 31st day of March 1967 five soldiers from B Company were killed and sixteen wounded!

Kenneth Breshears Killed-in-Action 03/31/1967
"Pappason"

\* \* \* \* \*

There were forty-five men wounded-in-action this month.

The following eleven men of the Battalion are alive in our memory:

    Gerald Breen           Kenneth Breshears

    Gary F. Schuler        John A. Todi

    Thomas Sullivan      Jerry L. Borgens

    James Vadbunker     Robert S. Liszcz

    Viril L. Austin         Charles M. Douglas

    Charles C. Dickey Jr.

We, the survivors, Honor these Gallant men who performed their duty by making the Supreme Sacrifice with their lives on that day.

They paid for the Freedom we enjoy today.

# April 1967

The 31st of March 1967 was a sad day for our unit with the loss of good men brave and true. Heroes in every sense of the word! Of course we were not given a moment to reflect on the tragedy of the situation. We had a job to do every day.

April 1, 1967 was business as usual without even a little time to mourn our loss. Companies A and B conducted Search and Destroy operations in the area without enemy contact. Company C secured the Battalion Forward Base while Recon Platoon secured a Re-supply Drop Zone.

We had a special permanent visitor to B Company in the field, our First Sergeant. He was the type of person, who abused his rank and made life unnecessarily difficult, a real Hell for enlisted men. The "Top" acted gruff and tough, and he treated the grunts as his personal servants. I know that this was nothing new for any of the services, but he did it in the most odious manner. To say that most of the men disliked him would be a gross understatement.  I have never liked people who take advantage of others.

Well, every dog has his day, and today was First Sergeant's turn. A special order had come down from the HQ Battalion Commander stating, "All First Sergeants will accompany the troops in the Field of Combat." We were surprised to see our Top Sergeant out with us in the field. What an "April Fool's Day" joke on him. He didn't look too happy and was rather subdued. We didn't really want him out in the field, but it was a big kick to see him squirm!

The newest, lowliest private barely weaned from Mater (Mother) looked as brave as Hercules in comparison to "Top" out in the field. The term "Chicken Shit" came to mind. Hell, I thought the big man was going to cry. One thing never changed, he still took advantage of his position. But at least he didn't make so much noise out in the jungle!

```
April 2, 1967 the Battalion conducted Search and
Destroy missions in the area with negative enemy
contact.
```

Those Viet Cong bastards didn't want to play, so they hid as usual. We had been without a squad leader for about five or six days. Today Sergeant Kenneth P. Newton became B13's new squad leader. Kenny Newton was from New York City, and you know how New Yorkers can be. Or do you? Sometimes they seem to be arguing just for the sake of arguing, and if you get two of them together, it could last all night!

My first recollection of him was that most people reacted to his manner as being difficult at best, and he was hard to get along with on a personal level. This was probably somewhat of a misunderstanding caused by an apparent Air-of-Superiority. He had a wry, dry sense of humor. I recall that he laughed a lot, but you couldn't tell if he was laughing with you or at you.

The only picture we have of him is the one "Chief", the Hopi Indian mechanic, had taken of him. That picture shows Newton with a shit-eatin' grin on his face sitting in the Track Commanders hatch. He was actually a pretty good guy once you got to know him. The best story I remember was when he got himself a good case of sunburn during a hot period. This happened because he went without a shirt and paid the consequences. This was particularly amusing to me because I thought that black people never got sunburned! He didn't like it one bit, and he didn't mind letting us know how miserable he felt. We all had a good laugh at his expense. That was a side of him that made him seem human.

April 3, 1967 was a quiet day for B Company. At 1:37am Company A engaged Viet Cong at XT210945 and located, 23 60MM Mortar rounds, 23 82 MM mortar rounds, documents and, misc. equipment.

April 4, 1967 at 2:00pm, an Armored Personnel Carrier from Company C hit a mine. After striking the mine it was hit by a LAW fired from a bunker. Six Bobcats were Wounded-in-Action. At 3:50pm while searching an area some 8,000 meters due west of Katum an Armored Personnel Carrier from Company A detonated an anti-tank mine resulting in five Bobcats being Wounded-in-Action. At 3:58pm Company A located a communication wire line at XT240906. While checking out the line, an unknown number of Viet Cong opened fire with small arms and automatic weapons. Fire was returned and the Viet Cong broke contact at 4:15pm. One Bobcat from Company A was Killed-in-Action and one Bobcat was Wounded-in-Action.

April 5, 1967 the Battalion conducted Search and Destroy operations in the areas of XT1582, 1588, 2182, 2188 with negative enemy contact. The Recon Platoon conducted convoy escort for Battery B, 2/35th Artillery.

(Maybe their union steward finally represented them and got them time off for bad behavior!)

April 6, 1967 the Battalion conducted Search and Destroy operations in the previous day's area with negative enemy contact.

While some of these days seem to be uneventful, we still started each day wondering about our fate. The mere challenge of staying alive still existed, and there were constant thoughts of an enemy out there ready to strike given the opportunity. You see, we didn't have peace or security under those conditions. Those days we also had Listening Posts and Ambushes to be performed in spite of the type of day it was. Imagine going to school and having a final exam in every class every day, and if you flunked, the results would be life threatening!

```
April 7, 1967 the Battalion continued Search and
Destroy operations in the general area of XT2188.

April 8, 1967 the Battalion secured a Landing Zone
for the extraction of the 2/1st Infantry, and then
moved over land to Tay Ninh. We arrived at Tay Ninh
base camp in mid-afternoon.
```

The Battalion had now been in the field from February 1st to April 8, 1967. That amounts to 67 days in harm's way. We set our B Company base on the outskirts of the 196th Light Infantry Brigades base camp for the evening. We were separated from the 196th by 3 sets of barbed wire and 3 sets of rolled concertina wire.

### Tay Ninh Trip Up
The base camp at Tay Ninh was a lot more secure than where we had just been for the last two months. They gave us the evening off that day, and so we attended to some of our personal things like shaving and washing ourselves. This did not mean showers, but just water in your helmet, wash cloth and soap. That's how we had bathed for the prior two months, so it was nothing new. But it was still nice to be able to take your time and not worry about surprises from the Viet Cong!

We also had the evening to rest up free from Listening Posts, Ambushes and watch duty. Very little rest, considering we were going back out to the bush early the next day.

We were fed a hot meal at around 5:00pm, and after that there was a little surprise. No, not women, although that would have been nice! There were a couple of large tubs with ice-cold beer to

*April 1967* 189

quench our thirsts. The ice-cold beer was like Heaven. I think I can still imagine how refreshing that felt. I probably had more than my fair share of beer. That night we had no duties, so who cared?
We had a couple of guys in our unit who had transferred from the 196th at Tay Ninh (during our three day break back in January). They still had friends in their old unit, so they thought why not visit? It sounded great to us. We hadn't been under any kind of a roof for over two months, not even canvas. So let's go!

I don't think this little trip was authorized, but do you think we gave a damn? Not us. What could they do, shoot us? I remember walking through a maze into the base camp. I vividly remember how I got back out (more on that later).

We walked down a long dirt road alongside the base camp headed south for about one mile. Along our left was nothing but the base perimeter for half of our walk, but there were hooches on our right. As we continued, there were rows of hooches on both sides. We had gone about another half mile, and then we turned to our right through another row of hooches until we reached about the sixth one down. When we opened the door to that hooch it sounded like Party Central!

Music was blaring and the room was filled with smoke. The Environmental Protection Agency would close it down today! We met the buddies of our fellow soldiers. They were friendly and good hosts. It would have been a super party if only there were some girls added. We had to settle for music, booze and more booze!

Luckily there were the ingredients for my favorite alcoholic drink, rum and coke. The first one went down smoothly and the second one ended the boredom. I remember speaking with two guys from Puerto Rico in Spanish. I'll bet they got a kick out of it! Some guys had casually been smoking weed and offered some to me. I said no and decided to have another rum and coke instead.

Well, the last drink must have loosened me up, because when they offered it again, I thought what the hell, it couldn't kill me!
I took a drag on that roach and held it in, and then exhaled. It did not seem to have much of an effect. I never had approved of the use of any drugs and had never tried anything. They showed me

the correct way and I tried again. I took a drag (more like slurping through a straw), and then I let it out. Well, after a short while it took effect, and I was very mellow. I continued conversing with my new Puerto Rican pals. Boy, did I speak uninhibited Spanish that night!

The party started to wind down about 2:00am, so we decided it was time to get back. We said our goodbyes to our hosts and started back. I was the last one in line. Someone decided to take a short cut diagonally back to the road. I was following north when I got too close to one of the Hooches. There in the darkness was a tent guide wire or something stretched to the ground. I tripped and must have hit pretty hard because I passed out into sleep, or was it booze and pot induced coma? It didn't really matter.

I woke up over an hour later, a little dazed. My mouth felt and tasted like I'd eaten a whole jar of white school paste, and my head felt as big as a basketball! It was still dark and I didn't know where I was. Thanks to Butch Petit's teachings I soon found my bearings. I got back to the road and sheepishly started walking in the right direction. It was still dark as the Ace of Spades and I felt like hell. Boy was I worried about my future!

I plodded along dragging my ass down the road. I felt like a big bear was stalking me and ready to pounce. I then realized that the bear had headlights. It was a jeep! In a short while they caught up with me. It was the Military Police. I had visions of a firing squad or Leavenworth. Neither option appealed to me. My ass was grass!

When they approached me I told the MP's my tale of woe including how I had tripped over the guide rope or wire and passed out. They got the biggest kick out of my dilemma, which didn't make me feel too secure. They asked me what unit I was in, and I said, "I'm with the 5$^{th}$ Mech from Cu Chi." They had me hop in, and then they told me they were taking me to my unit and not to worry. That was easy for them to say, they didn't know our First Sergeant. I had mixed feelings about what was going to happen at the end of my ride! They dropped me off at the spot where the Company had been, but it wasn't there. I thanked them and they wished me good luck. They were the kindest Military Police I've ever seen.

I got out of the jeep, and when I looked up, there before my eyes was a painful obstacle course. Remember the three sets of barbed wire and the three strands of rolled concertina wire I talked about earlier? Here they were between me and my unit! I felt like Hell, like there were a thousand little creatures in my mouth jumping around, and my head was pounding louder and louder.

No Guts, no Glory. I began my trek through "Wire Land"

How I made it through in the dark is a mystery to me unto this day. Finally I navigated through all three sets of barbed wire, safe and sound. I got off the ground after getting out of the last one. It was starting to get a little lighter as I walked to where the unit had been and it was definitely gone.

I wondered where the hell they had moved to. I had visions of a trial, then a wall, a last cigarette, a blindfold, and a firing squad, my own squad. Was that going a little too far? I hoped so. But going A.W.O.L. (Absent-With-Out-Leave) was a very serious infraction. They shoot deserters in war, don't they? Oh, it wasn't called a war at that time. Maybe I was safe on a technicality!

I continued my brave walk, when it was interrupted by the First Sergeant yelling at me. "Antinni, where the hell have you been?" (It's Antti, ant tee!) He could never pronounce my name! At this point I was scared shitless at the possibilities. I was reaching into my mind for an answer, something smart, not flippant, just smart. I was just desperate to think of something that would work.

I was really worried and still felt like crap. I needed a miracle to get out of this predicament. Help! Help! Please! Please!

Aha, a brainstorm! "First Sergeant, I tripped into a hole and was knocked out!" It worked. He didn't say a thing but, "Get your sorry ass in the track!"

You know when you tell the truth it'll set you free? Well, all right, it wasn't exactly the truth. But I did trip, and that's why I was late. I had actually pulled one over on the First Sergeant. I sat there in the track rather smugly as I heard him call in "All the chicks are in the roost".

As we drove off the sun was rising in the East and the sun's rays lit up the morning with bright hues of orange, yellow and red kissing the morning sky! Ah, another beautiful morning in Vietnam. There goes my promotion!

```
April 9, 1967 the 2nd Brigade began participation
in an operation in Ghia Dinh Province with the
mission of interrupting the flow of supplies in
and out of Saigon. The Viet Cong had been very
active while we were up around and past Tay Ninh
and north to the Cambodian Border.
```

I left the Tay Ninh base camp as the sun was rising. I had been scared to death that I was going to be shot as a deserter. As it turned out, I didn't even get punished! Who supplied the beer?

We were following about an hour behind the Battalion. I had no idea where we were going and the officers never bothered to consult with me. We were finally onto Highway 22. It was morning and the sun was on our left side, so we must have been heading south. After 1½ hours we caught up with the Battalion and B13 my track. I moved to it and left the First Sergeant. We rode for about four hours with a couple stops, and we were nearing a town.

The Battalion came to the town of Go Dau Ha where Highway 22 road ran into Highway 1. We made a left and continued south towards Trang Bang and Cu Chi. We must be heading home! The thoughts raced through my head like a Formula One racing car. A shower (aaah), a shave, and clean clothes. Several cool beers with snacks at the Enlisted Men's Club. Maybe even a movie. Yea!

I hated every second of writing the following account, but I felt compelled to tell the truth of what I had heard so that you may understand who the villains were that we faced every day in the jungle.

We continued for about 1½ hours, and we came to Trang Bang. Passing through took 45 minutes. The Battalion was going south at the end when I saw on the right a soccer field with white goal posts about 50 meters off the road. The field was bordered at the back by trees. Just as I saw it, I felt a strange sensation. Then it hit me! I had heard a horrible story about that soccer field.

When I first went out in the Armored Personnel Carriers during my first days in Nam in October 1966, someone told me about a very terrible and brutal incident that had taken place several months before. The Viet Cong for years had been going into villages and terrorizing the inhabitants. Sometimes they would kill, rape, beat and kidnap people to make them slaves of their unit, make them fight by threatening to terrorize their families!

They especially hated people who would assist civilian personnel. That was their game, not ours! This is not a fictional story. It was told to me by an eyewitness after the fact. The Viet Cong slipped into the village during the dark lonely night when everyone was sleeping peacefully. They snuck into the house where a young lady teacher lived. They grabbed her and dragged her out of the house kicking and screaming into the dark night.

The soccer field was like a park a little way off the road. They took her to the area where the trees were, then each of the men beat and raped her. The people could hear her screams but were powerless to help! They had prepared a hanging rope. Just before they hung her, they slit her breasts and then hoisted her up and left her there to die! This was not an act of War. It was a sadistic and barbaric act of brutality! The Viet Cong then threatened the traumatized villagers that if they cut her down they would get more of the same. Someone who was on a detail sent to take care of cutting down her body told the story to me.

The Battalion continued to roll down the road and I was in silent reflection remembering that evil deed. That young lady teacher was a real hero to all the Vietnamese people.

The terrain began to look familiar and we rode for almost another 2 hours. We were just about to the Cu Chi base camp. Hurrah! We were going back home to Cu Chi.... Well, as we kept on riding and waved goodbye to Cu Chi, we were really waving our middle fingers, and they weren't pointed at Cu Chi!

We all used some pretty vile and abased adjectives, vocalized in anger and disrespect! Should we have smiled? We were pissed off. We had been out in the field for 67 days straight without rest and a decent shower, and now no wine, women or song. We continued another three hours longer until we reached the appointed destination.

This area was quite pretty and lush with dark green vegetation, which means we didn't have to lie down on dying grass and Agent Orange when we were tucked in for the night. Yeah, right! This was the most populated area we ever had an operation in, so we moved off the road and into a more secluded area, closer to our natural enemy.

We were in the Ghia Dinh Province. This was the most challenging operational area I had been in because we were close to a larger number of civilians. We knew Charlie's tricks when it came to the use of civilians! Fighting in a remote area was bad enough, but fighting around a lot of noncombatants was nerve racking.

> Contrary to popular opinion, we were very responsible in our actions regarding civilians. You see, the Viet Cong didn't care if civilians died, because civilians didn't matter to the Viet Cong. The Viet Cong would sometimes use civilians as shields, and then they would sneak away. How about that? The difference is that we did care about the

people of Vietnam. Put yourself in our shoes. You might be on a daytime patrol and you are walking in an area that has houses. Suddenly, automatic weapons rounds are flying all around you. What would you do? The obvious thing would be to hit the dirt. Then what would you do? I would return the fire and you probably would too! That could be very dangerous for innocent bystanders. Would this have been an irresponsible action on your part, or your duty?

Think this over, and over again before you get the urge to judge. When you are confronted with situations as important as your own life and the lives of your fellow soldiers, there is not a hell of a lot of time to deliberate. I thank God that we never had to face that issue even when we were in the Ghia Dinh Province.

April 10, 1967 the Battalion conducted Search and Destroy operations around the roads which the Viet Cong were suspected of using.

April 11, 1967 thru April 14, 1967 the Battalion had little contact with the enemy. The activity and our presence were effective in slowing the flow of supplies to and from the area.

April 15, 1967 the Battalion was in Ghia Dinh Province, and short-circuited the Viet Cong's Supply system.

One Shattered Elbow
I can't remember exactly where we were, but I do know that Sgt. Kenny Newton was the leader of the 3rd Squad, the "Pretty Boy Squad". The unit was working out of a field base camp for a couple of days. On the 15th, we had a brand new platoon leader for the First Platoon. He was either a 90-day wonder or a West Point Graduate Second Lieutenant. He was so green he resembled the bright green Bamboo Viper, and he was possibly just as dangerous. Whatever the case, he was as fresh as he possibly

could get, and as a combat officer he was not even dry behind the ears (and especially in between).

The 3rd Squad was chosen for a night Ambush. How lucky! Darkness had reached the right hue and it was time to begin our evening soirée. We were assembled and ready to go. Our brand new platoon leader was present, so we started out. We began walking about five yards out across a dark dry rice paddy when suddenly a mortar flare was shot up into the dark-dark sky. When we heard that noise, we hit the ground. It lit up the sky and us like a Christmas tree.

Sgt. Newton yelled "get down!" Now, anyone with half a brain hit the dust and made an impression as deep as possible into the ground.

The flare seemed to hang up in the night sky, forever, lighting up the area. Everyone was hugging the ground for dear life. Then to our amazement and wonder, our brand-new Second Lieutenant yelled, "Everybody up and prepare to assault across the rice paddy"! That fucking flare was still in the air! I can remember staying down and remaining as small a target as possible. That flare was still lighting the ground and revealing our positions. You should have heard Sgt. Newton yell his refusal and began cussing him out, telling us to stay down! "You stupid Mother Fuck'n idiot, what the hell is wrong with you? Stay down!"

He yelled out something like, "When I give an order I expect it to be obe...." As he was getting his sorry ass up we heard the zing of an incoming rifle shot. We heard a yell. It was the Idiot himself, and then the flare went out. We never saw the man again. We were told he got it in the elbow.

That kind of sounded like insubordination because we were given a direct order by a "superior" officer and didn't obey. Do the regulations really say that we must obey a "stupid" order? He got his Purple Heart with an *Idiot Cluster* and probably went home with a disability. I respect everyone who even went to Nam and especially Purple Heart wearers, even him! Please don't tell me his name, its better he remains anonymous! Sgt Newton could not believe what had just happened and couldn't stop talking about it for days.

## April 1967

The Battalion for the period of April 16 thru April 21 was without enemy contact (as of book printing). This was lucky for us and lucky for the enemy. The Battalion had been in the field since the 1st of February. That's 80 days without a break, so the fact that we had negative enemy contact was a big blessing. According to the Tropic Lightning Newspaper we stayed out in the field.

April 22, 1967 the 1/5th Mechanized Infantry began Operation Manhattan in the Lower Boi Loi and Ho Bo Woods. One Bobcat from Recon was Killed-in-Action when his Armored Personnel Carrier detonated a mine.

I don't know if this is another example of Military Intelligence, but the practice of sending leaflets to warn citizens that we were to begin an operation in a certain area seemed very polite, but those leaflets also pre-warned the Viet Cong. The Viet Cong were able to evacuate the area long before our arrival. They employed booby traps, anti tank mines and anti personnel mines. This was an aid to 2-and-3 man sniper teams to sucker our troops to enter areas without exercising proper judgment. The Viet Cong had extensive supply bases in the area, probably since we had such a large presence in the other operations.

The Objective of Operation Manhattan: destroy the Viet Cong elements, supplies, and bases along the Saigon River.

April 23, 1967 the Battalion secured a Landing Zone in the area of XT5331 for the 1/27th Infantry. The battalion secured the routes of communication. Three Armored Personnel Carriers from C Company detonated mines resulting in two Bobcats Killed-in-Action and three Wounded-in-Action.

April 24, 1967 the Battalion conducted Search and

The Viet Cong set a lot of booby traps before Operation Manhattan

Destroy operations in the area of XT5131 resulting in negative enemy contact.

April 25, 1967 the Battalion continued Search and Destroy operations in zone. An Armored Personnel Carrier from Company A detonated an anti-tank mine resulting in one Killed-in-Action & eight Bobcats Wounded-in-Action. B Company had no contact with the enemy but destroyed three bunkers during the day.

April 26, 1967 at 3:10pm B Company came upon a Viet Cong who was in the process of setting up a Chicom Claymore Mine at XT520324. He was killed in the exchange of fire. Because the Viet Cong were forewarned they were able to rig the area with many booby traps. As a result, in the Boi Loi eight Bobcats were Wounded-in-Action.

*April 1967* 

April 27, 1967 the Battalion was conducting Search and Destroy in the Boi Loi Woods when at 1:25pm and discovered a tunnel complex. The units encountered mines and booby traps during the day; one Bobcat was Killed-in-Action and fifteen were Wounded-in-Action. (See Map A #7 on Page 314)

This activity could have been going on just before our Company arrived

We discovered that the complex was more than an escape system because we found an underground Hospital just like the one near the Cambodian Border on the 7th of February. The Hospital had an operating room that had been used recently because the blood on the dirt floor was still fresh. My best guess was they evacuated it about 4 hours earlier. It contained what appeared to be sleeping quarters, an eating area and ammunition storage. There were 2 booby traps set up in their hasty retreat.

April 28, 1967 the Battalion conducted operations in that same area with no enemy contact. Some bunkers and tunnels were destroyed.

April 29, 1967 the Battalion took responsibility for the security of the engineer unit activities in the area.

Women Viet Cong were fighting in the jungle as well as men

April 30, 1967 the Battalion conducted Search and Destroy operations from XT538338 to the Saigon River and back with negative contact with the enemy. Company C was OPCON to the 1/27th infantry. At 10:05am the unit made contact with the Viet Cong at XT578285 while conducting a sweep. The units remained in a firefight until 1:15pm. At that time The Viet Cong broke contact because artillery fire was employed. One Bobcat from C Company was Killed-in-Action and two were Wounded-in-Action.

*April 1967*

\* \* \* \* \*

There were thirty-eight men wounded-in-action for this month.

During April 1967 ten fine men from the battalion were added to the list of our fallen comrades in arms:

    James K. Lindsey        James P. English

    Stephen L. Colopy      James L. Russell

    Gary L. Doose          Rom Worley

    Gene D. Smith          Terry L. Anton

    Antonio Flores Jr.       George Obermeir

By the reading of their names we bring them back to our collective awareness.

# May 1967

The highways of Vietnam continued to be used by convoys as our primary mode of supply to the Base Camps at Cu Chi, Tay Ninh and Dau Tieng. There were 448 convoys for the last three months between Saigon and Cu Chi. Between Cu Chi, Tay Ninh and Dau Tieng there were 172 convoys, which, by the way, brought us our beer and snacks for the Enlisted Men's Club.

A point of interest was that between July 1966 and April 1967 there had been 27 Viet Cong agents taken into custody from among the Division Base Camps' civilian work force. Maybe your favorite barber who cut your hair in January was out in the Ho Bo Woods last week looking to cut your throat. Probably the screening process needed to be reviewed and improved.

May 1, 1967 the 1/5th Mech continued conducting Search and Destroy operations in the Ho Bo Woods with negative enemy contact. Company C remained attached to the 1/27th Infantry.

It's important to remind you that although we'd gotten used to the foul odors, we were out in the land of decay and humidity. Certain areas emitted stronger smells, sometimes like dead, and rotting animals (or humans!). Areas that had stagnant pools of dirty water took on their special odor. So remember to put on your nose plugs!

May 2, 1967 the Battalion conducted Search and Destroy Missions at XT5333, near the southern section of the Thanh-Dien Forestry Preserve. The Battalion also provided supply convoy escort.

May 3, 1967 the Battalion commenced a two-day sweep of the Ho Bo Woods. At 9:25am Company A made contact with an unknown number of Viet Cong at XT604267. Four Bobcats from Company B were Killed-in-Action when their Armored Personnel Carrier hit an anti-tank mine. There continued intermittent contact with the enemy throughout the day.

One of the casualties was Specialist 4 Jim Flickenger, my friend. The last time I saw him was on our last Listening Post duty. It's strange that you could be right there and still not know when it happened. I guess our leaders wanted to keep it as low key as possible. (See Map A #8 on Page 314)

Jim Flickenger, Killed-in-Action
Courtesy of Denis McDonough

## May 1967

May 4, 1967 the Battalion continued the sweep through the Ho Bo Woods. Six Bobcats were Killed-in-Action in the day by mines and booby traps (four from Headquarters Company, one from Company A, and one from Company B.)

While I am writing this I am feeling sad and angry because this information isn't just statistics, it's about people's dreams and lives. These men were our brothers!

May 5, 1967 the Battalion was still conducting Search and Destroy operations in the Ho Bo Woods, and also a road sweep to Trang Bang. There was negative enemy contact that day.

The fact that we had no enemy contact didn't mean we had it easy. We still were subjected to the mines, booby traps and the threat of sneak attacks. The human body is sure amazing. It can constantly manufacture adrenaline. Even with all the adrenaline we used up daily, it was still able to produce more.

We used adrenaline like cars use gasoline!

<u>Careful Communication</u>
From this title you probably expect this story to be about a secret military communication system or code. Guess again. Actually it's a far more important form of communication since it has to do with our sanity. We knew little about what was going on in the "World" (That's a euphemism for Home, Apple Pie and MOM!), and home seemed more important than military matters because we were doing things that were far from normal human activities.

A letter from a stranger would be welcome. Sometimes just an envelope with an address from the USA would have been welcome. A letter from a family member was a mechanism of balance in our lives, and helped keep us grounded to what normal life <u>used</u> to be like. The idea that someone, anyone, cared helped with our feelings of rejection from the United States about the War. Just knowing that normal living was occurring in most of the world gave us hope. All those things fed our minds and helped keep the connection alive.

What really caused excitement was a CARE package, you know, goodies. Yeah! The excitement wasn't only when I received one, but when anyone received one. Why, you might ask? The answer is because we shared! When we had Mail Call this day, I received a Care Package from my sister, and it couldn't have come at a better time. I had been doing the same thing for the last 5 months, and it was getting depressing. This Care Package didn't come with a ticket home, although they would have put one in if they could. Goodies consisted of several different candy bars, canned Chili, canned Pears, BBQ Potato Chips, Beef Sticks, cookies, gum, Kool-aid, some newspapers, personal items, and toilet paper. You name it! These items helped change my attitude immensely. I felt better already. This was a great Friday. All those things served as a reminder of Home, just the little things of life everyone else takes for granted except...for the GI away from the "World".

Sights, sounds, taste, and smells all helped keep the connection alive and brother, we needed it. The REMFs Rear Echelon Mother F (figure it out) could get some of that at the Post Exchange daily. But remember, we were out in the bush for 60 to 90 days or more at a time and weren't able to do that. And guess what? The "Roach Coaches" (Lunch Wagons) hadn't found their Mercenary Hearts out in the jungle, at least not yet! (Did they ever?) We couldn't buy and bring enough snacks to last for the amount of time we stayed in the jungle. A Care Package out in the field wouldn't last long because we were desperate men, and if we didn't share....

If you are reading this and have either sent or received a Care Package under similar circumstance, then you know how important they are to the receiver. Please remember this, and, if possible, find a way to send one to a GI in need in a war zone or any out-of-country location. The Care Packages will be appreciated! Support your troops, for they support and defend Freedom in the world.

## May 1967

We didn't have Cell Phones, Telegraph, Tell a Woman, Land line phones, Carrier Pigeons, or smoke signals to communicate with. Did I say smoke signals? Well, we had Native American Indians, so there! All kidding aside, we were limited in our ability to communicate with the outside world. Remember, this was the 1960's, and we were out in the jungle, (AT & T and Ma Bell didn't service remote areas.).

Close your eyes and think for a moment, then imagine yourself a long way from home in a dark, scary place where there is someone who is trying to kill you. During the day, you're doing the hardest work you'll ever do, and behind every bush and tree is the potential for death. The evenings are spent in terror where just sleeping could bring about your end. Every little noise seems like danger. The dark brings a thousand terrors and the daylight isn't much better. Can you imagine yourself living like this every day? Well, we did!

Right now there's a soldier somewhere as you read this experiencing these feelings. Please find a way to help.

May 6, 1967 the Battalion conducted operations in the middle of the Boi Loi Woods around XT5533. We also were providing security for an engineer unit operating in the area with negative enemy contact.

May 7, 1967 the Battalion continued Search and Destroy operations during the day and provided security for engineer activities. At 8:40am an Armored Personnel Carrier from the Recon Platoon hit an anti-tank mine: one Bobcat was Killed-in-Action in the explosion and three Wounded-in-Action.

May 8, 1967 there was negative enemy contact and negative causalities.

May 9, 1967 the Battalion continued security for engineering activities until 3:00pm. At that time moved to the Cu Chi Base Camp, ending the 1/5ths participation in Operation Manhattan.

I am writing this on the 30th of August 2007, and with the coordinates from the 2nd of May 1967 and the one for the Boi Loi Woods May 6 1967, I now know exactly where on the map these places were where we fought and lost so many of our Brothers-In-Arms. I can pinpoint where most things took place. Our superiors didn't exactly share the exact locations with the "grunts"!

That night, we had movies at the theater area followed by time at the Enlisted Men's Club drinking and listening to the jukebox in the left rear of the club. The back of the bar was on the side facing towards the Mess Hall. We had been in the jungle for 98 days of combat, which I verified in the Tropic Lightening Division's newspaper. We had left Cu Chi base camp on February 1, 1967.

May 10, 1967 the Battalion conducted maintenance in preparation for future operations. The unit was released at 4:30pm for the evening. The time was spent at the various personal pursuits.

May 11, 1967 the Battalion continued maintenance and preparation for future operations.

Ann Margaret
It was still May 11, 1967, and the Battalion was in from the field on one of our usual short breaks, one or two days at the most for a little rest. I was told I was going to have an all-night date with Ann Margaret in the evening. Boy was I excited. Yeah!

Well, my bubble burst when I actually got to see her. It was a real big letdown. Ann Margaret wasn't pretty in person. She had sagging bags (about 150 musty and moldy sand bags that is), large slats for eyes, a woodenhead, and big butt about seven feet wide. She was living in a bad neighborhood and hanging around with the wrong crowd (Victor Charlie)! Ann Margaret was the name for the Cu Chi Base Camp Outpost Bunker, across the Ben Soui Moung River.

Cu Chi Side of the river

We left B company around 8:00pm and headed east on foot. The trip was equivalent to about 4-city-blocks to the Cu Chi perimeter. We walked through the perimeter. There was a bunker in front of us about 50 feet away. The ground was higher on the Cu Chi side than across the Soul Ben Moung River, about 5 feet higher. Ann Margaret was on the lower side of the river. The bunker was about 9 sand bags in length, about 5 sand bags high, and about 6 sand bags deep from the back to the front. The entrance was in the middle about 2-3 sandbags wide. This all sat above a hole dug in the ground about 4 feet deep. The front had a 5-foot wide opening for us to look out and fire an M-60 machine gun. The roof was a thick pallet board supported by the sides, back, and a partial front piece, and then covered with two sand bags.

When we first got there we could see that our butts were on the line. We were the first line of defense for the Cu Chi base camp. The bunker was hardly hidden. There was a bridge that we had to cross to get to Ann Margaret. It was located on the other side of the river inland about 15 meters. The bunker was 1.5 meters higher than the surrounding area. Considering Cu Chi base camp produced a shadow of light to silhouette our little bunker, even on a very dark night we were a viable target for sniper or mortar fire. Welcome to Ann Margaret!

We surveyed the landscape before us to memorize any ridgeline for Viet Cong activity and likely small arm fire positions. The evening was peaceful and it was still light outside. The lay of the land stretched out before us. It was an open, flat area except for about 3 short ridge lines between us and the wood line. The wood line paralleled the river as far as we could see north and south. That was our field of vision and responsibility.

Ann Margaret across the river from Cu Chi

We were the back door into Cu Chi at the entrance to the infamous Fil Hol Plantation. It had been the end of the line for too many GI's. I remember climbing down the rear entrance in the middle and then around a corner. The area wasn't very big, but big enough to accommodate our squad. An M-60 machine gun was right in the middle of the bunker with a radio and a starlight infrared night scope. We settled in for the evening in our little bunker away from home.

We were gabbing as we looked out towards the plantation. Soon the night sky darkened like the inside of a tunnel without a flashlight. The more we talked and bullshitted, which we were well versed to do, the quicker we all came to the same conclusion. What if Charlie snuck around behind us? He could sneak up quietly and kill all of us! We turned our thoughts on how to best protect ourselves from the potential negative events.

That was an unnerving thought and a very possible event. Some of the guys got the brilliant idea to go outside and get up on the roof for a better view. This solution proved to be a less than great idea, since they were such good targets because of the natural light behind us. They received sniper fire almost immediately. The guys on the roof came dropping in like relatives to the home of a Million Dollar Lottery winner!

Well, now we knew that Charlie was out there. That probably helped keep us on our toes and on the infrared scope. We settled down after a while. Eventually we decided to stretch a wire across the back entrance attached to some soda cans. Now we had a warning device. That felt much better than being targets without warning.

We weren't used to going to bed early, so we stayed up later than we should have. Well, the bullshit got deep, deeper than a dairy farm at milking time. Now I know that's cow shit, but it all smells the same.

By that time I had learned to bullshit on a very high level on a variety of subjects. I could talk about anything from art to zebras, once I got started. Otherwise I was quiet. Sergeant Kenny Newton was our squad leader at the time. This night he was in fine form with his dry and sarcastic sense of humor. This sometimes would piss people off. Well, I could overlook it for what it was. This night he wanted to hear the speech made by Brutus. I quoted it from Shakespeare "Cowards die many times before their deaths, the valiant never taste of death but once". He got a big kick out of that. Then he decided to give me a nickname. He called me "The Professor". It didn't bother me that he did it with his usual manner, which could be considered a slam. From then on he would call me Professor every chance he got. The price of fame!

I know it was starting to get late, because we decided to take turns at watch. The rest of us went to sleep or stayed up and snacked. When it was my turn at watch, the evening was dark and still and creepy. I remember using the Starlight Infrared Scope and scanning the area for "Victor Charlie". Except for our initial sniper fire, the rest of the evening went without incident.

As the morning dawned in what would become another hot and

miserable day in Vietnam, we made our way back to the Base Camp. At least we felt safer there. We had made it through another watch!

May 12, 1966 the Battalion continued maintenance. We were to have another day to rest up and take care of personal business. This was the third day we had in our Home, B Company, and sleeping on cots and not the ground. After noon chow, the First Sergeant called a formation of the company and conducted some business, and then he asked if anyone had experience in Motor Pool Operations.

I had taken my Advanced Individual Training as a motor pool clerk in an armored unit at Fort Hood, Texas, so I answered the call. The First Sergeant told me to see him after the formation was dismissed. I went to talk with the First Sergeant, and then I was assigned to the Motor Pool starting that day. I was supposed to remain at Base Camp to procure parts and supplies that they needed. I stayed in the same quarters until I moved down to the motor pool.

I was ignorant about what was happening out in the field unless an Armored Personnel Carrier returned. You see, they didn't publish After-Action-Reports on a daily basis for distribution to GI's at the Base Camp. They'd rather keep us ignorant for our own good.

May 13, 1967 the Battalion left Cu Chi in the morning on Operation Kolekole.

I stayed behind at the Motor Pool and watched as my friends left on another mission after only three days' rest. Wow, three whole days out of 101 days!

FIELD-May 13, 1967 Company A provided the Cu Chi Base Camp reaction force. The other elements of the Battalion were conducting "Road Runner" operations on Highway 8A from Cu Chi to Bao Trai and Fire Supply Base Nickel located three and one half Kilometers east of Bao Trai at XT565045.

## May 1967

Operation Kolekole was concentrated in the areas of Duc Hoa, Bao Trai, Hiep Hoa, and Loc Giang as well as along the Oriental River. The Battalion was to conduct daily Search and Destroy, nightly Ambushes, Listening Posts plus extra night-time Road Runner operations as an additional danger.

BASE-I was back at the Base Camp Motor Pool trying to figure out how the hell to get the job done. So far I wasn't even able to find my ass with both hands. I was frustrated. Still it was better than being out in the field.

FIELD-May 14, 1967 the Battalion continued "Road Runner" operations to Bao Trai and security southwest of Bao Trai at XT527043. An Armored Personnel Carrier at 12:25pm from B Company detonated an anti-tank mine resulting in four Bobcats being Wounded-in-Action. Company A was Cu Chi reaction force.

BASE-That same day I finally found my butt with both hands and was able to get things going. Darn, now I have a Parts Order to process because of that mine.

Who do you think had the best day? I understood how important this part was, and even if they had one in the field, it still needed to be replaced. I got the parts number, then I had to find the part and pick it up.

Oh shit, I didn't know how to drive!

My problem was twofold. First, I had to teach myself to drive, a minor detail. Secondly, I had to navigate the road that had just been sprayed with diesel fuel to keep the dust down. The road was slicker than Owl Shit! We've all seen someone on ice skates for the first time. You know, they slip and slide all over the place. Well, I didn't have a pair of skates. I had a 1,500 lb jeep. I felt like an Octopus on ice skates.

The last time I had piloted a car was my junior year in High School. The vehicle I tried to drive was a 1960 Buick (the one with the big fins in the back that looked like wings). I didn't do so well with that Buick. I had a little meeting with the garage door molding. Those of you who were born after 1975 don't realize that those cars were made of "real" steel and were almost armored tanks. The score was the Buick 1, the garage door molding 0. As for me, the whole experience was too much.

Those were my friends out there in Viet Cong Land and I couldn't let them down. So I taught myself to drive. By the way, the 1960 Buick had an automatic transmission and the jeep had a stick shift!

I put my left foot on the clutch pedal, pressed it down, and turned the key. I introduced my right foot to the gas pedal and said, "Let's go guys". I let the clutch out and it grabbed the gear. That jeep just jerked back and forth violently several times and died a horrible death! Second try I got smart and decided to give it some gas gradually. I started the process again and it started fine, but then I popped the clutch and it jerked dead again. I weighed the successes and failures of the two attempts and decided to let the clutch out gradually. As it caught the gears, I gave it a little more gas before letting the clutch out a little more. It worked. There I was, behind the wheel of the jeep skirting around the Motor Pool Parade Ground in circles, and all was well until it came time to stop. What do I do now? The common mistake is to push your foot on the brake pedal and stop the vehicle, which is what I did. The jeep died another violent death. Oops, I won't do that again. I must remember all these things so I don't kill anyone!

I took a deep breath, fired up the jeep, and off I went, pretty smoothly, too. I drove up to the main road, almost forgot to put in the clutch, everything was fine. I very cautiously turned right on the main road and started to go a little faster until I realized I was driving on a road slicker than Owl Shit! Then I slowed down and poked along, trying to avoid a run in with the Military Police. I made it to the supply depot and got my part. Now I had to get back!

The "Jeep and I" (kind of sounds like the title of a Musical) made it back to the motor pool safe and in one piece. Whew! Where there is a" Willy there's a Way"! The mission was accomplished and the part made it out to the field. I was ready to collapse from all the energy release, but it was nothing compared to the field.

## May 1967

FIELD-May 15, 1967 the Battalion was still out in the field around Bao Trai conducting Roadrunner and Security operations. There was negative enemy contact, but continued with Search and Destroy.

Motor Pool Jeep

BASE-That same period I had started working on the Motor Pool Records and organizing the parts inventory. As I recall, it was all one gigantic screw up! The hooch was a disaster area because the mechanics barely had just enough time to get the Armored Personnel Carriers ready for the field before we went out again. I've seen them work on one all night until just before the unit pulled out on the next mission. I didn't, and wouldn't, straighten up their personal belongings.

The picture on the next page shows what the hooch looked like on the outside, with the Motor Pool garage tent to the right. I must point out the ice chest to the right that always contained cold beer for thirsty men when the company was in from the jungle. The term "my office" conjures up all kinds of euphemistic images of a big desk, cushy easy chair, wood paneling, beautiful accessories and "air-conditioning"! Well, my office, all four sides and roof was made of corrugated steel. It was Hell! (The perfect Word) The

Japanese used to put POW's Prisoners of War in those same types of cages as a punishment!

During the dry season it got so hot that you'd think you were in a lake of fire. I dare you, no, I double-dare you to try working in my office all day. I couldn't stand it any longer. I had to clean up the place. It was too cluttered to even move around my "office". First, I tried sweeping out the room, and it actually made things easier. The next thing was to organize the parts by type and then by location on the Track for quick reference. That put the place into a logical state and saved time. These feats were accomplished the first three to four days of my tenure in the Motor Pool. The difference was, I was busy and safe, and my unit was still in danger!

My office is in the background

FIELD-May 16, 1967 the Battalion continued Roadrunner, Security and Search and Destroy operations in the area of Bao Trai. Company A continued its mission of base camp reaction force.

BASE-I continued to work on the Motor Pool records.

FIELD-May 17, 1967 the Battalion conducted Search

## May 1967

and Destroy operations in the area of Ap Dong Hoa, 7 kilometers west of the Oriental River. There was negative enemy contact.

BASE-the work in the motor pool was progressing. I was bored and feeling frustrated with the mess of the records. At least I could drown my sorrows at the Enlisted Men's Club.

FIELD-May 18, 1967 the Battalion conducted Search and Destroy operations South, North, and Northwest of Bao Trai. At 2:50pm the Battalion Commander's Armored Personnel Carrier detonated an anti-tank mine on Highway 10, one kilometer north of the junction of 7A. One bobcat was Killed-in-Action and four were Wounded-in-Action.

BASE-I spent the day sorting the papers and forms into piles during the day. I sorted the paperwork into piles by titles including Record Item Cards, Requisitions, Receipts, and Returns. This took all day, as there were records for over a year to sort and organize. I don't remember exactly what the Record Item Cards looked like, probably a card with columns including date, document number, receipts and returns, issues, and a column for current balance. The top of the card had Part-Number, and name.

All this data had to match up and appear to be accurate. The military, i.e. Army in this case, had a system that was laden with paper work with forms in triplicate and forms about forms, all with their own acronyms.

Aside from Emergency Parts Orders for the field, this was basically a nine-to-five job, which was something this GI was definitely not accustomed to! Much of the time my attitude was that of a combat soldier, so all this free time was actually a catalyst for trouble. Somehow I managed to get in my share of trouble, even though I desperately tried to maintain a low profile. I learned to stay in the Motor Pool area during the day, so they almost forgot that I even existed. When it came to Guard Duty my name was still on the list! This was normally a type of position we called a "Kiss Ass Job", but that wasn't my style. I didn't want to be known as a "Rear Echelon Mother Fucker", as they were referred to. We had very mixed feelings about the REMF's. We accepted that they were necessary for our needs and really appreciated what they did, but we still didn't hold them in high regard. There was no comparison between what we endured in our tour of duty and what they had to endure, as hopefully you can gather from my comparisons.

FIELD-May 19, 1967 the Battalion conducted Search and Destroy operations east of Bao Trai in the area at XT5604. There was negative enemy contact.

BASE-This day I sorted each type of form by date, including record cards, requisitions, receipts, issues, and returns. I did not quite finish because there were a lot of papers. The field still had me beat because they were doing things that attracted the attention of the Viet Cong.

Field-May 20, 1967 the Battalion was in the same area doing the same operations. During the day C Company had one Bobcat Killed-in-Action by enemy small arms fire. Later that day C Company assumed the role of Cu Chi Base Reaction Force and closed the day at the 25th Infantry Division Base Camp.

BASE-I worked this day without any interference except maybe for a cramped hand.

FIELD-May 21, 1967 the Battalion conducted Cordon and Search of Ap Duc Ngai, with no enemy contact. One Bobcat from C Company was Killed-in-Action by an explosive device during the day.

BASE-I was pissed off all day because they tried to put me on KP Kitchen Police Duty. There was a lot of work for me to accomplish in the Motor Pool, and I had to be available to get parts when called for. Again, I knew nothing of what was happening until I read the After-Action-Reports while researching for this book. Human beings usually look and react at the things around them, and don't stop and think of how fortunate they should feel. I admit I usually look and react in relation to my reactionary feelings. My point again was I needed to be available to order parts as there was a need for them, without any delay. Lives could be at risk!

FIELD-May 22, 1967 the Battalion conducted Cordon and Search operations with the 1/49th Infantry ARVN (Army of the Republic of Vietnam) east of Bao Trai in the area of XT5903. The Battalion conducted Search and Destroy operations from this area to Fire Support Base/PB Nickel with no enemy contact.

BASE-I was safe and sound at Cu Chi Base Camp, working on the record-keeping mess. That is tedious and sometimes quite boring. Boring and tedious compared to what?

FIELD-May 23, 1967 the Battalion conducted "Road Runner" night operations and took turns to sleep during the day at Fire Support Base/PB Nickel.

BASE-While I slept passed-out, brave men were running up and down the damn roads looking for trouble from an unseen enemy.

The taller man was from Chicago standing next to me the one with sunglasses. He was wounded 03/31/67 and had just left the hospital.

FIELD-May 24, 1967 to May 31, 1967 the Battalion conducted various night "Road Runner", Search and Destroy, Cordon and Search, & Security operations in the Bao Trai area, with light and intermittent enemy contact.

BASE-My daily activity during this period was tedious, but I was about 50 percent done with the reconstruction process. For some strange reason we combat veterans carry around tremendous amounts of unwarranted guilt. Humans are strange. Before May 12 I was a grunt in Harm's Way with no real hope of getting out of my circumstances. Now that I was in the safety of the motor pool, I reacted to my current stimuli as if I were still out in the field! I guess those experiences wouldn't fade quickly.

The potential for me to make it home alive was greatly increased by my working in the Motor Pool.

* * * * *

There were eleven men wounded-in-action for this month.
May 1967 claimed the lives of seventeen of our Brothers-In-Arms. They were:

| | |
|---|---|
| James H. Flickenger | Chester G. Jordan |
| Glendell Morgan | Lee H. Russ |
| Thomas A. Brynelsen | John S. Cartwright |
| Ralph W. Crytzer Jr. | Jack R. Lenner |
| James N. Law | William E. McGinnis II |
| Daniel M. Kasten | Ronny L. Palmer |
| Mack E. Gregory | David A. Haraldson |
| Roy L. Branham | James E. Coleman |
| Randall Abogast | |

They answered the Call-To-Arms not because they wanted to die, but because they believed that we all have the Right to Live. Let no man tarnish their memory otherwise.

# June 1967

FIELD-On June 1, 1967 the Battalion was on Operation Kolekole. Various operations were continued in the Bao Trai, Duc Hoa, and the Cu Chi areas.

BASE-I was working on the records at the Motor Pool in safety.

FIELD-June 2, 1967 Company C had an Ambush Patrol outside of the perimeter. An Armored Personnel Carrier was on Road Patrol near the Ambush Patrol. It hit an anti-tank mine and flipped over onto its top. The Ambush Patrol went to help and secured the area. The Platoon Sergeant had his legs pinned underneath it. The driver was dead, still inside the driver's hatch.

BASE-I had to process and pick up parts for the field from supply. I spent the night at the Enlisted Men's Club. It was pretty quiet at the Cu Chi base camp with very little to occupy my time. Idle hands are the devils workshop.

FIELD-From June 3, 1967 through June 6, 1967 the Battalion was conducting various operations in the Bao Trai, Duc Hoa, and the Cu Chi areas.

BASE-I continued working on the records at the Motor Pool. The evenings were spent at the Enlisted Men's Club and writing letters.

```
FIELD-On June 7, 1967 the Battalion conducted
"Roadrunner" operations on Highway 8A, between Cu
Chi and Bao Trai these were nighttime "Roadrunner"
operations. An Armored Personnel Carrier was by
RPG Russian Rockets and burned. Six Bobcats were
Killed -in-Action. Two of the bodies burned inside
of the track could not be recovered until light of
day. Elements of the Battalion also conducted a
Seal and Search of Tho Mo on highway 10, between
Bao Trai and Duc Hoa. Elements also continued
security missions in the area. (See Map B #13 on
Page 315)
```

I understand that the people in the villages were warned of the impending operation. I wonder why we would tell anyone where and when we were going to do something. Before Operation Manhattan in the Ho Bo Woods began on April 22, 1967, we dropped leaflets out of airplanes to warn non-combatants of the up-coming operation. As a result, the Viet Cong were ready for us with massive amounts of booby traps. They evacuated the area and had two and three-man sniper teams to delay us and lure us into traps.

This night it was really hot in the area of highway 8A. The Third Squad 1st Platoon, B Company B13 was conducting the operation. There were two Armored Personnel Carriers running at alternating running positions. The Viet Cong observed the pattern of the two units. In between runs, when the carriers were not in sight, the Viet Cong set up an ambush on the road that was being patrolled!
A little while later and down the road came the Armored Personnel Carrier B13. My former squad members and the ill-fated Armored Personnel Carrier were hit by Russian Rockets in the gas tank and it exploded. The B13 Armored Personnel Carrier was engulfed in flames, consuming six of my former squad members who were trapped in the fire. That evening they couldn't retrieve two of the bodies out of B13, so they had to wait until the next morning when there was daylight.

## June 1967

Sgt Kenny Newton B Co 1st Platoon, 3rd Squad Killed-in-Action 06/07/1967

---

This may seem like gruesome and unnecessary detail to you, but I want you to be able to get an idea of what it was like, and feel the type of things we as GI grunts endured every day in the jungles of Vietnam.

Imagine moving along the road in the early morning on the detail to recover the bodies of your buddies. Then you had to remove their barely recognizable remains. You could have possibly talked to some of them earlier the previous day. Think of this horrible experience and how those on the recovery team felt, and about the haunting memories that are captured in their minds.

It makes me cry for the men of B13, and for those on that detail to recover the bodies in the terrifying darkness! There are no nice words to mask this event. Here it is in black and white. Can you grasp the experience? Please, someone tell me, how does a person forget an event such as this? Imagine how Tim Fyle felt identifying those six bodies!

These are the types of experiences you cannot rationalize into acceptance. You cannot stop it from permeating your subconscious mind. How do you live with that, where do you go for help? It will eat at you and cause undue trouble and hidden reactions that rear their ugly heads when you don't even know why. One night can create a thousand terrors that will mask what you don't want to see.

Harris Vonzell Davis
Killed-in-Action 06/07/1967

FIELD-June 8, 1967 the Battalion continued various operations in the same general area. A detail was sent to recover the bodies from the last night.

A detail had to get the bodies remaining inside the Armored Personnel Carrier B13. More than likely the driver and the Track Commander were still trapped inside. Those men who did this detail had a doubly difficult task because they had to bring the bodies through those areas with the least accessibility, and the daylight made the forms of the brave men trapped there quite strikingly visible! Imagine looking on the two trapped inside and seeing them. How would you feel and react?

## June 1967

My heart goes out to those men who had been performing the detail to recover the bodies! I will never forget later that day of the 8th of June 1967. After lunch I returned to the motor pool to finish my daily work when I got the news of the deaths of my former squad members. I was in a state of shock!

This is the part that I had forgotten about until writing this book.

I returned back to work and later in the afternoon the wrecking unit couldn't bring B13 back to the motor pool. There wasn't even a shell of the B13 was a charred mess except for the place where the two bodies had been trapped. The track was melted into the ground and it was apparent that it wouldn't be coming back!

I had ridden many days and months in it, and I had experienced so much with some of those men. I can't imagine the event take place before me in my mind with the explosion and consuming fire lighting up the dark morning. I felt guilty for being alive. This was my squad, my friends, and someone else who had taken my place. My loss was great. My friends were gone. This remains a vivid part of the landscape of my memory.

Can you see how a person could feel guilty for being alive when brave men such as those who die instead of you?

My heart goes out to the families who lost so much that evening along a lonely road in a strange land. The civilians who travel that road today have no thought of what had happened there over forty years ago. I hope this story can help the families to heal old wounds. The details of where and how those men died have probably been hidden from them all these 40 years.

This is only my feeble attempt to tell what happened to the men of B13, but the story doesn't end here because a short sketch cannot fully describe these brave men. They had an experience that ended their mortal Lives. To really know them was to know the fear, doubt and pressure they endured facing death every day while out in the field.

Please understand that there were no battle lines drawn where two opposing armies faced each other on a battlefield of Honor. This was not a well choreographed movie, where the fear & trepidation built in anticipation of combat, the soldiers of both armies knowing that soon the battle would begin. This was not a planned event, where the call would be made and all hell would break loose when the fight began. There were no clear outcomes, where the two armies clashed. Each saw their objective and vied for supremacy out in the open, where the battle ran to its normal end and the outcome was decided, with victory for one and defeat for the other.

This was a real, ugly, destructive war. Consider those intense feelings before the conflict and the adrenalin expended on those levels of fear around the clock, day-by-day, for two-to-three-month stretches at a time. No clear beginning, no clear end, no decisive battles. Mix in lack of sleep, blistering hot muggy weather, wild animals, deadly snakes, countless varieties of insects and an enemy, hiding ready to strike and run! Those men endured that and more, so much more than you can fathom.

I knew most of those men at a time when glimpses of their deepest thoughts would occasionally surface. I was part of the brotherhood of the 3rd Squad of the 1st Platoon track B13. I was on Cu Chi Base Perimeter guard duty with them 25 days earlier! They had hopes and dreams. A life was waiting back in the "World" for them. These were good men, Americans from various races and ethnic background who had, in common, Love of Life and Love of Country!

All that ended for them in a second on a dark lonely road in a country they had never heard of two-to-three years earlier.

The Survivors of the Battle for Cu Chi of the 1st Battalion 5th Mechanized Infantry have an annual reunion, usually in July. We have them annually because we are getting older, and our time together is precious. The reunion in

## June 1967

July 2006 was held at Valley Forge, Pennsylvania from the 5th through the 9th.

On the evening of Thursday July 6, 2006 we had a meeting to go over business and also to honor our fallen comrades. The family of Luis Milan was in attendance to Honor their brother. Up to that evening, the family had no information as to what happened to their brother, for 39 years. The only thing they knew was that he had died on June 7, 1967. They wanted to know more about their brother.

I didn't remember until about 5:00pm, that I would be part of the Official Honor Party. I know that Butch had asked me about a week before, but in the excitement I forgot. See, we are getting older! This part of our program can get pretty emotional, as we remember those who didn't make it. Butch knew Luis just when his tour of duty ended, as he had arrived sometime before January 1967 and Butch had left mid-February. There only two who served directly with Luis were one other and me. It made sense that we should be the ones to share our knowledge of Luis.

To work out our duties for that evening, Butch met with the two of us about 5:30pm. Butch revealed that he had received a letter from the man who was the Battalion Commander during June 1967. The letter re-told in detail what had happened on that fateful night. The problem was that the information was quite graphic and blunt, and so Butch had us read the letter. This hit the other man pretty hard because he was there that night. The painful memories were too much, so we told him not to worry about sharing with the group and the family.

We were all reluctant to give the family the letter, but Luis's brother insisted. Remember, they knew nothing about the B13 Armored Personnel Carrier being hit in the Gas Tank on the road. The fact that it exploded and the six were consumed in flames might have been too much for them to take. It was understandably too vivid a memory to relive that experience since he was there that evening and has been affected by the event ever since.

Butch opened the Ceremony honoring those of our fallen comrades and then told about his remembrance of Luis.

I was next, and I had remembered the River Ambush in February 13, 1967. I had to do something to defuse the tension during this most difficult presentation, so I asked the audience for a big smile. It was a big help to me. I was drawing a blank on what to say about Luis, and then a funny memory popped into my head. It was a big relief to me, and the audience enjoyed the story because it was humorous and light, and revealed Luis's true character.

After my presentation, Butch presented the letter to Luis's brother, and introduced the rest of the family. I think there were five of them. The family was very appreciative that we honored the memory of their brother. There is some healing each time we honor our lost Brothers-in-Arms.

Today's popular political rhetoric includes the phrase "Freedom isn't Free"! It is a very eloquent and powerful statement. Those who know the true meaning will immediately add "It's been paid in full with the unfulfilled dreams by those who gave their lives to secure that freedom!"

This is my tribute to my comrades and friends of that ill-fated B13 Mission. Maybe they paid your and my price for Freedom the instant they were hit by the Russian Rocket on that dark Highway 8A between Cu Chi and Bao Trai.

Please stop and reflect on this for a moment. Don't take Freedom for granted. There are still those who would take it from you!

They weren't famous (more likely unknown men), except for the fact that they continue to live on the stone "Wall" in Washington, D.C. and in the Hearts and Minds of those who knew them.

These men of B13 have a Place of Honor we cannot touch or ever hope to attain. They achieved it by falling in the line of duty. I'll be greatly rewarded if you can, in a small way, grasp the experiences and feelings of a combat veteran of any war.

BASE-It was still June 8, 1967. I had done my usual work at the Motor Pool fixing records. That evening I had been selected to guard the Motor Pool. At about 3:00am I was diligently performing my duty while listening to a radio report about the Israeli Air Force bombing the shit out of Egypt. While I was not for either side per se, it was just cool to hear of an army somewhere being able to take charge and do what it needed to do, in spite of world opinion. This was the 6-Day War of June 5-10, 1967. Since I was on guard duty the early morning of the $9^{th}$ of June 1967, which would have been the $9^{th}$ at about 9:00pm for them in the Middle East.

Had our country had the balls to do what was needed, as the Israelis did in their war, the war in Vietnam would have progressed faster and with better results. Charlie's ass would have been in a sling! Sound familiar?

Did we pay lip service to Democracy or did we stand behind our words? In the field we did not worry about what the world thought. After all, no one was chastising the Soviets and the Chinese for their actions in South East Asia!

Here was Israel alone against the armies of Iraq, Egypt, Jordan, Syria, Algeria, Kuwait, Sudan, the whole Arab nation, and they kicked their Asses!!

Today I have a lot of friends who are Arab. Like I said, it was just gratifying to hear someone doing what our soldiers were fully capable of doing, if we had true leadership at home.

The war we were fighting was a war of frustrations with every enemy foreign and domestic hell-bent-for-leather to give us a bad time. The political football was being kicked around at home, but our efforts were only recognized as something wrong. Those at home really had no idea of the poverty that existed in Vietnam. Hell, it still functioned as a feudal state much like in the 9th century A.D. when ancient warlords were fighting for control. Most of life's simplest things we take for granted didn't even exist in Vietnam.

Here I was, alone on guard duty in the motor pool, listening to history, (probably the only one in the 25th Infantry Division). It was quite an experience now that I think of it. I was off guard duty at about 6:00am and went into the hooch to sleep, and as I drifted off to sleep I did so with a satisfied feeling.

FIELD-June 9, 1967, the Battalion was conducting Search and Destroy operations in Thoi Moi southeast of Bao Trai.

BASE-After guard duty I slept to almost 12:00 noon and woke up hungry. I was worried about my stomach and what to put in it. So I got up and hurried down to the mess hall! I wasn't needed for anything specific, so I took off the rest of the day. That evening I spent at the Enlisted Men's Club drinking and snacking.

FIELD-June 10, 1967 through the 12th, the Battalion was still at Thoi Moi conducting various missions.

BASE-I was back at Cu Chi and smelled the basic odor that wasn't too strong, probably because the Base Camp inside the perimeter was void of rotting vegetation. The rest of the Battalion was out in the jungle area and were subjected to that smell that resembled driving by a dairy farm, because the jungle was in a continual state of decay. This unpleasant smell was experienced by the GI's 24 hours a day. Whew! I wonder what effect the jungle gases were having on our lungs.

FIELD-June 13, 1967 the Battalion conducted a "Country Fair" Operation at Thoi Moi, southeast of Bao Trai.

BASE-I continued with record restoration at the Motor Pool. During the noontime break I went to the Post Exchange to purchase some snacks and personal items.

FIELD-June 14, 1967 the Battalion conducted night "Roadrunner" operations in the vicinity of Bao Trai. B Company had negative contact with the Viet Cong. One platoon of Company C conducted combined security operations with the 2/49$^{th}$ Infantry of the Army of the Republic of South Vietnam. They were conducting night "Road Runner" operations between Duc Lap and Duc Hoa. One of the Armored Personnel Carriers detonated a mine. Two Bobcats were Killed-in-Action from the blast.

BASE-I was close to finishing the motor pool record reconstruction process and was feeling very confident and competent. I spent my evening at the Enlisted Men's Club as a regular customer.

FIELD-June 15, 1967 Company B was in the field but had negative contact with the enemy. The battalion conducted local security in the vicinity of Bao Trai. Company C searched the road between Duc Lap and Duc Hoa with the 49th ARVN Infantry.

BASE-I continued to work on Motor Pool records, and spent the night drinking at the Enlisted Men's Club.

FIELD-June 16, 1967 the Battalion was conducting Cordon and Search operations in the area of Tho Mo, located on Highway 10 about halfway between Bao Trai and Duc Hoa. Company A conducted road security with the 49th ARVN Infantry.

BASE-I worked my usual day and wrote letters and visited the "Club".

FIELD-June 17, 1967 the Battalion was conducting security for an engineering detail. C Company conducted a combined sweep operation of the Fire

Support base Nickel perimeter with an ARVN Squad from Military Intelligence.

BASE-I had made considerable gains toward the completion of my initial assignment.

FIELD-June 18, 1967 the Battalion along with the 1st and 2nd Battalions of the 27th Inf. conducted a Cordon and Search operation of Loc Giang, located southeast of Bao Trai at XT6102.

BASE-I was in the Cu Chi base camp working in the motor pool. This job was beginning to drive me crazy.

FIELD-June 19, 1967 Company B conducted road security operations with elements of the 2/49th Army of the Republic of Vietnam ARVN Infantry. The remaining Company's of the Battalion conducted local security operations.

BASE-My record restoration at the Motor Pool was nearing completion.

FIELD-June 20, 1967 The Recon Platoon conducted road-clearing operations on Highway 8A south of Cu Chi, along with one platoon of The Army of the Republic of Vietnam from the 2/49th Infantry. The Battalion conducted sweeps between Highways 8A and 9A, moving from southeast to northeast.

BASE-The area had remained rather quiet at B Company with First Sergeant Densmore out in the field with the troops. I was able to work hard at the Motor Pool without his disruptive presence.
I had established a routine in my day and still got a lot of work accomplished.

FIELD-From June 21, 1967 to June 29, 1967 the Battalion conducted various operations with ARVN units in the area from Bao Trai and Fire Support Base Nickel. On the 24th there was a ceremony celebrating the reopening of Highway 10 between Duc Hoa and Bao Trai.

BASE-I was safe at Cu Chi doing my duty and my drinking.

FIELD-On June 29, 1967 the Battalion conducted "Eagle Flights" to four Landing Zones east of Bao Trai with negative enemy contact.

BASE-I was at work in the Motor Pool ordering replacement parts and correcting the records. The records were caught up to February 1967. My evening was spent writing letters and visiting the Club.

FIELD-June 30, 1967 the Battalion conducted Eagle Flights to the Bao Trai area with negative enemy contact.

BASE-I was working my little fingers to the bone in my "office" (more like a steam bath).

Messy Combat Mechanics?
Officers can be petty and sneaky too. A Lt. Colonel or a Major from HQ Company decided to inspect the Motor Pool. He took a spin through the inside of the hooch, looked outside in the ice chest, and declared our beloved home a "Den of Iniquity". Can you believe that? Just what does that mean?

He didn't look at the Motor Pool Repair area or the Parts Shed, and not even a peek at my wonderful records (I think he was on a military order and discipline vendetta). Obviously this officer had no idea of the schedule of the mechanics, and how difficult it was for the Mechanics to clean and tidy up their quarters when they were out in the field all the time. And when they were in from the field they worked 18 hours a day or more, while they were only back at Base Camp for one or two days at a time.

What I'd like to know is what did he think the guys were supposed to do? We were fighting a WAR. Battle is not "neat and tidy". It is hell-bent-for-leather, and the mechanics did it out in the field and back at Base Camp too. I know because I was there at the time.

An officer had all the comforts of home at his living quarters at Base Camp. Who was he to judge? I know it was his duty and his right because of his rank, but why fuck with brave men who are working themselves to distraction.

Military discipline had its place, but carried to the extreme it was not productive like intended. Our discipline was out in the field during combat where everything went to "Hell in a hand basket"! Which is most important, Combat Discipline or "neat and tidy"? I was fortunate to get to know many of the mechanics. They were great guys and soldiers. Most people think of a mechanic as someone working in a garage in relative safety. Not in this case.

They never gave the motor pool mechanics enough time to be "neat and tidy". They ran everybody night and day with less than acceptable sleep out in the field, which burned that habit into our physiological time clocks. This created scars and frustrations that have affected our entire "adult" lives, and the lives of our loved ones. And they did it to the mechanics too.

The mechanics had the same idea of the badge I wrote about above!
Back row: new driver, Al Biggs, new mechanic
Front row: George Spooner, Ron Priebe and Edward Goodman

Many times I saw mechanics working on an Armored Personnel Carrier out in the jungle all night, getting it ready to move out that next morning. I don't know if they ever pulled Listening Post or Ambushes or Perimeter Duty, and it doesn't matter if they didn't.
During the day, the combat mechanics were right there with the rest of us. If a track broke down and was left behind, they were there working on it, exposed to the same dangers of enemy attack. They were just like the regular grunts out in the field. They needed a special rendition of the Combat Infantry Badge, maybe with a Wrench Cluster.

I'd been on an Armored Personnel Carrier that had broken down or thrown a track in the jungle. The rest of the company would go ahead and leave us behind. It was a very scary time. The mechanics were right there with us working and ready to fight. The combat mechanics carried weapons and used them in the field on the Viet Cong. I had total respect for our mechanics as soldiers fighting a war. There were very few times they worked on Armored Personnel Carriers back at Base Camp. They did most of the repairs out in the field. They were in a different kind of combat out in the field. And guess what the mechanics were doing when we were in firefights. They weren't cheerleading!

Jack Pashano "Chief" Killed-in-Action 08/19/1968

I have several combat photos that were taken by the mechanic we nicknamed "Chief". If the mechanics didn't stay with us in the field I would not have any pictures of Vietnam. My pictures were from his negatives and why is he out in the jungle? Look at his picture, the one below, and you'll see he was out there with us. The web site has more pictures of him. Jack was a proud resident of the Hopi Indian Reservation in northeast Arizona. Our mechanics did fight!

Many times we came in from the field for only one day, and they had all those tracks to maintain and repair. While we would spend one to two hours doing maintenance on our weapons they would spend all day and sometimes all night at the Motor Pool working. The next day they would be lined up ready to go after a sleepless night and I don't mean "Sleepless in Seattle" (the name of a movie). I mean no sleep! Sometimes the mechanics spent three days in base camp. Three days may seem like a lot of time. But considering the mechanics had to inspect, repair, and maintain twenty or more Armored Personnel Carriers that had been abused in the last four to five months, it was hard work. The way the Armored Personnel Carriers were abused, it's a wonder they ran as well as they did, all thanks to those mechanics.

Michael Seidenari, Allen Biggs, and Edward Goodman.
Allen Biggs, in the middle of the picture, was the mechanic in the February 3, 1967 action story

## June 1967

Oh, by the way guys, make sure your hooch is neat, tidy and spotless. That's what true military discipline is, and it's so… important! It is obvious that this officer was new to this combat unit and the war, and had no idea of what these mechanics did. He'd find out when his Armored Personnel Carrier needed repair!
I would have cleaned up the hooch but because I was not given authorization to handle anyone's belongings I didn't. If something were missing, whom do you think would be blamed? The outside of the hooch and the Motor Pool area were neat and organized by me when I was back there.

\* \* \* \* \*

There was one-man wounded-in-action this month.

The month of June 1967 claimed the lives of ten our fellow soldiers and my former squad. They are:

| | |
|---|---|
| *Everdene Baker Jr. | *Harris V. Davis |
| *William L. Evans | *Rex A. La Duke |
| *Luis E. Milan-Anavita | *Kenneth P. Newton |
| Robert L. Hoffman | Joseph H. Urmann |
| Robert L. Holland | Paul E. Hale |

While the rest of the world went about their everyday business, these men worked hard and paid the price for our freedom.

# July 1967

FIELD- July 1, 1967 the Battalion was somewhere East of Bao Trai from the 1st to the 9th. Numerous combined operations were conducted with the Army of the Republic of Vietnam $49^{th}$ Infantry. They had also tried airmobile combat assaults without enemy contact; however, some enemy fortifications were located and destroyed. There were no detailed after action reports to draw from.

BASE-for the same period I was still in the Motor Pool; however, on the $5^{th}$ of July 1967 there was an experience I had nearly forgotten.

Trash Dump
I was still at the Cu Chi Base Camp, and there were several things that had to be taken to the military dumpsite. The only person who was unlucky enough to be around at Base Camp was Tim Fyle. He had also ended up with a base camp job of driving a jeep.

There were several large items piled into the small utility trailer. A few of them were so heavy that help was needed unloading. There was an old Staff Sergeant who was either supervising or going for a joy ride. I didn't really care. It just seemed funny that he needed to go.

We drove into the dump from the North (the dump area was in a shape like a horseshoe). The odor as we drove in wasn't too bad, but as we got in the middle we were surrounded by masses of stinking trash. It was amazing. It had almost every type of trash you could imagine. There were piles of trash in mounds everywhere in a mess. Did I expect it to be all neat and tidy? This area was a really large dump. Talk about government waste!

There were at least 30 Vietnamese rummaging around the dump, picking up just about everything and anything. The things you and I wouldn't even give a second thought about what seemed to be a treasure to them. They were walking around on top of the piles in search for "goodies". There was a small woman sloshing around at the bottom of one of the hills. She had an old pair of combat boots, about size 10. They kind of looked like clown shoes except they weren't very colorful or funny! It was such a shame to see the vast difference in the two cultures. Our culture had so much but saved so little. The Vietnamese did so much with so little.

Then the funniest thing happened. That old Staff Sergeant started talking to her, not in Vietnamese, but in Korean. He told us that she was from Korea. I think he said that they had a permit to take anything they wanted out of the dump. This site didn't have any weapons or ammo, so I guess it was ok. These people were very ingenious in making all kinds of things out of seemingly nothing.

The poverty level of those people was astonishing. It was sad that they had to find a living in a dump. There was food waste in this location, and some of the people were collecting bits and pieces of any food they could find. It was sad and depressing to see such abject poverty. I do know that the Vietnamese people were very resourceful and could make all types of knick-knacks out of things we thought were trash. Hell, they had even made a building out of soda cans!

We got out of there as quick as we could because it smelled so bad, and we weren't enjoying what we saw. No wonder some of them had bandannas over their mouths and noses.

The real truth is the leaders of countries hardly ever experience what we observed in the dump that day and during our tour of duty. It was like looking at their dirty underwear! The people were the reason we should have been there, not the politics. As for us GI's, most of us felt we were there for the poor people. Above all else we were there for each other. People care about people, not governments!

FIELD-July 10, 1967 the Battalion shifted its operation to northwest of Bao Trai along the Oriental River.

BASE-I was getting close to finishing the re-creation of the Motor Pool Records.

FIELD-July 11, 1967 the Battalion was continuing Search and Destroy operations along the Oriental River.

BASE-I was still safe and sound back at B Company Motor Pool.
I was told that the next day I would be on Guard Duty. Didn't these people know that I was a very integral part of the company? I tried to tell them, but they didn't buy it. I wasn't a very happy camper, so I decided to drown my sorrows in several beers at the Enlisted Men's Club.

FIELD-July 12, 1967 the Battalion conducted Search and Destroy Missions in the area encompassed by Highways 6A, 19, 7a and the Oriental River. Company B located 9 bunkers, one tunnel, supplies, and several booby traps.

BASE-It was my turn to pull Guard Duty in the Motor Pool, but during the day I continued to do my work on the records. While working, I was still griping and moaning about Guard Duty for that evening. Boy what a spoiled little brat I'd become. Not too often were parts ordered at night unless they got into a repair job in the dark and the field supply for a part was depleted.

## Off Guard Duty

It was July 12, 1967, just before they shipped me back to the land of Ambush and Listening Post. My sense of honor was offended because I was back at Base Camp, and they were out in Harm's Way. I wasn't a chicken shit or an REMF. I just had the training in the Motor Pool. So I was it. This Sense of Honor didn't stop me from making the best of it (or the worst of it, as it turned out)!

I must note that when I took over in May, the records for the motor pool couldn't pass a "short arm inspection" done in a WAC unit (Women's Army Corps)! By the time I was done those records were put together so well that they could pass an I.G. Inspection (Inspector General). You could consider them almost perfectly put together, with issues and inventory matching whether or not they were 100% accurate. (These talents were put to good use by me in business some 30 years later during a bank audit done by a Top 10 accounting firm. Everything was legal, but some minor items were not quite visible unless you really knew where to look for the information. And they didn't!)

While I had avoided things like Shit Burners' Detail and Kitchen Police, I was unsuccessful in avoiding Guard Duty. Drat!

Guard Duty was very boring and a waste of time in my estimation. I must admit I thought the Army did a lot of things that didn't make sense. I guess if the Viet Cong overran us, it would matter. Come to think of it, when you looked out the back of the hooch toward the Black Virgin Mountain, there wasn't much out there between the unit and Viet Cong Land. So, then I felt like an idiot.

Anyway, when I wasn't on Guard Duty that night, I was in the Enlisted Men's Club drinking beer. Not in the guard tent. Well, the beer, the boredom, the boiling heat and a tired Spirit got the best of me. I wasn't exactly in top military form, and not quite sober, when guess what? The damned Officer of the Day decided to make an inspection of the Guards and caught me "under the influence". Oops! Strange as it may seem, I wasn't replaced, just chastised! That incident helped me to sober up pretty quickly. I didn't understand why he didn't have me relieved.

I was a little too drunk to be scared and too tired to care much about it. The morning was a different story.

## July 1967

Normally, my butt would have been roasted over a slow burning fire if the First Sergeant had been back at Base Camp. Miracles do happen! About 2 or 3 months before this, our non-combatant chicken shit First Sergeant succumbed to the order of the Battalion Commander's "All First Sergeants will accompany their Company in the field". Yeah for me!

I was still scared to death of what First Sergeant Densmore would cook up to punish me the next day, and I was very uncomfortable about it. I continued that night on my Guard Duty, and I went to bed when I was done. Morning came too quickly for me. I was as hungry as a bear but still dreading the outcome of my previous night's guard duty.

FIELD-July 13, 1967 the Battalion had encountered light and sporadic enemy contact in the area of Loc Giang located southeast of the junction of Highway 10 and 6A. Two Bobcats were Wounded-in-Action and "Dusted Off", picked up by Medivac helicopters.

BASE-On the morning of July 13, 1967 as I was making my way to the mess hall, I was halted by First Lt. Sol Wainwright (the Executive Officer). He was in the process of herding the small flock back to Base Camp Cu Chi. As sternly as he possibly could (considering his non-stop laughter, which made me nervous), he relieved my anxiety. I might have gotten shit-burning detail. He just laughed at me, and told me the best words my little GI brain (Government Idiot) could have heard at that point. He said, "Relax, I am not going to tell the First Sergeant about this!" Whew, my ass was saved!

Combine this episode with the story about my earlier Tay Ninh Trip Up, and if I had stayed in the Army I would have held the record as the oldest, active, living PFC Private First Class soldier in the history of the U.S. Army! Promotion, what promotion???

I must say he really saved my butt that day. I wish I could locate him to thank him. Also, when I did get my promotion to E-4, Specialist 4$^{th}$ Class, guess whose name was on the paperwork? Right, First Lt. Sol Wainwright!

I had the evening off, so I went back to the scene of the crime, the Enlisted Men's Club, for drinks and snacks which kept us alive one day to the next. My drinking was interrupted by the sound of some incoming mortar rounds.

At 9:35pm the Viet Cong decided to attack Cu Chi base camp and showered us with 16 rounds of 82mm mortar fire. Fifteen soldiers were wounded in less than one minute. This may sound calloused and high-handed on my part, but one minute was hardly enough to get me excited since I was used to being closer to the incoming rounds. Besides, if it's not directed near your position, one could hardly notice.

FIELD-July 14, 1967 at 7:20am one Bobcat from B Company was wounded when an anti-personnel mine was detonated north of Highway 6A between Loc Hoa and the Oriental River. At 7:21am a track from A Company detonated an anti-tank mine with negative casualties. At 7:45am one Bobcat from Company A was Killed-in-Action and two Wounded-in-Action when a man stepped on an anti-personnel mine near Loc Thuan. At 9:00am Company C had four Wounded-in-Action from two booby traps.

BASE-The morning of July 14th I received word from First Lt. Sol Wainwright that things were going too slowly out in the field and the Company needed me to go back out and stir things up a little. I was devastated. I am not a coward, I just wanted to live. My chances of staying that way were better at the Base Camp. Ah, hell, it was getting pretty boring at Base Camp anyway, but where would I get my beer? And when? Inside I wasn't feeling all that great about the Land of Listening Post and Ambush, but I couldn't show it. So off I went like a good little GI back to the bosom of B Company. I wondered if this had anything to do with that Idiot Lt. Colonel or Major.

FIELD-July 15, 1967 Company B, working in the previous day's area, located a munitions cache. Among the things found were 60 81mm mortar rounds, 43 60mm rounds and 32 2.75-inch rockets.

## July 1967

It sounds like they didn't use quite all of their 4th of July fireworks.

BASE-I remember they whisked me away in a chopper to join my friends out in the field early in the afternoon.

```
July 16, 1967 the Battalion conducted Search and
Destroy operations in the area of Loc Giang. The
Search operation was conducted with the Trang Bang
Regional Forces Company. Elements of the Battalion
provided security for engineer activities in the
area.
```

### My First Day Back In the Field - ARVN Ambush
Sometime earlier we had teamed up with the (ARVN) Army of the Republic of South Vietnam units on field operations. We just happened to be working in the area of Loc Giang with the Trang Bang Regional Forces (an ARVN unit we'd been working with in the area that day). We were closer to "civilization" than during most of our field time spent in Viet Cong territory.

ARVN unit preparing for Ambush Over-niter

We were looking forward to a little easier evening because we weren't going out on any Ambushes this night. We had set up our evening Base Camp, eaten, and had settled down for an evening of luxury. We were free from Ambushes or the Listening Post because others were taking care of those things tonight. Another luxury was that we weren't in the total darkness and quiet like when we were on Ambush.

I am totally unaware which "ARVN" unit we were near at this time, but our Vietnamese allies were going out on an Ambush that particular evening. I guess we were on hand to rescue them if they should get into trouble.

What we saw kind of surprised and bewildered our "Western" sensibilities. Here we were, seasoned and tough soldiers going out on a dangerous mission. As they walked by us into the unforgiving bush, we saw something that you would never expect in combat. Some of ARVN soldiers were holding hands as they marched out.

We all thought that was very strange, as you can well imagine. Our ignorant minds went into the judgmental mode until someone who had been exposed to their culture set us straight. He told us that traditionally some Vietnamese men do this as a Sign of Friendship or Solidarity for one another, nothing more, nothing less! 'When in Rome, do as the Romans do" wasn't going to apply in this case, so what did it matter?

Most of us had never seen this behavior before, so our shock was understandable. I initially was just as pissed off as everyone else who experienced that behavior. Do you think this is that much different than the Scots wearing "Kilts", or the men of Indonesia wearing skirts called "Kain"? It is just their culture, nothing more.

It's amazing how things that we previously experienced have a way of re-appearing. Somewhere around 1998 I was living in Citrus Heights, California and was at the local mall. I noticed four-six younger Vietnamese men walking through the mall holding hands. To most Americans this behavior is definitely odd, but due to my prior experiences some 30 plus years ago, I was able to accept it for what I knew it was.

There was a group of "macho" natives that were making fun of those young men by whistling, making catcalls, and harassing them to no end. Armed with knowledge and my generally protective nature, I interceded on their behalf.
I explained to those boys that if they understood or knew of the Vietnamese, they would have been more tolerant. I re-counted to them my experience in the Vietnam jungle, many years prior. I asked them to leave the young Vietnamese men alone, and as I walked away the harassment stopped.

The 17$^{th}$ to the 23$^{rd}$ of July 1967 we continued as Security for engineer activities.

On July 24, 1967 the Battalion was continuing Local Security with Search and Destroy operations in the Loc Giang area. At 8:00pm B Company had four Bobcats Wounded-in-Action when an anti-tank mine was detonated.

Until 8:00pm happened, it seemed like the Viet Cong had been on R&R (Rest & Rice) for about the last week. Then we heard that at 10:28pm, the Dau Tang Base Camp received 70 82mm mortar rounds inside the Perimeter and 30 rounds on the outside of the Perimeter. One aircraft was destroyed and 24 were damaged. Fifty GI's were Wounded-in-Action in the attack!

We were pissed off and wanted to go get those sons of bitches!

July 25, 1967 the Battalion was working the Loc Giang area providing Security for the Engineer and Artillery units. During this period, four Airmobile Combat assaults were conducted along with personnel from Hiep Hoa. Enemy contact was light and scattered.

Two weeks earlier I had requested that my R & R (Rest and Relaxation) be in Taipei, Taiwan, and it was granted. This was a little later than usual, but because of my absence from Mid-November to Mid-December 1966 and my moving from the field to the Motor Pool, it wasn't approved until July 24th for the 27th of July. Talk about great timing. I had to leave the field on the 26th so I could leave Cu Chi for the airport. Yea!

Field-July 26, 1967 the Battalion was conducting Search and Destroy operations and Security for Engineer and Artillery units in the Loc Giang area. At 11:15am Company A suffered two wounded from a detonated booby trap the area of XT435175, north of Highway 6A. At 1:20pm Company A had a Bobcat Wounded-in-Action from a booby trap.

I left the field for Cu Chi Base Camp in the afternoon so I could be ready to catch a plane for Taiwan the next day.

Typical Booby Trap setup in the bush

FIELD-July 27, 1967 the Battalion conducted Airmobile Combat assaults (Eagle Flights) made on the East and West Banks of the Oriental River.

## TAIWAN- Day One: The Joys of Flush Toilets
As part of the benefit package for American GI's we received a 3-day Rest and Relaxation Holiday, supposedly after 6 months! I had taken some time in deciding where I was going for my R & R, but I finally decided on the island of Taiwan, at its largest city, Taipei.

I can remember leaving the hooch for my 3-day vacation. I went to the 25th Aviation for a chopper to the Air Base in the Saigon area. I boarded the helicopter in Cu Chi. The flight didn't last too long, but while it was landing it seemed to be coming down much too quick! Oh no, not now, don't crash! Well, it landed pretty hard and jolted us, but there we were safe on Terra Firma. Whew, still alive and raring to go!

I don't remember getting on the airplane in Saigon, but I didn't flap my arms and fly under my own power. It was a pleasure to fly again on a modern jet airliner instead of an old propeller plane. As we approached the island, it looked very beautiful with its dark rich greens and purples sitting in a liquid pool of bright blue ocean. The hills were beautiful and the scene was refreshing. I got off the plane carrying one big bag (with little in it.). That bag is now in my garage all torn apart except for the 5th Mech stickers on it. We arrived about 3:00pm in the afternoon. The temperature and humidity was just right.

The next logical thing was to find a taxi to the hotel. Mind you, I'd just spent months on end in an aluminum coffin (APC-Armored Personnel Carrier) at death's door. That was a picnic compared to the taxi ride. To make a short story long, a TT Taipei Taxi is usually a short trip. You get in, tell them where you need to go, sit down, put your head between your legs and kiss your ass good-bye! Taipei Taxi Drivers drive with two things, on two different surfaces. They drive with their horns and their gas pedals...on either the road or the sidewalk! Traffic lights, what lights?

I arrived at the hotel in one piece, registered, and went up to the room. It was nice, real nice compared to what I had become accustomed to in Nam. The hotel was an older building but clean and comfortable like an average hotel in the states. It didn't even occur to me until I looked into the bathroom that there, before my eyes was a FLUSH TOILET! WOW!

Imagine yourself spending a whole year either in Base Camp, occasionally taking a crap on a wooden slab into a metal can below, or in the field digging a hole in the grass and squatting in front of everyone else with your bare butt smiling at the others. Talk about "Mooning"! Since we spent all but a few days a month or less at the Base Camp for our total tour, this meant that most of our necessary toilet functions had been taken care of in the open. I know this seems a little foolish and silly, but we take for granted the modern conveniences we enjoy every day. You can imagine that a flush toilet was a huge luxury.

While not long, the trip was tiring because we left our home in Cu Chi, got to the airport and took off. I was very tired, so I decided I could use a nap. I had been too excited to sleep on the plane. I would need all the rest I could get for the upcoming indulgence that evening!

I almost forgot to mention the glorious SHOWER/TUB in the bathroom. I had gone a long time without the luxury of regular showers. There was also another forgotten novelty, a sink and a mirror. Hey, I still looked human! Come to think of it, I remember taking a long hot shower, then flushing the toilet a couple of times for fun before my nap. I called the front desk and asked for a wake-up call for 7:30pm. It was a wonderful feeling to lie down on a real bed in the safety of a hotel room. I slept like a baby!

The wakeup call came all too early, but the three-hour nap took the edge off my nerves. I was famished. So hungry I could eat a bear. For the heck of it, I took another shower and flushed the toilet a couple more times. I dressed and left my room looking for food. What I ate or where wasn't important. Real food, that's the life! I returned to my room to get ready to meet up with the other GI's I met on the plane to go clubbing.

Having been where I'd been, and where I was going back to, I guess the hotel arranged some entertainment. When I returned to my room at about 9:00pm there was a knock at my door. There at my door was a girl. I was a little surprised, but I invited her in.

## July 1967

I don't remember what she looked like because it didn't matter too much. The rest is history.

I met the guys around 10:00pm and we hailed a Death Taxi. We gave the driver our destination, got in and prayed! We made it to the club in one piece. This was something that resembled Real Life. The club played Rock and Roll music, had plenty of booze, and of course girls. We had a great time, but decided once the club closed to head for the hotel and that real bed. The last thing I remember is my head hitting the pillow. That night was more than welcome, and boy was it restful just being there in safety.

```
FIELD-July 28, 1967 the Battalion was conducting
Search and Destroy operations in the Loc Giang
area. Company C had one Bobcat Wounded-in-Action
from a booby trap explosion.
```

TAWIAN-Day Two:
On July 28 I slept until 10:30am. What a luxury. I took yet another shower and got dressed to start my second day of R & R. It occurred to me that food was the First Order of the Day. I went to the same restaurant as last evening. I was able to have real eggs (not powdered), hash brown potatoes (fresh, not dehydrated), wheat bread toast, (not rice bread) with jam and coffee. This was almost like being home.

I had passed a swimming pool provided for American Servicemen on my way to the restaurant. The pool didn't cost too much. I decided to go back to the hotel for my swimming suit. The water was cool and refreshing, and lo and behold, a diving board! I used the low board to do my warm up Swan Dive with perfect gymnastic form. That was followed by an Inward Cutaway Dive, a standing Back Flip, and then I finishing with a 1½ Front Flip Piked. Wow, I hadn't forgotten how to dive.

There was a bus trip to the ocean, what the hell, why not! The bus ride was a great trip. It left the city and wound its way through the verdant hills and down to the sea. The day was nice and warm, the ocean inviting. I was hungry after my trip to the ocean, and some real food again sure hit the spot.

That evening some of the GI's, who for some reason gravitated together, decided to go to another nightclub. I wasn't much of a dancer then, but I could drink. We met some of the bargirls (or taxi dancers, as they were called in the forties). They were nice to us and invited us to their house the next day. I think we made it back to our hotels that night.

```
FIELD-July 29, 1967 the Battalion conducted four
Eagle Flights along with one Company of CIDG
personnel from Hiep Hoa. Enemy contact was light
and scattered.
```

<u>TAIWAN-Day 3:</u>
I got up late, showered and flushed, ate breakfast consisting of real food, and did some site-seeing. Later that afternoon my GI acquaintances and I decided to take the girls up on their offer. It was like a party and we had a great time (with no hanky-panky, thank you). We watched TV in the Chinese language. It might have been a Soap Opera, and I actually started to understand what was being said. In spite of the language it reminded me of being back home where things were normal. Our "normal" life was to kill or be killed and the hell with everything. The fact that this was our last day away from Death's Door made going back a lot more difficult.

We were scheduled to leave the next morning, the 31th of July 1967. It was time to get back to our hotels, back to Vietnam, red and black ants, Bamboo vipers and all the other things we'd been putting up with. All good things come to an end, and this R & R was no exception. I packed up what little I brought, flushed the toilet good bye a couple of times, and walked out the door....

I checked out of the hotel and caught a TTT (Treacherous Taipei Taxi) to the airport. I renamed the taxis because I think it may be safer to ride in the Armored Personnel Carriers in Vietnam! The wait for the plane going back to Vietnam seemed like an eternity. I had nothing to look forward to where I was headed. We boarded the jet at the airport and said good-bye to Sanity and back to Folly. I was so depressed that I don't remember the flight back to Vietnam and how I got back to Cu Chi.

## July 1967

FIELD-July 30, 1967 during that day the Battalion continued to provide security for Engineer and Artillery units. Three Bobcats from Company C were Wounded-in-Action when a booby trap was detonated.

VIETNAM-I arrived on the 31st (about 12:00 or 1:00pm) and then in Cu Chi around 2:00 pm. I was back in the Land of Ambush and Listening Post by late afternoon (oh, by the way, don't forget Search and Destroy!)

FIELD-July 31, 1967 the Battalion continued to provide Security for Engineer and Artillery units in the same area. The Battalion conducted Search and Destroy operations. There was negative enemy contact that day.

"Mrs. Cong, can Charlie come out and play?" I guess he has his piano or tap dance lesson today.

July 1967 was a successful month except for one Bobcat Killed-in-Action. To us grunts, one man was as important as twenty, for we were all diminished by the loss of one of our own!

\* \* \* \*

There were fourteen men wounded-in-action this month.

The only Killed-in-Action soldier for July was:

Guillermo Munoz

He served His Country and the Cause of Freedom and paid for it with his Life.

# August 1967

August 1, 1967 the Battalion provided security for Engineer and Artillery units. B Company conducted Search and Destroy operations in the Loc Giang area, and an Eagle Flight combat assault was made into a Landing Zone 4 kilometers south of Trang Bang

It was the evening of August 1, 1967, and we got word that the next day's mission would be an Eagle Flight in the morning.

The title of this book, Landscape of My Memory, came to me forty years to the day after the Search and Destroy operations described above. Here's that story from my recent diary.

"Today is August 1, 2007. I left Sacramento, California at 4:45pm. I am writing this while I am flying on a US Airliner to Phoenix Arizona on the first part of a journey to Atlanta, Georgia. The captain just announced that we are flying at an altitude of 6.5 miles or 34,320 feet. As I am looking out the window there are thick elongated clouds whisking along below the plane. I am reflecting about my last three months in my Vietnam experience, trying to piece together bits and pieces of that time, trying to dig deeper into what I remember, which is very little. I stare out the window desperately reaching back to 40 years ago, and things are whisking by, just like those clouds. My mind is blocked!"

"I need a picture or some description from someone who was there at the same time to provide information to jump-start my memory. I don't know if that time was so dull and uneventful or too horrible. The After-Action-Reports give sketchy facts that don't connect with my memory."

"An interesting phenomenon is occurring! Every so often there are brief openings in the clouds, revealing glimpses of the landscape below. As quickly as this happens out the window there are openings in the clouds of my mind, brief pictures like glimpses of the landscape of my memory...."

"I remember two pictures from my collection. One shows the combat mechanic named "Chief" kneeling down on the ground by the Armored Personnel Carrier, the other is a picture of a Chinook CH-47 Transport Helicopter taken from another helicopter at the same altitude."

"I suddenly perceive the memory of one operation where we rode on a Chinook CH-47 on a mission to a Landing Zone. But how did "Chief", a mechanic, fit into this glimpse of time and space?"

"The After-Action-Reports for July, August, and September recount several helicopter assault missions. I remember only two of them, but I hadn't been able to recall when or where we went. I close my eyes, ears and conscious mind to what's going on in the plane, and I try to get in touch with the internal mental landscape. I try to fish out some factual memories, or maybe it'll be a nap." "Now on August 2, 2007, and I'm on another airplane on the second leg of our voyage. The clouds are once again spread out below.

They look like a giant blanket of soft spun white cotton. I see a thick billowing tower formation of massive clouds on the horizon ahead, built up above each other, extending high above our altitude. It was very menacing looking in its strength!"

"Quickly, just after penetrating this massive tower, when we pass through into a sky of scattered and broken clouds which reveal pieces of the landscape below. At the same moment, more of the vague pieces of the landscape of my memory are revealed to me. Like a flash in my mind, I recall a long-ago flight on a small Huey helicopter into a dense jungle area. I don't quite remember where or when, but I do remember the area because it was a dense and wooded area with three or four small clearings where we landed. I now have some information to search the After-Action-Reports (as sketchy as they are) and find where it was located."

I later found the link to that first revelation about the CH-47 transport helicopter. It was located in the After-Action-Reports, and enabled me to remember and recount more details. To this day I believe it's no coincidence that I was writing these diary entries on the same days as the events took place 40 years ago. What a gift it was to have the landscape of the clouds reveal to me the Landscape of My Memory.

August 2, 1967 airmobile combat assaults were made into three different Landing Zones southeast of Loc Giang along route 10. Enemy contact was light and two Viet Cong were killed. Security for the activities of Engineer and Artillery units in the area were provided by C Company.

We made sure that we had our weapons in good order and then checked our gear and ammo status. I can't remember what we did about chow. I think we had the usual field breakfast. We were ready at 6:00am. They called for a formation of those who were on the mission and got us into groups by platoons. The First Sergeant gave us some instructions which we could hardly understand. Because he was so ignorant it was difficult for him to string more than five coherent words into a sentence (Can you tell I didn't like or respect him, only his rank?). There were three groups, one for each of the CH-47's. We waited. It wasn't long before we heard the faint sound of helicopters nearing our position. The big helicopters made a lot more noise than the little Huey's.

The Ch-47 Helicopter Giant

The CH-47's were quite large, with much bigger propeller blades because of their tremendous weight when loaded. We entered from the rear of the vessel, as it had a large ramp similar to the Armored Personnel Carriers we rode. As we got inside, we sat on built-in benches on either side. These ships were large enough to carry vehicles and even some artillery pieces. When we were all on board, they used hydraulic motors to raise the ramp and we waited to take off.

The pilot revved up the engines to a fever pitch and began the take off. As it was lifting it made quite a racket. All that noise made the take off quite exciting. When we began cruising through the air, the rotation of the blades sounded much louder than the "wop, wop" you hear when driving down the road in a car or van that has an open sunroof. I remember "Chief" was sitting across from me taking pictures (that's why his image came to me forty years later).

This book would probably not have been written if it weren't for Jack Pashano "Chief's" pictures.

## *August 1967*

Once we were in the air, the pilot headed his ship toward the North about 15 minutes from Loc Hoa with Loc Thanh on our right side, just past Loc Thanh. He made a turn to the right or east for about 5 to 8 minutes, then Southwest to just past Highway 10 southwest of Loc Giang to our Landing Zone.

The CH-47 circled once, then came in for a landing. We got up & quickly disembarked and spread out from the helicopter. The pilot did what all pilots do, he got the hell out of there!

We were on one of three Landing Zone's that day. We did search and destroy all the morning with very few discoveries. The early afternoon we encountered the enemy, and after an exchange of weapons fire the Viet Cong broke contact. The search of the area revealed two dead Viet Cong by body count. No US soldiers were killed or wounded. Elements of the Battalion had provided security for Engineer and Artillery units.

We had been on this Search and Destroy operation all day and finally arrived at the original Landing Zone area. We moved into this area anticipating a possible Ambush by the Viet Cong. We secured the area by 6:30pm and awaited the return of the Chinook CH-47 Choppers. About a half hour after securing the Landing Zone we could hear the choppers nearing. When they were in sight, we called in our security. As the CH-47's landed, the men ran to get on. A few soldiers provided security for the Out Post Security group to get on the CH-47's, and then the ones providing security were able to board. As the security personnel boarded, the ramp was lifted and secured. The pilots revved up the engines and took off as fast as they could. A successful extraction!

The trip took about 20 minutes, and we arrived at our base camp area around 7:00pm. It was good to get back to the Armored Personnel Carriers after being ground-pounders all day long!

August 3, 1967 we conducted Search and Destroy operations around the area until around 4:30pm.

August 4, 1967 at 10:25am a grenade factory was discovered 1 kilometer north of Highway 6A, along the Oriental River at XT4016. At 2:20pm a second grenade factory was located several hundred meters to the northeast of the first factory's location.

August 5, 1967 the 1/5th (Mech) Infantry conducted a Cordon and Search of the junction of Highways 10A and 6A. That evening at 9:45pm, three Bobcats were Wounded-in-Action by enemy mortar fire.

August 6, 1967 at 2:30pm a munitions factory was located in the area of XT4118. This was only a couple of hundred meters north of the grenade factories located on August 4th.

August 7, 1967 at 3:30pm a large ammo cache was located in the area of XT4016, near the banks of the Oriental River. The Battalion continued to provide security for engineer and artillery units in the area.

When we provided security, sometimes we were able to stay in one spot for the day. That duty enabled us to do things we couldn't do when we were on the go.

C-Ration Gourmet
This isn't the first time I've talked about food in this book and it won't be the last. Since we were out in the jungle and bush for most of our time in-country, we didn't have three square meals a day. (Why do they call them square?) I was lucky to begin my stay at B Company after Captain Robert Vanneman had instituted hot meals for the Company in the field. I guess his predecessor didn't care about his men and whether they got decent chow. Just imagine, three C-Ration meals every day?

I think we had one, rarely two hot meals in the field, depending on circumstances. For example, this wasn't possible if we got back into a night base camp way after dark. Breakfast was the easiest meal to prepare because most of us, besides Ambushes and Listening Posts were already there. I've been on a few Ambushes where there wasn't any chow left when I returned!

## August 1967

We were providing security for the engineers all day, so we stayed in the same spot that day and took turns on watch. This gave me a little time to become creative, exercising my culinary expertise in the field.

My story about baked bananas that took place February 1967 was a true story and it showed how some GI's were very creative. To this day, I can eat the same thing for many days in a row, probably because of the US Army. But that doesn't mean I'll enjoy it.

A few of the entrées that were available in C-Rations were Ham and Lima Beans, Spaghetti and Meat Balls, and Beef Steak (I believed it was Salisbury Steak). I remember a few of the snack items such as Cheese Crackers with Peanut Butter sandwiched in between, Caraway Seed Crackers with Processed Cheese in a flat container can, Pretzels. Desserts were also available like Pound Cake (my favorite), Fruit Cake and maybe Chocolate candy. If these aren't right then some of my memories about food aren't so clear.

The C-Rations were in green cans that came in a beige cardboard box. (They didn't know about esthetic colors and food in the Army.) Included were things like cigarettes (in case the Viet Cong didn't get us!), matches, chewing gum (we wouldn't want to deprive 'Charlie' the joys of stepping on a wad of chewed gum and dealing with it), and napkins. Did they supply condoms, or was that too long ago? (It's interesting how things change.) We used napkins in place of toilet paper. That beige cardboard box served two needed purposes. First it was for packaging the C-Rations, and second it was for heating the entrees. Tear up the box and then put it in the makeshift pit with sticks crisscrossed to hold the can, use the matches provided, light the box and heat your food.

We didn't tear it up because it would take time, so we used C-4 Plastic explosive wads to heat our meals. We were convinced that the C-4 wouldn't explode if lit with a match, so that's what we used when we could. This leads me to believe that we had some lighter Claymore Mines that were probably the source of the C-4. This war supposedly the only way to ignite C-4 was thru an electrical impulse, so we were right! Or maybe we were just damn lucky.
I never heard of any explosions from cooking with C-4 and I know it was used extensively by GI's in Viet Nam.

## Chef Boy-R-D-A

I am certain that I wasn't the only creative cook in the unit, although what we had to work with made it a challenge.

My specialty consisted of ingredients from a far away country: The USA.

### Combat Lasagna

Ingredients:
>Canned Spaghetti and Meat Balls, Caraway Seed Crackers, and Processed Cheese.

Equipment:
>One extra empty can, one cooking platform built from sticks, extra sticks, C-4 explosives, matches, can cover, P-38 can opener.

Directions:
>Open can of Spaghetti and Meat Balls (use P-38 Can opener)
>Open Caraway Seed Crackers container
>Open Cheese container (that took a lot of luck!)
>Take Meatballs out of can, place in box
>Crush Meatballs in to pieces
>Place a one-half inch layer of crushed Meatball on the bottom of the empty clean can
>Smash up the noodles and sauce
>Place a one-half inch layer of "sauce" over the crushed Meatballs
>Place one-quarter of cheese container over the Sauce
>Place 1 and ½ crackers over the cheese
>Repeat the above until ingredients are used up.

Note: Having 2 Cheese containers (obtained through any means necessary) provides extra insurance for a successful meal.

>Cook the masterpiece by placing the can on the stick platform (There are many sticks available.) over the C-4 and place a cover over the contents of the can, and light the C-4 with a match. The contents should cook for about 10 minutes; add combustible materials as needed into the fire. The cheese melts and runs down and mingles with the

other ingredients as it heats. When the top layer of cheese melts, the dish is done! Bon Appétit!

Hey, this shit is good!

A great accompaniment to the Lasagna could be made if you had a recent Care Package from home. We would put some water in our canteen cup, add Kool-Aid with sugar packets and stir. Time to chow down until it is all gone, sipping some of that "nectar of the gods" as we ate. Save some of that Kool-Aid for dessert. The pound cake was the crowning glory of this once-upon-a-time extraordinary GI fare.

After such a gourmet lunch we would light up a smoke and put up our feet. Isn't life grand!

Remember, we were still in the jungle and 'Charlie' had a pretty good "sniffer". I'll bet that aroma from the Lasagna drove him wild! Whoever said C-Rations were boring?

When the Vietnam combat soldier was fortunate to get a hot meal, it was usually in the early morning hours at breakfast since that was about the only time we were all in the same place except Ambushes and Listening Posts. We had C-Rations to eat for most of our meals, but the timing of meals depended on when it was convenient to the operation, not exactly when we were hungry! During the day we were scattered in all directions. Throughout the day when in the jungle with trees and thick bushes, there usually was little visibility, so it was a little safer to take some time and eat.

I have always been interested how different eras have handled basic field problems. I was talking recently with a young man who was a US Marine from Iraq, Sgt. Keith Arnold (a Combat Warrior and Veteran who was awarded the Purple Heart for his wounds). Eventually we discussed one of the most important things to us grunts, Food! I thought it would be interesting to compare this important subject matter. I was curious at the time about his war experiences with food compared to our experiences with food forty years ago. The talk did not revolve around whether we should or should not be involved in war. We were concerned at that moment with what our troops ate.

Food is very dear to the hearts and minds of GI's, in combat especially. We who were in combat in Vietnam had fewer hot meals. For lunch and dinner we ate mainly C-Rations with various combinations of goodies including one "main course" in a can. The C-Rations were fairly good, with some being better than others. They were hot because we heated them with the box or a small ball of C-4 explosive.

The guys in Iraq had more hot meals, especially when they did sectioned operations. They got their meals at six "mini" cook camps dispersed within a three-to-four mile area. The meal times in the cook camps were within a certain range, so I guess you could say they had more scheduled meals. Hurrah for them!

They also had "to-go" meals called MRE's ("Me Reluctant to Eat!"). Actually, they were meals in aluminum sacs containing dehydrated food that you add hot water to. I think Keith's word to describe most of them was NASTY! Considering both set of circumstances of eating, you could say it was a draw.

One axiom has never changed. The solider from Valley Forge to Iraq complained, but endured the weather and the food!

August 8, 1967 the Battalion continued to provide security for Artillery and Engineer units.

August 9, 1967 Company C had one man Wounded-in-Action from a booby trap. The rest of Battalion units during the day had negative enemy contact.

August 10, 1967 Combat Eagle Flights were made into 5 different Landing Zones. Contact with the

enemy by the Battalion was light. At 11:45am A
Company had four Bobcats injured by a charging
water buffalo in the area of XT4713.

Water buffalo ready to attack

## That Ain't No Bull

Do you know that bulls are color blind? During a bullfight they respond to the motion of the red capes rather than the bright color. I guess it's the same with water buffalos. The four men who were assaulted by water buffalo were from Company A, and I'll just bet that they were 1st Platoon 3rd Squad and their track was A13. One of those water buffalo was probably that little calf that escaped our shots back in February when we killed those six water buffalo south of Katum. I guess he was still holding a grudge.

Being color blind, he didn't know that 13 in gold was Company A and not the blue 13 of Company B. Sorry, you guys of Company A. we didn't know water buffalo were color blind and that they could hold a grudge! I wonder if those water buffalo really were relatives of the ones we killed in February who were seeking revenge.

August 11, 1967 the Battalion continued Search and

Destroy operation in the same area. At 12:15am the Recon Platoon had an Armored Personnel Carrier detonate an anti tank mine, causing two Bobcats to be Wounded-in-Action.

August 12, 1967 a munitions cache containing 268 Chicom grenades, 12 grenade launchers and assorted small arms ammunition was located at XT414172. This was in the same general area as the munitions factories that had been located earlier in the month.

Enemy weapons cache found during Search and Destroy

August 13, 1967 at 6:30am a Bobcat from Company C was Wounded-in-Action because of a detonated booby trap and was "dusted off" by Medivac Helicopter.

August 14 & 15, 1967 the Battalion provided

Security for the engineer and artillery units with negative enemy contact.

August 16, 1967 a small weapons cache was located along the Oriental River at XT397184.

August 17, 1967 Company C engaged four Viet Cong and killed all four by body count. The Battalion conducted daytime and night Ambushes in the area.

Ants in Your Pants
I went on one of those daytime Ambushes. We left the perimeter at 8:30am. We went east for about two hours. We crossed flat open territory with scattered bush lines very carefully. We came to an area that was dense with large bushes almost like a wall. We looked up and down those bushes trying to find an area we could cut through with machetes. After hacking away through the bushes for about one hour we made it to a small area that was flat. The flat area had tall bushes that looked like a raspberry patch only taller. We hacked through another section into an open area with elephant grass with a trail cutting through.

Typical elephant grass was about 4-6 feet high. We thought we could use this area for our Ambush site. The tall grass would make a perfect cover, as we could almost blend in with the grass. We made sure we left no evidence of our presence as we moved into the grass. We hoped we might even get some rest if the Viet Cong didn't show up.

I laid in the grass for about twenty minutes and felt quite rested and comfortable, just waiting for the Viet Cong. It started very slowly, and then my skin began to itch a little. I felt something on my neck and I slapped my neck! Then I pushed myself up a little off that smashed grass, and looked down at the Ground, and it was alive with Red Fire Ants! When I pushed myself up my Fatigue Jacket opened up a little and let a clump of Red Fire Ants down my jacket. It wasn't long before my body was teaming with ants just like the ground. Those damn things were stinging me like everywhere, and I started to go crazy!

I jumped up to my feet like a rocket, started ripping off my Fatigue

Jacket. I was hopping up-and-down, twisting and turning. I threw

Look at the relationship of GI standing and the Elephant Grass

off my jacket and started squashing those red bastards like a madman! I tried everything to get them off my body, because those monsters knew how to hurt you.

I looked for insect repellant spray, which was nowhere to be found. We didn't carry large spray cans with us on Ambushes. My skin felt like a pincushion with sharp pins sticking me everywhere!

When they started to go down my pants I fought valiantly! This went on for about five minutes, and I didn't give a rat's ass if the Viet Cong heard it or not. I was busy with a live enemy. I sure hope the guys enjoyed my suffering, because I could hear some laughing. I hoped they were still keeping a lookout for the Cong. I finally got my hands on a little white plastic bottle of insect repellant and used a lot of that STRAIGHT DDT (Now illegal to use for anything in the United States) over my body to kill the ants and sooth my injected ant wounds. The repellant started to work and I calmed down, but then I started to feel a little sick. Those aren't called Red Fire Ants because of their color, but because their stings feel like fire!

All that hopping around and the noise made me a big target for the Viet Cong. So either they weren't around or they got such a big laugh over it that they didn't have the heart to shoot me.

We've talked about ants a couple of times. You've probably seen an anthill or two before, look at the white mounts in the picture. Those aren't anthills, those are ANT MOUNTAINS!

There were 120 CRA's (Crushed Red Ants) for that day from our Ambush. I don't think they counted dead ants as enemy Killed-in-Action, although if REMF's ever battled them I'll bet they'd count!

What the "protected" don't know is the Black Ants and Red Fire Ants can be very dangerous. If someone were to get knocked out and lie unconscious long enough while covered by a colony of ants, they could become paralyzed, and in time they could be devoured! You could become their stored up food for winter. That didn't happen to me, or else you wouldn't be reading this story. However, I did feel a bit woozy from all the bites.

We settled down to a new location and stayed for about three hours without enemy contact. At 3:00pm or so we pulled up that Ambush and started back to the Field Perimeter. I felt better but the trek back was a bit rough with heat and humidity making everyone sluggish. The further we went it really took its toll, we finally made it back by 5:40pm. All in a day's work.

August 18, 1967 at 12:41pm Company A located a

weapons cache at XT432146. At 3:45pm Company C located a weapon and ammunitions cache XT430127.

Chief's track when he was Killed-in-Action August 19, 1968.
It's here to honor him. Notice the Indian Headdress on the track.

August 19, 1967 the Battalion continued to secure Engineer work areas and provide Security for artillery units. At 5:15am an Ambush Patrol from the Recon Platoon that was set up on the Oriental River had one Bobcat Wounded-in-Action & evacuated due to a gunshot wound.

August 20, 1967 Company A and Company C conducted Eagle Flights into eight different Landing Zones. Enemy contact was light and sporadic. B Company performed Security operations and Search and Destroy for the Engineer and Artillery units.

August 21 the Battalion conducted Search and Destroy operations in the area with negative enemy contact.

We had been in the Loc Giang general area since the 13th of May around Highway 10, 10A, and 6A basically conducting Search and Destroy operations, Ambushes, Listening Posts, Security for the Engineer and Artillery units, and providing Eagle Flights to several different locations. August had been rather dull compared to other operational months, which was all right with the GI's.

Pump You Up
Mechanized Infantry Units used lots of fuel (Fossil to be exact). In the beginning we only had gasoline engines in the Armored Personnel Carriers. The main problem with gasoline is it has a propensity to explode when stimulated with flame or spark! Near the end of my Tour of Duty we started to get diesel engines in the new Armored Personnel Carriers (Chrysler Mopar V8's). Diesel tends to burn up rather than explode which would be the GI's preference!

This story has little to do with explosions or fuel volatility. It simply deals with Fuel. I only remember one time topping off the Armored Personnel Carriers (no, they didn't get very good of gas mileage). In fact, I think they probably got feet per gallon because of the types of terrain they had to travel upon. Anyway, I only recall this one instance.

Viet Nam Service station

When we were running low on fuel, we didn't drive into our local Shell or ESSO service station and ask for full service. No siree!

We did, however utilize, pumps and full-service personnel. The full-service personnel we used were the cheapest labor we could find. You're right, we used GI servicemen.

---

This was before we extensively utilized female combat personnel, unless I am mistaken. In that case we would have to say GI service personnel. My great niece, Private Kylie Antti, graduated from Basic Training in July 2008 with the U.S. Army. Her chosen Military Occupational Specialty (MOS) was Refueling. She will be driving a tanker truck. Interesting how the army has changed (Go Army). Her father Jim Antti was a Jar Head (Marine)! We finally discovered that women could be a most formidable fighting force!

Have you ever seen a mama bear when someone gets too close to her cubs? If not, just use your imagination!

---

Talk about driving into a service station for fuel. How about the service station driving to you, now that's service. That's exactly what we had. An Armored Personnel Carrier pulling a utility trailer with eight 55-gallon drums filled with gasoline. People have been spoiled over the years. I've been in stores when the electrical service has been interrupted and everything comes to a halt. The stores can't make a sale, and if they could, no one would know how to compute the proper change! If I am wrong, I humbly stand rebuked.

You can't even get a drink at a fast food restaurant because the machines need electricity to work. The service station would be out of business unless they had a gasoline or diesel generator.

Where there is total dependence, there is no Freedom!

Well, we in the Military had an independent system. It was called the Hand Pump, and if you had about 45 minutes then you too, would be Independent and could pump your own. GI power, not electricity was used, and the 45 minutes equals refueling time.

## August 1967

Of course we had lots of time. It brought a whole new meaning to "Time on My Hands"!

The US Army mobile gas service station with hand pump

August 22, 1967 at 11:00am one of our Chieu Hoi (a captured Viet Cong turned informant) directed Recon Platoon to a location where several weapons were discovered. At 2:25pm another Chieu Hoi led Company C to a 1,400 pound rice Cache at XT453147.

August 23, 1967 the Battalion conducted Search and Destroy operations in the general area of the weapons and rice discovered on the previous day. There was negative enemy contacted.

August 24, 1967 an Ambush Patrol from C Company engaged a motorized sampan on the Oriental River at 2:55am. The sampan was shot-up, and the boat sank into the River. Some B Company elements conducted Eagle Flights into various locations. Company A had two Bobcats Wounded-in-Action from a booby trap at XT459039. After an hour of searching Company A located 3 small caches in the same area, containing small arms and mortar ammunition.

Prisoners of war, some were repatriated

August 25, 1967 the Battalion continued Eagle Flights in the Loc Giang area. Early in the afternoon eleven detainees and one Viet Cong prisoner were apprehended and turned over to Vietnamese authorities.

August 26, 1967 the Recon Platoon was led to a tunnel at XT412165 by the Viet Cong prisoner of the previous day. One Chicom carbine and 200 rounds of ammunition were found inside the tunnel located several hundred meters north of Highway 6A. Eagle Flights were conducted to an area where a Chieu Hoi (defector) stated that a weapons cache was located. No weapons cache was found.

August 27, 1967 the Battalion conducted Search and Destroy operations in the same area with negative enemy contact.

August 28, 1967 at 3:35pm, Company C with the assistance of a Hoi Chanh (returnee), located and destroyed 2 tunnels and 4 hidden spider holes. At 7:00pm a Company C Ambush patrol engaged 2 sampans and five Viet Cong on the Oriental River XT406143. The sampans loaded with cargo were sunk and five Viet Cong were killed in the engagement.

August 29 the Battalion continued to provide the Security for Engineer Units working on Highway 10 and conducted Search and Destroy operations in the area.

## Signs of Evil

B Company was sent on a mission up Highway 10 about 5 miles towards Loc Thanh. We were just about a mile away from Loc Thanh when we went off the road near a temple. As we pulled around to the front of the temple and stopped, we saw something strange. Humans tend to react without thinking, and as a result we get into trouble. We were from the "Baby Boomer" generation born in the 1940's.

We grew up with the images of certain symbols burned into our memories, the "Hammer and Sickle" of the USSR, the "Rising Sun" of the Imperialist Japan, the "Red Star" of Communist China and the "Nazi Swastika" of Germany. These symbols signify evil enemies from World War II and the Cold War.

Everything evil pops into your head when you see the symbol of the world's most evil person, Adolph Hitler. He and his monsters committed sick, sinful and sadistic acts against oppressed people in many countries. The crimes of Adolph Hitler and Nazi Germany are embodied in one symbol, the twisted cross the "Swastika"!

The picture accompanying this story is a picture of a Buddhist temple in South Vietnam. If you look at the roof you will notice a symbol that is similar to the Nazi swastika. At first glance it gives you an eerie feeling of an evil presence.

Notice the symbol in the middle of the roof

Maybe you don't have the same reaction; if not maybe you need to learn more about it. I say that because there is a group of Neo Nazi's in this country, the Good Old USA, who would revive and lift up that symbol along with the same evil intent to rule the world!

The symbol on this temple represented a different meaning than its hideous use by Adolph Hitler and his gangsters. However, both Nazis and Buddhists display it the same on buildings.

Before writing this, I did what I couldn't have done in Vietnam. I researched the meaning of the "Swastika" and found some interesting information. The Swastika is an ancient symbol used centuries before the Nazi's got a hold of it. The Nazi's changed the symbol slightly by tilting it on an angle. That version can be seen on the Nazi soldiers during marches it represents their conquering the world. In Vietnam, we saw the symbol with a straight on view as on the picture of the temple.

The use of the Swastika can be found on Byzantine buildings, Celtic Monuments, as a Buddhist religious inscription, and it can be found on Greek coins.

Obviously, we had a very strong reaction to seeing this symbol on a religious building. Take a good look at the picture to the left and you will see in the lower left of the picture a 50-caliber machine gun pointing at the door of that temple. Notice the gentleman at the bottom of the picture nervously eyeing the barrel, wondering if it will be lowered toward him.

Even today in Iraq the enemy has no qualms about using sacred buildings as safe firing positions.

The person in the Track Commander's Hatch in the prior picture was either resting his head by supporting it with his hand and arm, or looking through binoculars to get a closer look. We learned to be careful because Death could come at any time and any place!

I don't remember if it was part of our Mission to check out that particular building. We were seldom enlightened of our purpose on most missions. We left there a short time after arriving, and we had no enemy contact that day. We turned back towards whence we came, and then we got off the road and began Search and Destroy operations in the area of the Battalion Base Camp.

August 30, 1967 Recon Platoon engaged and sank a sampan on the Oriental River. B Company assisted S-2 Personnel in apprehending a female who was identified by a Hoi Chanh as a Viet Cong Nurse.

August 31, 1967 the Battalion continued Security for Engineer and Artillery units in the Loc Giang area.

* * * * *

There were twelve men Wounded-in-Action this month.

During August 1967 no Bobcats lost their lives in Vietnam!

# September 1967

September 1, 1967 the Battalion conducted Search and Destroy operations. This was in the Loc Giang Area and provided Security for Engineer Unit work area and Artillery Units. Three Bobcats from C Company were Wounded-in-Action when a booby trap was detonated at 9:25am near Loc Hoa at XT 419180. Company A was led to a tunnel by a Hoi Chanh at Xom Mia at XT453163, several weapons and a US Claymore mine were found in a tunnel. C Company went OPCON to Task Force Hodson.

September 2, 1967 elements of B Company conducted Eagle Flights to assault Landing Zone at XT414149. No enemy contact was recorded. Some detainees were apprehended by Company A near XT4417. The First Platoon from B Company secured a bridge about 5 kilometers West of Trang Bang at XT453191 during the night. C Company, while OPCON to TF Hodson, conducted Security, Search and Destroy operations in the sugar cane fields near XT438078.

We hoped that we could stay at that bridge for a while.

September 3, 1967 at 12:10am B Company's First Platoon was securing the bridge site and received one round of mortar fire. One Bobcat was Wounded-in-Action. The rest of the Battalion conducted Search and Destroy operations in the Loc Giang area as part of Election Security for the Republic of Vietnam. Company C conducted Search and Destroy operations as part of TF Hudson.

I was at the M-60 foxhole on the perimeter, snugly surrounded by two Armored Personnel Carriers. We were just sitting and jawing. We talked a lot about different things, mostly about getting back to the "world" and what we were going to do.

The subjects ranged from food, family, friends, and girlfriends. Then we switched to important things like fast cars, fun, even some hopes and dreams. I think it would have been interesting to have had a tape recorder to preserve some of those "enlightened" conversations. Given our situation, most of us just wanted to get back home upright.

Incoming
Then at about 12:15am we began to hear a sound of something flying our way that made kind of a loud warbling sound. Then we recognized the distinctive sound of mortar. It was over our heads as we yelled "incoming", and then we heard an explosion!

It hit the ground about 50 meters behind us. It exploded and then there was silence, except we could hear the distant murmurings behind us from the Perimeter. That was our excitement for the evening. We sure hoped that no one was near where it landed!

Things settled down after about 10 minutes, and then a visitor stopped by to tell us the news. We had none of the basic personal advantages of civilian life which led to the following. Some poor GI was in the dark taking a crap, and before he was finished and could pull up his pants, that mortar exploded and sent a sliver of shrapnel into his butt! Double ouch! What kind of a war was this where a guy can't even take care of business without getting attacked! I could imagine the poor fellow being asked "and where did you get your Purple Heart wound?" They told us that it wasn't too serious, but they weren't the one with the wound! A speedy recovery was their prognosis.

Most of the basic human needs weren't available, and as I settled down for my turn at sleep I realized that I didn't even have a pillow for my head. We slept out in the open on the dirt like wild animals of the jungle. Talk about wild parties!

We took our turns at sleep and watch, and when the morning became a new day we were hungry as usual. We did get to eat that morning, and we remained at this same position the rest of the day as Bridge Security.

September 4, 1967 the B Company platoon remained at Bridge Security and the rest of the Battalion continued Search and Destroy operations in the Loc Giang area. Company C remained OPCON to TF Hudson and conducted Search and Destroy and Security operations in the Ap Dong Hoa area.

September 5, 1967 C Company returned to the Loc Giang Area at 8:00am and continued operations with the rest of the Battalion.

From the 5th to the 9th of September 1967 there is no mention of B Company in the After-Action-Reports. Maybe we continued to watch that bridge. I don't remember.

September 6, 1967 the Battalion continued to conduct Search and Destroy operations in the Loc Giang Area. The purpose of the operations was to bring protection and stabilization to the area after the election.

September 7, 1967 the Battalion conducted several

Saturation Patrolling and Security operations in the area. At 12:37pm Recon Platoon apprehended a female detainee who was identified as a Viet Cong intelligence agent. At 2:15pm an Armored Personnel Carrier from Company A detonated an anti-tank mine resulting in four of the nine Bobcats Wounded-In-Action and they were "dusted-off" by Medivac Helicopters. (How did they get to have nine?)

September 8, 1967 the Battalion provided Security for Engineer and Artillery Units. Eagle Flights were conducted to various Combat Landing Zones. At 1:10pm one Bobcat was injured when a helicopter crashed due to a lost rotor blade.

**This may seem laborious, so it probably was (especially to the GI's), but it was always preferable when there were no deaths or injuries.**

September 9, 1967 the Battalion was continuing to provide Security for Artillery and Engineer unit operations. Day and Night Ambush Patrols were also conducted in the area. At 4:20pm Company A had an Armored Personnel Carrier detonate an anti-tank mine with negative casualties.

September 10, 1967 the Battalion was conducting Airmobile Combat Assaults "Eagle Flights" with negative enemy contact. **Yeah!**

September 11, 1967 the Battalion conducted Mounted Sweep operations, as well as Dismounted Search and Destroy operations.

September 12, 1967 the Battalion conducted Airmobile Eagle Flights and established a Blocking Position west of Go Dau Ha at XT2532. Company A remained in the area of Fire Support Base Diane providing security for engineers. At 2:45pm one

Bobcat from Company C was Killed-in-Action by a "friendly" artillery long round. Recon Platoon provided Security for Fire Support Base Carol located northwest of Go Dau Ha at XT334357. At 3:15pm Company C led by a Hoi Chanh (captured informer) to a small arms cache at XT252324. At 6:00pm the Battalion completed Airmobile Movement back to Fire Support Base Diane. The Recon Platoon provided security for Fire Support Base Carol located northwest of Go Dau Ha at XT334357.

### Huey Eagle Flight
September 13, 1967 the Battalion was slated to go on Eagle Flights to three Landing Zones. One detainee was taken into custody by Company A at 3:45pm.

We must have been part of another Unit's operation. There was a group of men left behind to man the Armored Personnel Carriers. We were already lined up in anticipation of the helicopters arrival. As they were coming in toward the ground we moved in quickly, ducking our heads because we always felt like they were going to cut our heads off. We boarded quickly.

When the last men were on, the pilots took off with haste as they were easy targets on the ground. They climbed quickly and then headed northeast.

Landing, loading and leaving as fast as they can

The area looked like a flock of geese heading south for the winter on their annual migration. But the Hueys made a hell of a lot more noise! They tended to cover the sky like a blanket. We flew for about 20 minutes and the ground became more densely covered with the vegetation and trees. Five more minutes and I could see a large area broken up in three large fields. As we approached, our altitude lessened and we prepared to disembark. When they landed we jumped out and ran to assume positions about 35 feet away from the helicopters. Those pilots got the hell out of there, like the Devil was on their heels!

We really didn't know what the hell we were supposed to be doing. (What's new? We were seldom informed.) We kind of felt naked without our Armored Personnel Carriers. This was probably the brainchild of some Military Strategy Genius or a mad man. Who could be sure. We were told to carefully move into the trees about 20 feet away and set up a position. We moved there and then we waited there a couple of hours. Then they sent a couple of Patrols down two trails farther into the trees while the rest of us watched and waited for their return, or perhaps for a visit from the Viet Cong.

Those Patrols returned in about two hours all intact, which meant they didn't encounter any Viet Cong either. We waited about a half-hour and then we heard the faint noise of choppers coming in the distance, which meant "get ready to get the hell out of there!" We lined up the same way as we did in the morning as the noise indicated that they were getting closer. We were eager to board again.

Those egg beaters whipped up a lot of dust with plenty of wind and loud noise, so keep our big mouths shut to avoid eating dirt. They came closer and closer, noisier and noisier, and dustier and dustier, with those blades whipping around ready to lop off our heads. Gee, wasn't this fun?

The moment the Hueys landed we ran like the Devil was on our heels, jumped on, and when fully loaded those pilots sped out of there like they were late for dinner! After about 30 minutes we were back at the Field Base Camp Area and the relative safety of our Armored Personnel Carriers. We landed outside the Perimeter, jumped off the choppers and ran as fast as we could to avoid the

## September 1967

rotor blades. The pilots revved up the engines and lifted out of there quickly. Thanks for the joy ride. Why don't we do it again sometime? I sure hoped the strategy employed worked for some greater good, because I was starting to get worried about my taxes increasing to help pay to fly us around in circles some more. We were the grunts so we did what we were told, even if it didn't make sense to us.

September 14, 1967 the Battalion continued the Security operations, as well as, Saturation Ambush Patrolling in the Loc Giang area. B Company had no enemy contact. At 5:15am the Ambush Patrol from Company A engaged two Viet Cong with negative results. At 10:20am another Ambush Patrol located 500 meters south of the junction of Highways 10 and 6A, received small arms and automatic weapons fire at XT435157. One Bobcat was Killed-in-Action and two were Wounded-in-Action.

September 15, 1967 the Battalion continued with operations of the previous day.

September 16, 1967 B Company returned to Cu Chi Base Camp and assumed the role of the 25th Infantry Division's Reaction Force. Company A continued to provide security for Engineer units at the laterite pit and west of the junction of Highways 1 and 7A. A Hoi Chanh led the Recon Platoon to 5 anti-tank mines, which were destroyed in place. At 7:30pm an Ambush Patrol from Company C engaged and killed three Viet Cong in a sampan on the Oriental River. Company B went OPCON to the first Brigade at 8:15pm.

What that meant was a double edge sword, because if nothing happened, you could basically goof off if in base camp for very short while, but when something happened anywhere, anytime in the 25th Infantry Division's Sphere of operations, guess who came to their rescue anywhere and anytime, day or night?

It was no fun being out in the field. But it was also no picnic back at Base Camp, since the Military Geniuses would think up all kinds of stupid things to do. Most of OPCON we were out in the bush!

```
September 17, 1967 the Battalion continued their
operations in the Loc Giang area. At 5:15pm B
Company was released from OPCON to the 1st Brigade
and continued as Cu Chi Base Camp reaction force
in the field.
```

Bath, What Bath?
When B Company came in from Loc Giang and became the Reactionary Force, the Company had been out in combat 129 continuous days! That's a long time without a proper bath or even a shower.

---

Whew! I read in the After-Action-Reports that the 25th Division quartermaster "Bath" unit reported that "extensive support" was given to the 1st of the 5th Mechanized Infantry and to the 4th/9th Infantry during field operations for the quarter ending July 30, 1967.

Now, maybe the 4th/9th Infantry had some baths or showers, but for the 5th Mechanized Infantry, we consider this to be a bunch of "Bull Shit"!

---

We only had a bath one time in the field and that was in a Water Buffalo watering hole by Cambodia in February 1967. That water was full of mud and crud at the bottom. Maybe their services were reserved for Officers because the Low-Life Grunts never saw any of those "Bath Unit" facilities.

We arrived at the motor pool at 8:00pm, and by the time we got all our crap out of the tracks and then into the Hooches it was now 9:00 pm. It was a little cooler than usual and getting dark, so I believe that thirst won over cleanliness. A contingent of us went to see if the Enlisted Men's Club was open. To our joy, it was open and they were ready for our big thirsts. We were looking forward to some smooth, cold, refreshing beer. Several of the beers went down pretty easy, then a few more until I had my fill. I decided it was time to catch up on some sleep.

I left the Club for my hooch. My cot beckoned me to visit for the evening. I hoped there wouldn't be any emergencies out in the field tonight. Ah, sleep, perchance to dream! (Hey! I might get about 7 hours sleep tonight.)

Hair and Nails
I don't know how, but I actually did get 7 hours sleep. That hadn't happened since the 13th of July! Imagine after all that time how absolutely grungy we were, as well as terribly unkempt. The Company gave us some time to go to the Post Exchange to buy supplies and food, and to take care of personal grooming and other necessities. I was lucky to find a decent set of "fatigues" in my footlocker, probably because I had a lock and key. I also found a razor that wasn't dull. I shaved and showered. You have no idea what a luxury this was for us to wear clean clothes. I felt like a million bucks and human again, except I felt and looked like a shaggy dog.

All the GI barbers had left the Company, so we had to settle for the Vietnamese barbers at the gate. I was surprised to see the sign Chicago Barber Shop. Not home but close enough. My money was burning a hole in my pocket, and being so shaggy, the barbershop was calling me. I also brought my dirty laundry with me.

The main road into the Base Camp ran northeast to southwest, and the 1/5th (Mech) was close to the Northeast end of the Base Camp. A little to the left or further North was B Company. Where the main road ended at the East was the outpost Ann Margaret.

If you went southwest toward the entrance you came to the Post Exchange, and farther down was the Ambush Laundry and barber shops.

Vietnamese entrepreneurs owned these businesses. When we had the chance (we certainly had the need), we would go up to the Front Gate and bring what little laundry we had to get it clean.

I dropped off my dirty laundry at the Ambush Laundry and then off for a long needed and wanted clip job because I felt like a shaggy dog. When I saw Chicago (as in Barbershop) I knew I was going to make it home!

I didn't remember if they had regular barber chairs or not. I only went there once the whole time I was in Nam. You got a little surprise the first time you ever used the services of the barbers.

The Chicago Barbershop

When they were done cutting your hair, they started doing a neck massage on you. They held their fingers together loosely, and then they proceeded to do a series of light rapping karate-type chops. They charged extra for that service, and you had to tell them no or else they would charge you. Those treatments could be very beneficial; they helped take out the kinks. (Like right now while I am inputting this information I could sure use a treatment.)

The barbers were not occupied, so I sat down in the chair. I asked for the works. This might sound funny when you consider that we spent a lot of time roughing it out in the field, which is not what you could call a "genteel life style". They had manicurists, and you'd see Combat-Hardened Soldiers sitting down at a table getting a manicure. It felt good to have your nails trimmed and your cuticles cleaned up, even if the next couple of days you'd be back abusing your hands as well as the rest of your body (It won't make you less of a man unless you think that way). I indulged myself and had my nails done. It was almost time for afternoon chow, so I paid my tab, and started toward the 5$^{th}$ Mech and lunch.

I learned recently that before I got to Vietnam one of the owners of the shop was found dead in the Fil Hol Plantation. He was killed in a firefight the night before as a Viet Cong Colonel!
(This wasn't an uncommon occurrence as the Viet Cong were sly.)

I was distracted into going further to the Cu Chi Base Camp Front Gate. Some new cars caught my eye that some company was selling on the right side of the road. You could buy and pay for most of it from your army pay (it might take 10 years, but you could pay for the car). I remember one of the cars was a midnight blue 1967 Pontiac GTO, and another was a 1967 black Chevrolet Camero. I continued on my way to lunch.

I arrived at the mess hall just in time to eat. Once I was finished, I decided to go back to the hooch and lie down for a short nap to rest my weary and clean bones. This was a luxury, and I would have liked to make it a habit.

Even though I took a nap I still made it to evening chow. Of course I don't remember what we had, but it was probably ok. After dinner I decided to catch up on some letter writing to the folks at home. I always let them know I was doing fine. It was good to connect with home, for their sake and for the sake of receiving future letters or even some goodies. I remember receiving some Care Packages which I shared with the other guys. My family really supported me emotionally and with goodies.

September 18, 1967 Company B remained at Cu Chi as Base reaction force in the field, the Battalion with Company C 2/22$^{nd}$ Infantry continued operations in the Loc Giang Area. At 6:21am an Armored Personnel Carrier from Company C detonated an anti-tank mine. Four Bobcats were Wounded-in-

```
Action and the Armored Personnel Carrier was a
combat loss.
```

## Stormy Weather

The last couple of weeks we'd been sporadically blessed with rain and had some accumulation around the Base Camp Area of the 1/5$^{th}$. Vietnam has seasons like just about everywhere in the world. The dry dust of the dry season stuck in your teeth and permeated everything. The humid temperatures made it a very uncomfortable season. About the time you thought you couldn't stand it, it got worse until the seasons started to change. Relief was on its way, or at least we thought it was relief.

Most people live in areas where it rains, but unless you've been where there's a monsoon season, YOU AIN'T SEEN RAIN!!! Imagine something like a fire hose unleashed on you, the force of the spray falling from the sky!

Well, we went from bone dry to wet and then wetter. Being in a war zone in an Infantry Line Unit was not the most comfortable place to be. Comfort didn't exist. It was hot and sticky as hell, or wet, cold and sticky as hell. So you see, war is hell!

I've mentioned earlier in this book about drainage ditches around the hooches, which are dangerous in the dark, but very handy in the monsoon season under normal conditions. The picture on the next page shows how useless ditches could be in the monsoons.

By the middle of September the weather had started to change. The sky was getting darker and darker, and the storm clouds were building higher and higher to a beautiful but menacing strength. A good wind came up and cooled the dry, parched earth and its vast inhabitants. Then we heard plop, and then plop, plop, again plop, plop, plop, plop. And then all the Wrath of the Rain Gods spat out their Vengeance on us, their poor little subjects. It was a deluge that formed "Lake Cu Chi"!

The rain lasted all night at a steady downpour. We were lucky that our roof was corrugated steel, not like the tent I had when I first arrived in 1966. The tent would accumulate too much water, and it could have collapsed on your head!

September 19, 1967 the Battalion was conducting security operations and preparing for Nighttime Saturation Ambush Patrolling. Company B remained at Cu Chi as Base reaction force and provided one platoon to secure Engineer operations 6 kilometers northwest of Cu Chi.

The Battalion after an all night and day monsoon rain. "Lake Cu Chi"

The rain continued into the morning of September 20th until about 9:00am, when the storm appeared to be breaking up. I was at B Company's Base Camp at Cu Chi, and B Company was still Base Reaction Force. I decided to check out the grounds to see what the storm had done to the area.

The rain had been pouring down in buckets of liquid refreshment. It created a swamp-like atmosphere around our "home". I still remember those wooden sidewalks and some metal gratings we used to walk on without slipping in the mud during our rainy season. Well, they were nowhere to be seen. They were under water, drowned. The main drainage ditch was somewhere under "Lake Cu Chi" (as I dubbed it!).

I was outside, so I guess the hard rain had stopped. I know I have enough sense to come in from the rain. Actually the sun started to peek through the clouds and blessed us with a beautiful rainbow to remind us that God wasn't going to destroy the earth with another flood. I was walking at the end of First Platoon's Hooches toward the Motor Pool, close to where the little bridge crossed the creek or drainage ditch. It was also under water. I saw someone walking down the path on the other side of "Lake Cu Chi".

This person wasn't really walking. He was sloshing along on the West shoreline of "Lake Cu Chi"! I was on the East shoreline looking toward the Motor Pool. As he got closer, I saw that he was a Lt. Colonel or a Major. My stress level began to build. He then changed directions and started to cross "Lake Cu Chi" even closer toward me. Then whoosh! He disappeared into that great body of water. He wasn't down long, but his hat started to float away down-stream while he was under water. It was the funniest damn thing I had seen in a long, long time. I laughed my head off, and then quickly shut up as he bobbled up to the surface. It was only a few feet deep. The moment he popped back up I got my ass out of there, back to the hooch to hide. I laughed my head off again when I got back to the hooch as I tried to recount the event to those who were in the hooch.

It was very gratifying for me, a mere enlisted man, to see an "Officer and a Gentleman" indisposed in such an ungentlemanly manner! I don't remember seeing that Officer ever again. Remember, my luck with officers hadn't been very good. The joy of witnessing that officer's episode kept replaying again and again in my head with much satisfaction. Oh well, "into each life a little rain must fall". This incident was the comedy highlight of my stay in Vietnam!

The rest of the day was dry. Slowly the lake began to drain. After several hours of afternoon sun it had become a pond. I quit concerning myself about it.

Our focus became fixed on food, so off to the Mess Hall we went.

The next focus was entertainment, so after letter writing we were off to the Enlisted Men's Club for beer and snacks.

(I had told my friend Keith Arnold about this episode. He said he'd like to have seen that.)

Most of the weather we endured was very hot and very humid, adding to the already unpleasant circumstance of not being able to see our enemy.

The story above is true and still tickles my funny bone! I have been interested in combat weather conditions ever since September 20, 1967.

The motor pool five days after the rain

Our combat forces in Iraq and Afghanistan have equally miserable weather conditions. There they have a variety of climates, including Mountains where it snows in the winter, the Upper Plains with dry rolling grasslands, the Lower Plains with the fertile delta between the Tigris & Euphrates Rivers, a humid area and marsh lands with average temperature at 94F degrees. They also have swamps in the southern part, and the Desert region with average temperatures at 99F degrees, and highs above 130F Degrees at times. I believe that my friend Keith was around the Lower Plains region of Iraq.

Most regions of Afghanistan had better visibility than in Vietnam's jungles. Keith was no stranger to hot and sticky conditions, and the hot times were Hot, Hot, Hot! Keith was part of a ground-pounder unit.

Their Search and Destroy operations were conducted mainly in urban areas, which was extremely difficult because of the house-to-house searching they did in the cities.

Imagine that you are on a mission with them and you broke open a door. When and whom do you shoot? The idea that you're going to be able to accurately discern this in the second it happens is very crazy. Try it on for size, CNN!

## Stupid Ideas

Since the rain had stopped, all the creatures came out of their holes including the "Top". Isn't it funny how "Top" First Sergeant William Densmore ties into this story so easily? I mentioned earlier about the Army coming up with something irritatingly stupid for us to do, and they didn't disappoint me. Some super-intelligent person had the idea to beautify the area (Operation Beautification) and make us look like a "real" Military Unit. Egad! Whose stupid idea was this? I'd been here for almost a year and no one ever gave a rat's ass if we ever had comfortable surroundings. Now they got the idea to paint rocks white, and line the walkways with the decorated rocks.

I recalled the rock idea wasn't new, because back in January 1967 the First Sergeant had put Sgt. Lampa, the older man from the Philippines, in charge. He had us start to straighten out the rocks one day, but then we had to leave the next morning on another operation in the Tay Ninh Area. Now some dumb jackass came up with the idea to continue, only this time to apply white paint!

Come to think of it only a Rear Echelon Mother Fucker could have come up with an idea like that. It smelled of the First Sergeant. You see, before the colonel made all First Sergeants accompany the troops out in the field, "Willy" had been a Combat Virgin. He was the one who coerced the guys to wood panel his hooch. Who else but an REMF would have come up with an idea like that? We would rather have had beds with sheets and pillows for our heads first.

They almost had a mutiny on their hands. Remember we were Hardened Combat Soldiers, not pansy-ass landscapers. Oops! I didn't mean to mention a pansy... that's a flower! (Damn, I don't want to give them any more stupid ideas.)

September 21, 1967 one platoon from B Company provided Security for an Engineering Unit. The remainder of B Company stayed at Cu Chi. At 7:30am an Armored Personnel Carrier detonated an anti-tank mine near Xom Thap at XT543169. Two Bobcats from B Company were Killed-in-Action and four were Wounded-in-Action.

September 22, 1967 B Company provided one platoon for engineer security. The other platoons remained at Cu Chi as reaction force. The Battalion was to continue Search and Destroy operations and Ambush Patrolling.

The operations helped us to break the REMF's focus on that stupid landscaping idea. We were fighting men, not exterior decorators. I never heard another word about it before I left, so Good Luck Fella's!

September 23, 1967 B Company returned to Cu Chi at 10:00am as Base Reaction Force.

No one thought about sprucing up the area that day.

September 24, 1967 B Company was still the Base reaction force.

No mention about the "B" word "Operation Beautification."

September 25, 1967 Company B went OPCON to the 1/27$^{th}$ Infantry in the bush. The remainder of the Battalion conducted Search and Destroy operations and Night Ambush Patrols in the Loc Giang area.

September 26, 1967 Company B was still OPCON to the1/27$^{th}$ Infantry. The Battalion continued Search and Destroy and Ambush operations in the Loc Giang area.

September 27, 1967 B Company and the Battalion continued operations of the previous days.

September 28, 1967 at 7:00am B Company was released OPCON to the 1/27$^{th}$ Infantry and secured Rome Plow between Highway 1 and 7A at XT5416. The Battalion occupied blocking positions along the Oriental River at XT4116 and XT4114.

September 29, 1967 the Battalion conducted Search and Destroy operations and Night Ambush activities in the Loc Giang area. B Company continued to provide security for Rome Plow operations.

September 30, 1967 the Battalion had occupied night positions at Fire Support/Patrol base Diane at XT424166. During the day the Battalion began movement to Cu Chi Base Camp, arriving at 1:55pm. Company B remained until later at XT545155 to provide security for Rome Plow operations.

The Security Duty worked out pretty well without any incidents, and we ended that operation at XT545155. That evening the battalion moved back to our "Home" at Cu Chi Base Camp. This was my last time in the field. I was a short-timer, and that was nothing short of a Miracle considering at least five to six different close calls that I remember!

## *September 1967*

The Battalion had been in the field since May 13, 1967, that's 136 days. We had 98 days prior, so the overall total was 234 days with 3 days rest in between. Think what that would have done to you? Think of the effect that this had on our minds and bodies! These figures were verified in the Tropic Lightening Newspaper.

I was such a short-timer that you'd need to get on your hands and knees just to speak with me, however still wasn't as short as Butch Petit! For all practical purposes this was the end of my combat tour of duty in the Republic of Vietnam.

My life had been forever changed. The young man, wide-eyed and hopeful, was now an old-timer in the Unit! What has life in store for me?

* * * * *

There were twenty-four men wounded-in-action this month.

September 1967 claimed the lives of four of our Brothers-in-Arms. They were:

    Evaristo Sandoval       Harold J. Canan

    Michael A. Roberts     William Swensgard

These men were heroes because they stayed to fight while others hid or ran away. Those who hid and did not go owe a debt they cannot pay. The valiant gave it all that day their journey ended. No guilt or shame can remain but on the hands of those who hid or ran away!

# October 1967

Last Days in Vietnam
The next best thing to leaving is being a "short timer"! At the beginning of October I had about 12 days left in Vietnam.

What I am about to tell you might be as big a shock to you as it was to me, (unless you've skipped the rest of the book to see how it all comes out).

Sometime on October 1st the First Battalion Mechanized 5th Infantry Division and B Company in particular arrived at Cu Chi Base Camp, and, hold onto your seats, remained there until the morning of October 8, 1967 (a Whole Damn Seven Days!). Well I'll be! I never, ever, never, never, ever, ever remember the Battalion being at Cu Chi for that many days in a row! Wow! The U.S. Army must have started to get soft!

Entertainment
From October 1st to October 7th, 1967 this is where and how the boys and I spent our time at Cu Chi Base Camp as well as the few times in the past.

Entertainment for the 1/5th Mechanized Infantry was very limited, not because there was nothing to do, but because of the few days we were not in the field. When we weren't in the field, the types of entertainment for us in Vietnam was limited to some occasional movie, radio (Armed Forces Radio that is, and even an occasional Vietnamese station), television (very limited), reading (not most of us), and our favorite meaningless pastime, drinking anything that would get us drunk and help us pass out or fall asleep.

Unless you had your own stash of booze (hard liquor), or a good friend's stash, the Enlisted Men's Club was your only chance. The only alcoholic drink was beer. Ice-cold Beer was available for purchase, and I don't remember them putting any limitation on how much we could drink! Mostly we would drink and pee and drink and pee. On and on, all night, until they kicked us out. At any given time we might be drinking Miller High Life, Anheuser Bush, Lone Star, Balmity Balm (beer made by the Vietnamese with embalming fluid), Hamm's "The Beer Refreshing", Lucky Lager, Foster's "Australian for Beer" or OB "Off Brand" a Korean Beer.

The Enlisted Men's Club also sold snacks like pretzels, shoestring potato sticks, Beef Jerky, Slim Jims etc. Snacks were very, very important items because they served two different purposes. First they were salty and they helped keep you thirsting for more beer. Second, we needed salt for our bodies two white tablets daily to counteract the dehydration of the heat, snacks for alcohol. Besides those reasons, they tasted good together and we enjoyed them.

The club also contained a juke box that played songs like "The Green, Green Grass of Home", "Sugar Shack", "Unchained Melody", "California Dreamin", "Leavin' on a Jet Plane", "Who'll Stop the Rain", "I am a Rock", "The Beat Goes On", "Bridge Over Troubled Waters", "The Sound of Silence", "Blowin' in the Wind", "Where Have All The Flowers Gone", "Eve of Destruction", "Soldier Boy" and other favorite songs of the day. I don't know if those songs helped us connect with our former lives and made us feel more at home, or if they made us feel more homesick and or miserable than we already were. We did enjoy listening to those songs, and I guess they worked to our benefit. Beer, food and music made up our favorite available combination for a Base Camp evening.

The club was located at the farthest Northwest corner of the 5th Infantry's Battalion area. As you entered the club, the bar was on your left. The building was about 10 feet X 14 feet, and the bar was about 7 feet long. The walls were made of plywood up to about 4 feet high, with another 5 feet of frame with bug screening. I think it had a tin roof. The jukebox was in the Northeast corner of the room.

The Enlisted Men's Club provided two basic functions, it gave us a little bit of the good old USA, and it provided a place to relax from the daily terror we faced. However, since we were in the field so much, I could count with one hand the number of times I was in Base Camp and used the facility from January 1967 to the end of April 1967. The fact that we didn't spend much time in Cu Chi worked in my favor, because personally I would have become an alcoholic if I had spent more time at the Enlisted Men's Club.

My most vivid recollection of the Club was giving instructions to the bartender. First, I would draw a line on the bar midway, running from my left to right side. I would put several beers worth of bills on his side of the line. This would be my tab. I told him to give me two beers, and when I had put one empty can over the line, he was to give me two more beers. When the money ran out, I would put more bills over the line until I decided to stop. Then I would let him know I was finished. It was easy to run through 20 to 25 beers a night! The horrible heat and humidity supported a terrible thirst.

Unfortunately we had two basic types of drunks, those who became Melancholy and those who were Happy. Take the type of a melancholy drunk and a sad song and you had one Depressed GI. But take a Happy, up-beat song with a Happy Drunk and you had a party! I believe I was a Happy Drunk. "Let's Party" was our in Camp Motto!

Occasionally we had the opportunity to watch outdoor movies at the Battalion Movie Theater with benches for seats. The only movie I remember was The African Queen. If you've seen the TV show Mash, with the episode where they're watching a movie and the film continually breaks, you'll get an idea of my Vietnam movie-viewing experience. You would be sitting back enjoying the movie of the night, and the film would break. Different war, same problem!

The world is indeed a small place, because about five days before my exit I ran into one of my younger brother Steve's friends from the Chicago neighborhood where we grew up. I sure hope that he made it back Home. The next day another familiar face popped up at B Company. It was one of the sons of our Landlord where I lived with my stepmother in Chicago. Talk about it being a small world!

I said my "goodbyes" to those going out the next day to knock on Death's Door and planned for my journey back to the WORLD!

```
October 8, 1967 in the morning, the Battalion
departed from Cu Chi and moved to an area 4
kilometers from Trang Bang at XT537168. The
mission was to establish a Fire support/ Patrol
base at that location. Platoon-sized Search and
Destroy operations conducted in the area during
the afternoon.
```

Guess what? I didn't join my unit in the field. If you were in my shoes, would you feel good or bad about that?

```
October 9, 1967 B Company and C Company set up
separate night base perimeters to the south and
north of Highway 7A. Platoon sized Search and
Destroy operations. At 9:16pm B Company engaged
and killed three Viet Cong 1,000 meters from base.
```

For the next five days the company was up by Trang Bang. B Company, I am proud to say, killed seven of those Viet Cong bastards, three on the 9th and four on the 11th. Thanks for the great send off!

I was extremely thankful for all the times I remained unharmed by the Forces of Evil during my stay in Vietnam. We should count our Blessings every day and remember the ways in which harm has passed us by.

My last two days at camp were a drag, with nothing to do but wait and hide from Sergeants and Officers and I didn't want to give them too big of a target to shoot!

## October 1967

I left the company area on the afternoon of October 10, 1967. I was leaving Cu Chi for the last time, and it was a glad yet a sad parting. I was glad I was going, and I was sad that there weren't more of my friends and buddies coming with me!

I had said my goodbyes several days before I left. My good friend and rescuer First Lieutenant Sol Wainwright B Company's Executive Officer (who I've not seen or heard of since October 10, 1967), signed my Final Release Papers from the Company. I was eager to begin my adventurous journey back to the WORLD!

I don't remember how I got from Cu Chi to the Out-Processing Center at Bien Hoa. I got there in the evening and spent the night visiting at a Base Nightclub, listening to rock n roll with a Vietnamese accent, and drinking many beers.

The next day, October 11, 1967, I was processed out for my return to the WORLD. When they were finished with processing, they decided to take one last crack at my tolerance. I know for a fact that the term "Military Intelligence" is an Oxymoron! This day before I left Vietnam, they had us building a defensive position.

There was a small hole very close to the inside of the Perimeter, a foxhole. There was probably the most ignorant and dumb Sergeant in charge. He had us fill sand bags twenty feet away, carry them to the foxhole, and place them around the front and sides. That was the stupidest fucking thing I had ever seen. Why not fill the bags with the sand from the hole as it was being dug? I was so mad I could have shot him in the ass, but I wanted to get the hell out of country so bad that I tolerated this insult to my intelligence!

Why did they have to fuck with us? We served our "Time at Death's Door" almost daily. Why, Why, Why? "This is the Army Mr. Jones!" (World War II movie song)

Since I had the remaining evening to get emotionally prepared to fly away, I took another crack at drinking beer to escape the boredom. I don't think I've listened to another Vietnamese rock n roll band since. The girls in the group sure were fine, though! I really enjoyed myself but after a few drinks I became reflective.

October 12, 1967, my final day in Vietnam had finally arrived!! Not only was I leaving Vietnam behind, but I also left behind some awful habits. The alcohol I drank the night before was the last I would drink in my entire life. That was forty years ago. I had quit smoking more than six months earlier.

The bright morning sun broke the Shades of Nighttime's Dismal Veil. A New Day and a New Beginning had dawned. I felt the excitement of the day. I had passed by the Edges of Death and was going to "The Green, Green Grass of Home".

The last thing I remember is walking up those stairs. Each step up the stairs was another joyous step toward Freedom's Winged Chariot. Joy swelled in my Heart as the final step brought me to the door. Please, please let this sight not be a mirage.... The stewardesses welcomed us as we boarded, and I went to find my seat. Sitting in those soft seats, the softest seats we'd sat on since in Vietnam, felt unreal. Hurry, close that door and let's get the Hell out of here before I wake!

Oh that magnificent Continental Airlines Jumbo Jet!! We waited to take off. It seemed like an eternity! It began to move.... Varoooooooom!!! As the jet lifted off the ground the entire group of passengers loudly yelled, "Hurrah!"

GOOD BYE VIETNAM!

Up, up and up farther into the clouds of my memory...

The terror, pain and even the laughter were physically over for me, and it was time to try and piece together a life. I felt utter joy and relief, but I still felt the closeness of many brothers for whom the terror and pain continued until they left Vietnam. The realities of war still continued for the $1^{st}$ of the $5^{th}$ Mechanized Infantry in the field.

*October 1967*                                          

\* \* \* \* \*

There were five men wounded-in-Action this month.

I must give honor and respect to our Fighting Boys who fought and died in the month of October 1967. There were seven men who made the supreme sacrifice:

    Frank A. Price III           Junior Burns

    Gary P. Pulley              Ralph J. Di Pace

    Gregory B. Hubbard      John C. Steer

    Jeremiah Sullivan

Most of these men were unknown to me. Not because I didn't care, but when you were a short-timer, it was difficult to want to get too close and make new friends you would have to leave behind.

All the men whose names you read at the end of the chapters deserve our Honor and Respect for their Supreme Sacrifice made in helping to secure our Safety and Security. They are the Heroes of this book.

# My War Never Ends...

A great number of Vietnam combat veterans have remained in their shells, staying silent and not wanting to remember "things" that have been eating away at their lives under the surface! Sometimes we react in exaggerated ways to seemingly minor events at the unexpected drop of a hat. Almost anything can trigger a memory or feeling from decades ago, and the result can be an exaggerated reaction. Surprise, surprise, surprise!

There were no exit interviews, no psychological counseling offered (or we didn't know of any) to help us assimilate back into polite society. No one even asked if we were OK. It was get out, go home, and make do! Now all they want to do is analyze us.

I am a big fan of old movies because of the images that are portrayed. There were big differences between our experience in Nam and the images portrayed in the movies of the World War II era. The biggest difference was the nature of the enemy. The enemy in the movies presented a clear and present danger to the safety of the whole world, a war machine that threatened our shores. Then the dastardly attack on Pearl Harbor whipped us up to the height of our zeal! The threat hit too close to home to ignore.

I've seen repeated images in songs, slogans, advertisements, radio, newspapers, and newsreels extolling our troops and actively supporting the war effort and our troops in World War II. This rousing support for the GI was seen in the treatment of our troops at home before, during and after the war.

Most young men of my time born in the forties and fifties grew up watching war movies showing Loved, Respected, and Honored War Veterans as Heroes during and after World War II. If I am wrong, someone please enlighten me. We went to war to die if necessary with those ideals burned into our memories. The silver screen of Hollywood showed defenders of freedom who were loved, respected, and honored as Heroes! Swelling with national pride!

Imagine our disappointment . . .

The movies about Vietnam have portrayed drug crazed, sub-human, sadistic civilian murderers unfit to walk the streets of your beloved country! Some accused our men in Vietnam of assaulting innocent women and children on a grand scale. We who served there are confused because, in our minds, we did just the opposite. We treated the Vietnamese people with respect. So, where did all these misconceptions come from?

We have not only been accused. We have been found guilty <u>AS CHARGED BY HOLLYWOOD</u> and by uninformed general public opinion. No trial, no justice? Do you actually believe that our boys, especially the ones you personally know, would have turned into rapacious monsters?

> We also wonder why no one ever has said anything about the countless murders and atrocities that were committed by the Viet Cong and North Vietnamese soldiers on the non-combat citizens of the Republic of Vietnam.

You come home with all those expectations burned into your

memory when soldiers were Loved, Respected, and Honored! Then people call you despicable names, spit at you, and curse you as baby killers and as crazy degenerates! Are we different? Yes we are different. We endured all that unjust slander and more remaining silent for all these years!

And on top of that, we lost our innocence. We are scarred. No amount of acceptance and thanks today can blot out the stains left on our hearts and minds. We've been hurt and have been living under a dark cloud ever since we left our war behind.

People tell you to let it go, but I tell you IT WON'T LET US GO! Considering the statistical differences between a Combat Veteran of World War II in the South Pacific and a Vietnam Combat Veteran there is a huge difference, as found in the Westmoreland Report.

World War II lasted four years, or 1,460 days. Due to rotational schedules of combat veterans the average combat days equaled 40 days for their entire tour of duty, which is about 2.7% of their time as combat soldiers. This will blow your mind! The average number of combat days served by a Combat Vietnam Veteran was 240 days of combat in one year, which is 64.9% of the time. That is 24 times more combat time on a percentage basis.

The number of combat days for our unit from October 1966 to October 1967 was about 330 days, or 90%. Quite a staggering and substantial difference!

Do you believe PTSD Post Traumatic Stress Disorder is just a puny excuse for Vietnam Combat Veterans for their difficult lives, or could there be a valid cause? Have you ever seen a 58 to 68 year old teenager? Talk about arrested development. A lot of us were just kids when we left to fight, many not old enough to vote or drink. But we were judged to be old enough to sacrifice our Youth, Sanity and our Lives. We wound up feeling abandoned by a nation that we love, respect, and honor.

THAT'S HOW AND WHY WE ARE DIFFERENT FROM ANY OTHER VETERAN IN OUR NATION'S MILITARY HISTORY!

Thankfully most of us are able to function quite well in society, we are able to hide the baggage that continues to affect our minds. The trend today is for people to live to an older age than previous generations, but Vietnam Vets are gradually falling apart internally from the effects of Agent "pick your color" Orange, including DDT for mosquito repellant and whatever! There have been many attempts to take away or forestall what little benefits are afforded our Vietnam Vets, adding insult to injury.

The last three years I have noticed the health of some of my brothers slip a notch or two. It has been painful for me to see. Some suffer from physical wounds and conditions, others from the effects of environmental chemicals. Yes, we were subjected to straight DDT used as insect repellent rubbed all over our bodies. A drug called Dapsone two orange pills daily was used for Malaria and is also used to treat Leprosy.

I have had the honor and privilege to attend several reunions of The Survivors of the Battle for Cu Chi Class of 1966, 1$^{st}$ Battalion 5th Mechanized Infantry, and 25th Infantry Division. These men have been through hell and back and are still teenagers trapped in older adult bodies. I can attest to that myself, because that's how I feel. My thought processes and my actions are often those of a much younger and less mature person. Normal development some-how has escaped me (or should I say us), and I imagine other people might wonder when we're going to grow up. So do I.

In spite of our scars, we have married, worked, and raised children. The normal things everyone does. No, we are not a bunch of drug-crazed killers, we are Americans living in the land we Honor and Love.

Nevertheless, a good number of us still have a teenage mentality. We focus on fast cars and fast women (sorry wives). Although this sounds bad, we're mostly harmless.... While college students were learning to cut the parental "apron strings", we were ripped from our mother's bosom!

These guys I am writing about are a great bunch of men. I would leave on a mission right this minute into the breach once more. It may seem unusual to hear those rugged looking men expressing their love for each other. There is a special bond between men who have experienced the heat of battle. I don't expect you to understand, but to accept and admire them.

We all suffer from PTSD (Post Traumatic Stress Disorder) laden with survivor's guilt! Can you beat that? Feeling guilty for being alive. What a thing to live with, all from serving your country. Plus we can't get a good night's sleep. We are still on our combat jungle schedule of two hours on two hours off watch, and function on two to six hours sleep in three days. This might not sound too bad. Consider that this schedule has been in effect day-by-day, week-by-week, month-by-month, and year-by-year for 40 some years. Try that on for size. Oh by the way, don't forget our ugly memories...

I have witnessed the high price paid by those brave men. Think of that war and then think of how many times lately you've heard comparisons with the Iraq War. I've heard many such comparisons in the last several years. Then remember that it was the American people who lost the Vietnam War, not the soldiers. It was lost on American soil and in the American press. Check it out for yourself.

<u>Don't do the same to our Honorable and Brave soldiers in Iraq and Afghanistan!</u>

The men of the 5$^{th}$ Mechanized Infantry have great attitudes and are staunch Americans. We sometimes get a little worked up when we hear other "Americans" putting down this country. I consider some acts done in the name of "Freedom of Speech" may be bordering on treason. It's rather difficult for someone to give aid and comfort to the enemy and then try and hide behind or use the precepts upon which this country was founded. Those things just don't settle well with us. You see, we see through different eyes because we have seen the Cost of Freedom. We make no apologies.

<u>An Excerpt from the Memoirs of General Giap, North Vietnam Commander</u>
"What we still don't understand is why you Americans stopped bombing Hanoi. You had us on the ropes. If you had pressed us a little harder, just for another day or two, we were ready to surrender! It was the same at the battles of TET. You defeated us! We knew it, and we thought you knew it. But we were elated to notice your MEDIA was definitely helping us. They were causing

more disruption in America than we could in the battlefields. We were ready to surrender. You had won!"

This was the ultimate test during the Cold War and although the United States (through internal pressure) ended the war just as the Communist North Vietnamese government was ready to give in.
The bombing of the north had brought them to the edge. Had we continued bombing they were prepared to surrender and just before we went to Paris and then pulled out!

There is a well-known military strategy called "Divide and conquer". Let's not allow the enemy, or anyone, to divide us again!

UNITED WE STAND, DIVIDED WE FALL!

If you don't know and understand the mistakes of history, you will be doomed to re-live them! Honor, Duty, Country, these were words used by that great American, Five Star General Douglas Mac Arthur at his final West Point address. They weren't just words, they were his way of life.

Thankfully times do change. I have had more young people come up to me and thank me for my service in Vietnam than any older people, and that is truly a blessing. I suppose they can see through all the false facts to the Truth.

America is still the best system to live under.

Else, why would so many want to come and drink FREELY from the WELL of FREEDOM? Please don't lose sight of that! Support your troops in word, deed, and actions! Freedom isn't free. It has been paid in blood by soldiers!

..."The Beat Goes On"...

# Epilogue

The flight into the Clouds of My Memory has been sometimes bumpy and sometimes smooth soaring. I have been repeatedly amazed at how many memories I had blocked for so many, many years. Thankfully, the thick clouds of my memory have whisked by, and openings in the clouds have revealed to me the landscape of my memory, showing the shape and pattern of our experiences.

We descend towards the end of our journey and have time to reflect. If I've done my job, then as we near the closing of this book you've experienced a taste of our horrendous wartime experience. Some of the writing has been extremely personally painful, but it was a Labor of Love. Love for my Brothers-in-Arms, Love for my friends, Love for my Country, and as the tears drop down onto this final page of the Landscape of My Memory, Love for my family!

I pray that you now have felt the terror of the nights and the uncertainty of the days in the jungle. That terror was experienced on a daily basis by the soldiers for the Cause of Freedom.

America is THE DREAM Come True (because of the Brave).

God Bless America

Thank you

Richard Daniel Antti

# Map A - Fil Hol and Ho Bo Woods

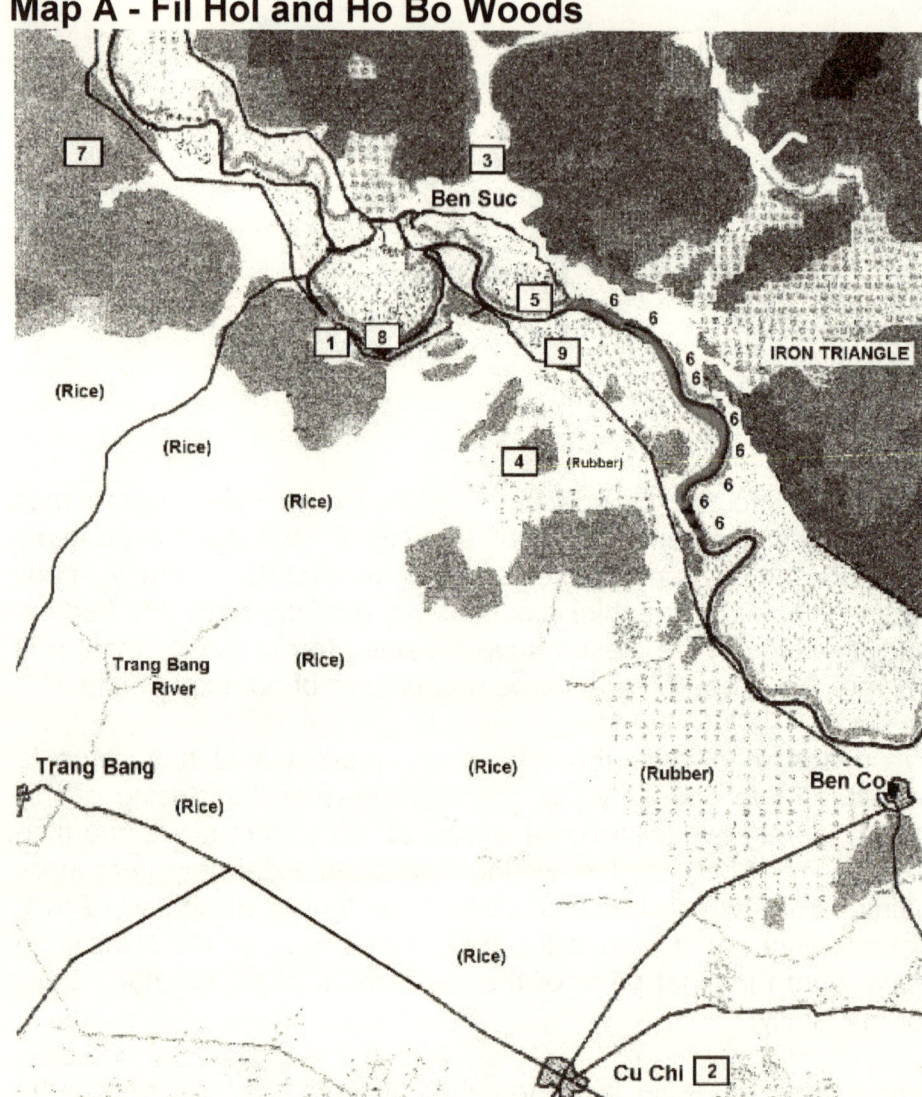

1. 10/22/66 – My first day in Field, my first Action
2. 10/31/66 – My first Ambush
3. 01/17/67 – Ambush
4. 01/18/67 – Company A tunnel documents
5. 01/19/67 – River Patrol
6. 01/19/67 – River Boat and blocking zone, follow 6's
7. 04/27/67 – Second tunnel
8. 05/03/67 – Jim Flickinger Killed-in-Action
9. 01/23/67 – Donut Dollies in field

# Map B - Tay Ninh-Katum north and Cambodia border

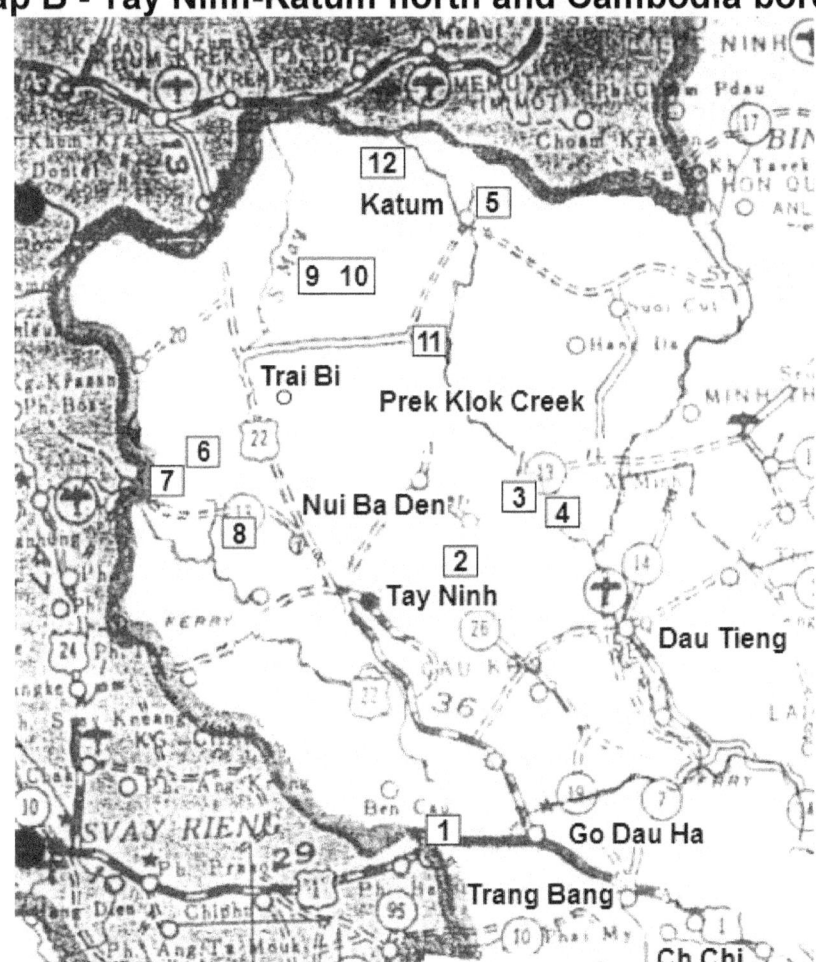

1. 11/05/66 - Convoy interception point
2. 11/08/66 - Night Ambush
3. 11/09/66 - Patrol to locate crossing point
4. 11/11/66 - Location where I received letter of my fathers death
5. 11/24/66 - Rainy Thanksgiving breakfast location
6. 02/07/67 - My first tunnel
7. 02/13/67 - River Ambush into Cambodia
8. 02/22/67 - Secured perimeter for Paratroopers
9. 02/27/67 - Watering hole bath
10. 02/28/67 - Water buffalo incident
11. 03/26/67 - Cooked banana's, water filled bomb crater, the dig
12. 03/31/67 – My trail blazing, B Company disaster with RPG2's
13. 06/07/67 - B Company 1st Platoon, 3rd Squad Rest in Peace

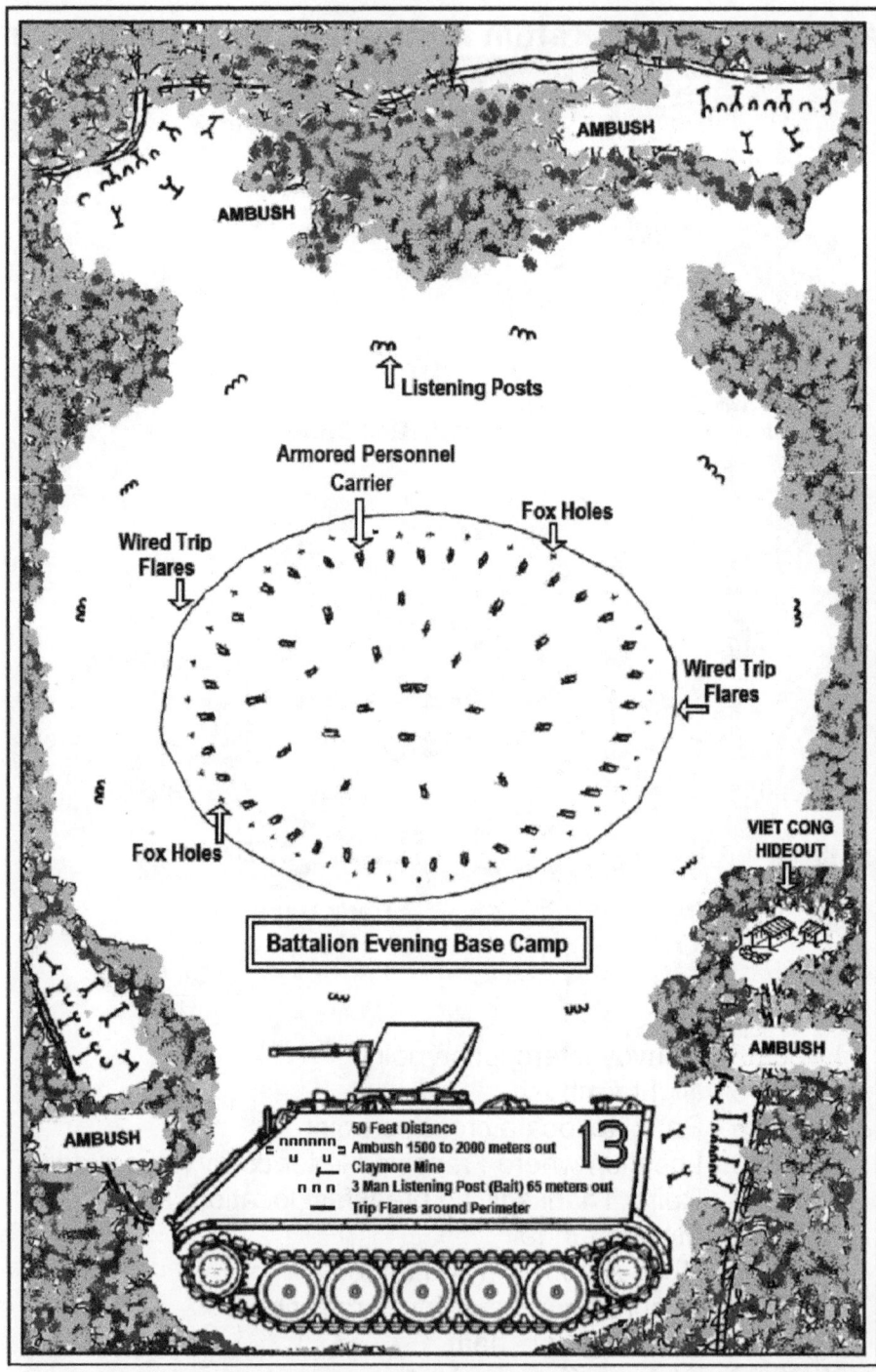

The layout could be by Company, Platoon and various sizes. 50 feet measure is for Perimeter-Listening Post area. Ambushes would be 6-7 times further away from the Perimeter to be accurate to scale. Ambushes were set from air reconnaissance and daily activity. Field Base Camp locations were mostly changed almost every evening.

## Front Cover Artwork

The airplane wing is that of a DC-6 propjet like one that carried me to the "land of Enchantment", Vietnam. It will carry you there too!

The first opening in the clouds reveals two Vietnamese farms as they are pictured on our unit web site, www.1-5th-m-25th-inf-1966.com. The farms give shape and form to the book. The second opening in the clouds shows some of the rice paddies that always seemed to outline the edges of the jungle, the killing fields that took too many of our good men. They beckon you to find out more!

The billowing cloud formations are taken from actual photos found on our web site. They provide cover for the lanscape, hiding dangers, awaiting your discovery.

The lone fighter soaring through the clear blue sky honors the Navy, Air Force, Marine, and Helicopter pilots. It also speaks softly of a loneliness we felt from the lack of moral support from our beloved country!

These elements are part of a powerful story of human emotional cost. Painting the picture was quite an emotional experience.

The concept and design weren't a creative idea, they just came to me out of the blue. I hope you were drawn into the story. I hope I have provided you a unique opportunity to experience what happened beneath the clouds!

www.ingramcontent.com/pod-product-compliance
Lightning Source LLC
Chambersburg PA
CBHW020737160426
43192CB00006B/228